Cele

brity

cate
interviews

by JUDY WIEDER

An Advocate Book

CREATIVE DIRECTOR: Craig Edwards

PHOTOGRAPHY DIRECTOR: Michael Matson

Manufactured in Hong Kong.

This book is published by Advocate Books, an imprint of Alyson Publications,
P.O. Box 4371, Los Angeles, California 90078-4371.
Distribution in the United Kingdom by Turnaround Publisher Services Ltd.,
Unit 3, Olympia Trading Estate, Coburg Road, Wood Green, London N22 6TZ England.

First edition: November 2001

01 02 03 04 05 ✳ 10 9 8 7 6 5 4 3 2 1

ISBN 1-55583-722-0

Library of Congress Cataloging-in-Publication Data
  Celebrity: the Advocate interviews / by Judy Wieder.—1st ed.
    ISBN 1-55583-722-0
    1. Homosexuality—United States. 2. Celebrities—United States—
  Interviews. 3. Gays—United States—Interviews. I. Wieder, Judy.
  II. Advocate (Los Angeles, Calif.)
  HQ76.3.U5 A38 2001
  306.76'6—dc21   2001046233

Advocate
BOOKS

Introduction

by LIZ SMITH

What makes celebrities talk to *The Advocate*?

Lord knows I asked myself that on the day I sat down, contrary to anybody's expectations—most of all mine—to dig deeper than I ever had before into my personal story for *The Advocate*. What possessed me, after all? Not only had I read many a probing *Advocate* interview, but I had especially noted those done by the magazine's editor in chief, Judy Wieder.

When you've been in business as long as I have, you never forget there's a tape recorder rolling. But something about Judy makes you want to. I can still see her leaning across the table listening to me. She's not pretending to be interested in you. She is interested. She feels that telling your story could do some good for others and for you. She's right.

Judy comes by her world-class listening skills naturally. She is a songwriter—make that a Grammy-winning songwriter—and was long before she ever started interviewing famous people. At first it was all about other musicians, starting with Michael Jackson in 1971 and followed by a succession of rock band interviews, especially heavy metal—music, she once joked, she couldn't really listen to, let alone write about. So she didn't. She wrote about the people. For Judy, it was always a portrait of the soul—the spirit of the rebels making all that noise. Maybe it was those years that taught her not just to accept the new and different but to celebrate it and to enjoy coming back to tell the tale.

From Aerosmith to Guns N' Roses, all the rockers talked to Judy. It was no different when she arrived at *The Advocate*—not the easiest place to corral celebrities back in 1993. There was a fear that just to appear in the pages of the magazine would pin one with a permanent lavender label.

Judy was unruffled. Her first week at the magazine, she did a cover story with Mark Wahlberg, who was in the doghouse with gay activists over an alleged spate of homophobic comments. From that best-selling cover story on, Judy perfected the art of *The Advocate* interview. Pointed, topical, intelligent, and yes, full of good gossip. But never vindictive. Always with a spirit of fairness and a genuine curiosity to learn the truth, not promote a prepackaged point of view.

And the stars respond. Judy has talked with Catherine Deneuve about making lesbian love in *The Hunger;* with Liza Minnelli about walking in on her husband, Peter Allen, in bed with another man; with Ellen DeGeneres about losing a significant other to a tragic car accident; with George Michael about falling in love with a man for the first time. When Chastity Bono came out and made headlines the world over, she came out to Judy.

Nowadays Judy is more than a celebrity interviewer. Under her guidance as editor in chief, *The Advocate* has become an essential source of news, the place to go for an evenhanded, sharply presented biweekly view of the world from the gay and lesbian perspective. That perspective turns out to be broad indeed—and a damn good read by the way.

I asked Judy once why those gun-shy and guarded creations we call celebrities are so willing to tell her what's really on their minds. She shook her head. "One of the people I interviewed told me that he told himself, 'This girl's not gonna hurt me. She'll do the right thing with what I say.'"

Having been on the other side of an interview with Judy, I have to tell you, it's true.

Liz Smith is a world-wide syndicated columnist and the author of Natural Blonde, *her best-selling memoir.*

George M

ichael

The first time I met George Michael

we were both in the closet. It was in 1986, and I was a contributing writer for *Creem* magazine. George was taking a break from the cold weather in London, where he was mixing his first solo album, (the brilliant, destined-to-be-Grammy-winning) *Faith*, and I was on assignment to interview him in Los Angeles. When I arrived at the lush canyon home of his then-manager, I was told that the platinum-selling pop sensation was waiting for me in the back-yard and that I would have only one hour with him.

Three hours later George walked me to my car. Even though a crucial piece of information never made it into our conversation, we knew we had bonded. I had learned more than I would have guessed about a "teen star" who was growing into a man. Shedding his bleached-blond locks and pushing away from the safe harbor of Wham! (the chart-topping duo he and Andrew Ridgeley formed back in 1981), the Greek-descended Georgios Kyriacos Panayiotou was beginning the first leg of his journey to "becoming real." He was no longer comfortable being a pop idol. He felt like a phony for many reasons. Some he mentioned; some he didn't. He thought there were important things going on in the world and didn't like being locked into an image that left him unable to address them. While George was grateful for past Wham! hits like "Wake Me Up Before You Go-Go," he had already begun staking out more serious music territory with songs like "Careless Whisper." Excited to be taking on the challenge of a solo career, he also had understandable concerns about leaving a sure thing. Would he be accepted on his own? What would people think about the new music he was making, songs such as "Father Figure," "Faith," and "One More Try"—which he talked about but couldn't share because they were stuck in the grasp of his legendary perfectionism somewhere far away in a London recording studio.

"It's like my hair," I remember him saying about his quest for authenticity. He ran his fingers through his thick dark locks. "I had dyed it blond for years in Wham! It kept getting blonder and blonder. I didn't know what I really looked like anymore. I come from a dark Greek family. Who is this blond boy? I can't do it anymore. That image isn't me, so how can I be proud of it? I've got to start showing people who I am."

That evening there was a dinner for the *Creem* staff in Los Angeles. Everyone wanted to know about my interview with George Michael. I vaguely remember a din of questions that suddenly ended when one of the editors silenced the restaurant with, "So is he gay or what?"

"Gay!" the magazine owner's 20-something daughter wailed, clearly horrified and disappointed. "No way! I'd throw out all his records if he was gay. I love him. That's gross." Being truly surprised by the question, I think I probably saved her George Michael record collection for a few years by saying "Nothing like that ever came up. He talked only about girls."

But to myself I wondered, *Is that what he was really trying to say?* Of course, why would he say anything to me? I never offered him any safety or opening. I was hiding too. And with the shriek of disgust from a George Michael fan still ringing in my ears, I could hardly blame him for worrying about the consequences of coming out. It would be devastating. Like all teen stars, he was the object of every young girl's heated affection. What a nightmare. If this was true—if George Michael was gay—what in the world was he going to do?

Twelve years later the charade ended in the bathroom of a Beverly Hills park (the details of which can be read in the following interview). Although George had fallen in love with a man several years before, lost him to AIDS, and written openly about it ("Jesus to a Child") on his stunning 1996 *Older* CD, he had never spoken about it publicly. Believing that it was enough to be out with his friends, the reclusive singer felt being gay wasn't something he wanted to do the "grand interview" about. He didn't have to share that too, did he? Whose business was it? Besides, the British tabloids had been outing him for years. Why cooperate?

There are two things I have learned about George over the years. The first is that he loathes being photographed. (The photograph that he sat for with Melissa Etheridge for the cover of *The Advocate*'s special commemorative issue for the Millennium March on Washington is, I like to say, "the picture of a miracle." Even his manager, Andy Stevens, offered me a job for pulling it off.) The second is that George often says no, then reconsiders. After a lifetime of having people at him all the time with requests, he has learned to throw up a wall so that he can have some space to find his own thoughts. He's very political and very serious. Things must have a point: something more than pop publicity, something deeper than vanity, something that will be life-changing, not just for everyone else but for him as well. Thus, just when I thought he would never do this interview or never perform at Equality Rocks (the Human Rights Campaign Foundation's "Concert for the New Century" at RFK Stadium in Washington, D.C., in April 2000), he said yes.

Actually, as the following two interviews with George Michael clearly show, he said a whole lot more than just yes.

The perfect introduction to this stubbornly candid interview with George Michael took place in Venice, Calif., a week before the actual conversation that follows. The 35-year-old music superstar was in the midst of filming his "Outside" video, using a public

bathroom in the sandy beach town to fill in for the Beverly Hills park bathroom he's been forbidden to go near since his April 7, 1998, arrest for lewd conduct.

Michael, born Georgios Kyriacos Panayiotou in north London, wore a baseball cap and buried his head in a video monitor while actors dressed as police dragged a struggling man out of the public toilet and into a van. Shading his eyes from the afternoon sun, Michael glanced up at the interviewer, recognized her from a 1986 interview they'd done right after his professional breakup with Wham! collaborator Andrew Ridgeley—and smiled, relieved.

"Sit with me and watch as I record the joys of outdoor public sex," he said with sarcasm. "But don't look over there!" He pointed to a lone photographer who had somehow slipped onto the set. A bodyguard shielded the star with a makeshift curtain. Soon clicking could be heard from a nearby parked car. Two paparazzi shouted to each other in Italian. Michael's manager rushed at them. A helicopter began to circle the area. Someone pointed to the top of a nearby condo. The roof was swarming with men aiming long-distance lenses at the pop star.

"Oh, screw it," Michael groaned. Let me just wrap up this scene. It kinda fits with what we're filming."

How did foreign photographers know Michael was filming a video in Los Angeles? Why, since the 1993 AIDS death of his first true love, Brazilian designer Anselmo Feleppa, has his homosexuality been belittled in British papers? Where do the tabloids always manage to find pictures of Michael's current boyfriend, Kenny Goss? Why, after a career-long battle to keep his personal life away from the press, is George Michael sitting down with *The Advocate* and doing what he swore he'd never do?

"People are still telling me to be careful," he sighed. "But at the end of the day, all I can do is be honest. I've reached a very good point of self-acceptance. I don't have any shame about my sexuality. I don't think people are going to desert me because they know more about me—"

Frantic voices drowned out the rest of his sentence as a van drove up to rescue Michael from the multiplying paparazzi. He leaned out and yelled above the din, "Come to my house on Saturday. I'm ready to do this."

And he was. The following interview took place in Michael's Los Angeles home on October 10, 1998.

Obviously your first single and video, "Outside" [from *Ladies & Gentlemen...The Best of George Michael*], deals with your arrest. Can you talk more about what went on in that Beverly Hills bathroom?

In the video I introduce the same situation that I was in but with a straight guy in a bathroom. A beautiful young girl comes in—the whole thing about police entrapment is that they don't send in someone you wouldn't even look at twice—so we send in a beautiful young girl. And the guy realizes she's available and kisses her.

She changes into a cop—an older, real mean, tough cop. Which makes you think, *That's so unfair. That's ridiculous. She came on to him.*

Why should people see it differently if it's a guy, if it's male-male sex? So I try to actually make straight people think about that. I try to make them see the basic unfairness of police entrapment.

Actually, we don't know what happened. What got you arrested?

That's exactly what happened. I think it'll be almost patronizing to most gay men to tell what happened. So many of them know exactly what happened.

At first we heard you were alone in the bathroom. Why were all the reports wrong?

Well, let's say it's fairly likely that there was some cooperation between the police and the paparazzi. I literally got arrested, called my boyfriend—bless his soul—to come pick me up, we went to dinner, and I said, "Darling, the lot will be there by the time we get home." And I was half right. At about 4 in the morning, they were at the house, and by 5 o'clock there were helicopters.

What do you mean by "cooperation between the police and paparazzi"?

There was interaction between the L.A. police and the paparazzi in London. I think the cooperation was between someone who sent the police there as soon as I got to that park because the police station was at the end of the road, literally 600 yards away. And I think the reason that the reports changed so much was because the police were freaked out that it was me they'd arrested. The Beverly Hills police don't want to be seen to be arresting celebrities.

Are you saying the paparazzi tipped off the police?

The person that directed the police there knew, and someone made a lot of money. When other bits of information started coming in and I found out that pictures had been floating around since last year because the guy hadn't been able to sell them—

What pictures?

The pictures that ended up in *The Globe,* the *Enquirer.*

Of this arrest?

No, it wasn't of the arrest. The pictures the tabloids used were taken of me in that park the year before. Obviously there was no story without the arrest. It was just me sunbathing in that park where I took my dog quite a lot. With an arrest, those pictures of me were worth somewhere in the vicinity of £100,000.

You were just sunbathing?

Yes, and the thing that's really upsetting about those pictures is that I took my shirt off. I *never* take my shirt off in public—ever. Even when I'm slim I never take my shirt off in public. And the day the picture was taken I was a little overweight. One tabloid headline actually said "Fat and Gay." I just laughed when I read it. I thought, *What does that mean?* I didn't understand it! It was like, "Here are two things you'd hate to be. And he's both!"

So what did happen in the park and the bathroom?

The truth is that it was just like just about any other entrapment case you've ever heard of. I walked into the bathroom, and literally 30 seconds later someone else walked into the bathroom. As I was leaving the bathroom, I saw this guy who was basically masturbating in front of me. It was the usual thing, a good looking guy. I certainly didn't look at him and think, *Oh, that must be a cop.* And actually, nothing happened at all other than me returning the favor in kind from about eight feet away. And then he walked straight past me and out, at which point I thought, *Oh, he obviously wasn't impressed,* you know? Something was not happening for him.

How insulting! What did you do then?

I left immediately. It's not even like I was loitering or anything. I left thinking that it was probably just as well anyway that he walked out. And as I was walking back to the car, they arrested me. It was standard entrapment. There was absolutely no one else around apart from the backup cop halfway through the park who I couldn't see at the time. I made that slipup, and they got me straightaway.

No one else observed this?

No, and the remarkable thing to me in that situation is, who's to know what really went on in there? I'm quite sure in their business—however they're trained to do this kind of stuff, and apparently they are—I'm quite sure the actual official training does not involve taking your penis out and getting that involved. But who's to say that he did that? Only him and me. There were only the two of us in there. Why does the word *policeman* in a situation like that mean more than the word *citizen?* I thought that in almost any kind of criminal situation there had to be some kind of evidence other than a policeman's word. I'm not saying for a moment that I did the right thing by responding. In the end, I responded, and there was a crime committed—however pathetically small I may think the crime was. But I was responding to someone who was already doing it.

Were you scared when they nabbed you?

People said I was crying, but I was furious. I said, "This is ridiculous. This is entrapment. I know exactly what this is. I'm gonna have to shout 'Entrapment.' "

Had you done that before, gone to that bathroom?

No. But I've been in that park.

I have since heard the park referred to as "a reputed cruising area for homosexuals."

I've since read that that was well-known, but I doubt it because it's a very quiet park in the middle of Beverly Hills. But how many bathrooms in L.A. are *not* well-known cruising spots?

Why were you there?

What do you mean! Oh, I'm not saying that I didn't go there to cruise, and I have to say, as far as cruising spots go, it's pretty glamorous—a beautiful park, beautiful people, you know. It's not a posi-

tion I would have normally put myself in. I saw the situation, I thought the guy was cruising, I walked straight into the trap—bang. And it was immediate; they were right after me.

Did you consider denying it?

No. I think to have denied it would've been stupid. I'm not sorry that it happened. I'm glad that it happened—which at the same time makes me wonder whether I subconsciously allowed it to happen.

Well, I was working up to asking you that.

Oh, yeah! Look, I'm 35 now. I don't think you can base your sexuality around anything other than the people you fall in love with. When I was younger I slept with men and women, and I didn't fall in love at all. I was kind of underdeveloped that way. I would have brief relationships. If you sleep with both sexes and you think you're having relationships, well, it's kind of confusing. The other thing is, as a celebrity, you're given all kinds of choices you really don't want.

Like?

I went from being a relatively unattractive child in school to becoming famous. I was suddenly given the opportunity to have sex whenever I wanted it. I had way too much sex with way too many people, most of them women but some men. And because I had no emotional understanding of myself, all of it was fairly unsatisfying. Also, I would choose men that were completely unavailable or who were similarly confused sexually. When I did finally allow myself to get into a relationship where there was real commitment going, I was 27. From then on I believed I was gay.

So falling in love was what ended your conflict?

Yes, exactly. I'm one of those people whose sexuality obviously was ambiguous to people. And I was attractive to young girls, so automatically I became a focus for them. But was that fake? No. So I had to contend with that. All the time I was trying to figure out why it was that I wasn't making relationships that lasted or why it was I felt so lonely. I never had a moral problem with being gay. Obviously, since I was a young man who was adored by millions of young girls, the convenient thing was to think, *Well, hopefully I'm going to find that woman that I'll fall in love with one day.* But I wasn't finding her.

You never fell in love with a woman?

No. I thought I was. I thought I had a couple of times. I also thought I had with men—and then I realized that none of those things had been love. I realized that I was just trying to work myself out.

You fell in love eight years ago. Why didn't you come out then?

Because I'm a very proud person, and I have a very hard time with authority, which has to do with my upbringing. I had a very strict father.

I don't understand.

If you tell me that I have to do something, I'm going to try *not* to do it. And what people don't understand in the equation of my relationship with the press is that I've had people talking and writing about my sexuality since I was 19 years old. Andrew Ridgeley and I were immediately the center of a lot of gossip, although Andrew is completely straight and I thought I was bisexual at the time.

I'm still not sure why your relationship with the press kept you from coming out.

If you think about it, someone who is as motivated as me to become a star is driven by insecurity and the need for recognition and autonomy—so that you can't be controlled, so that you have freedom. And once you get in that position, one of the only entities that tries to control you is the press. Because you don't have many people to answer to. But the press tries to make you answer to them and to the public all the time. So I had this thing of, "Fuck you! I'm not going to give you my private life! I'm just trying to work it out myself, thank you very much!" And by then it was like two dogs with a bone. I kept trying to see how I could be clever and retain my dignity, not denying my sexuality but not giving them the three words they wanted.

Ugh. How exhausting!

God, yes! What I've realized in this whole last six months is just how much energy I was giving them. Recently there were loads of pictures all over the papers just because someone spotted me holding hands with Kenny. When I'm out with Kenny, I'm very physical with him. When I was with my last boyfriend—the one that really started my gay life, as it were—I didn't hide. We traveled together, we shared bedrooms—we never hid. I just knew one day the press was going to go for it. I never thought it would happen this way. But I thought, *When it happens, it happens, but I'm not giving it to them. I'm not going and doing a special interview.*

Like this one?

[*Laughing*] Yes, well, then here we are. But what I realize is that I actually allowed people to think I was miserable, closeted, and that that was why I was reclusive—as opposed to being sick of the way these people write about me. I let people think, "He feels this is something to hide." I let people think the issue was my sexuality, not my privacy. And the interesting thing is that the moment there was no privacy, I realized that *that's* all the issue was. Not one part of me has any problem with people knowing I'm gay.

So did the press win?

Well…but I had my way because they had to drag it out of me. They had to go to that extreme. OK, it was humiliating, but I was not a party to it. I didn't go and volunteer it and say, "OK, I'm gonna give you what you want because I'm tired of it." Actually, it didn't change my life because from the moment I met Anselmo, I was out in my own life with everyone immediately.

With your parents too?

No, I didn't come out with my mother and father until immediately after my first boyfriend, Anselmo, died. It was horrible, but the day after he died I wrote my parents a letter. It was such an easy letter to write. I felt that when he died he was passing a gift, saying, "I introduced you to yourself, and I opened you up to everyone you loved except your mom and dad. And you have to deal with that." So I wrote them a letter and saw them as soon as I got home after I'd been to Anselmo's funeral in Brazil. And everything was fine; it was wonderful. Of course, they were more concerned that I had just lost my partner than that I'd actually finally said what they already knew.

Your father knew?

Yeah, because I hadn't had a serious girlfriend for three or four years.

When Anselmo died and you came out to your parents, were they worried about your health?

No, because I told them that I'd been tested immediately when I found out that he was sick. And my parents know that I wouldn't lie to them. Obviously AIDS would be a concern to any parents that haven't confirmed that their child is gay, but I think that my mom and dad weren't worried about that. They know I'm a very cautious person—[*smiles*] apart from the cruising.

I see. How did your father react to your arrest?

He was great actually. He called me the next day and said, "Tell them all to fuck off! You are who you are." I was very impressed with that.

Since he was the strict authoritarian in your life—and you say that anybody trying to control you reminds you of your experiences with him—was it liberating for you to tell him?

To be honest, that whole period was such a blur because of the grief. I know that by the time my mother died last year, I thought it was quite amazing that we hadn't actually been open with each other until three years before. There was absolutely no difference in the relationship. It didn't make us closer because we were already very close. I just thought of how awful it would have been for her to have died without knowing, without us actually having talked about it. But my parents were fine about it. I knew they would be.

Then why didn't you tell them before?

I think I was more worried whether my father would blame my mother, the usual things. You know? But when I told them I realized that the only people I was actually hiding from was the press.

Did the gay community appear to be annoyed with you for not coming out?

Yes, but I find that the people who think that way are not as connected with their families as the people who have a more moderate view of how they want to come out. For instance, there are people for whom it would be ridiculous to pretend that they're not gay. The way they grew up, their mannerisms—I genuinely believe that for some people, they never had a choice but to deal with it from a very early age. And it's easy to understand why those people don't understand the people who aren't that cut-and-dry. I think very often that people who are plainly gay don't understand when people who are not as plainly gay have other issues to contend with.

Choices come with problems too?

Yes. But as soon as I fell in love, it was all clear. All the choices that I thought I was weighing were gone. You can be proud of your sexuality only when it's bringing you joy. Until you love someone, it's not necessarily bringing you joy. But without love, all of these issues seem kind of murky.

Maybe that's why Boy George needled you for years about being closeted.

Exactly. And what were his choices? He makes it absolutely clear that he could never be anything else other than what he is. Boy George—since Wham!—has been trying to out me. He knew I had boyfriends. I refused to rise to the bait with him. I've always turned the other cheek. At the end of the day, his motives are so transparent. He's never said anything that really bothered me until his *Advocate* article this year ["Boy Will Be Boy," June 23, 1998].

"I still believe in monogamy as an ideal. I'm not saying that I'm perfectly comfortable with my sexuality in terms of my enjoyment of casual sex. And that's coming from someone who really would like to be monogamous—even though I've failed dismally."

Oh, dear.

He's always said horrible things, but in that article he said that I thought I was too good for the gay community. I felt like that was really over the top. He did an article directly after I was arrested—interestingly enough, he writes a column for one of the tabloids, which is exactly where I think he belongs. It's an English tabloid called *Daily Mail*. It's also pretty right-wing and homophobic. I think it's quite interesting that he writes for them, so I guess he'll go for anyone who pays him. For a gay man, his attitude toward me is identical to the paparazzi's. The first article he wrote was all about how concerned he was for me and that we were sisters under the skin and all this stuff. But he was just gloating and pretending not to gloat. And then I think he realized that people didn't care. So at that point he did that interview with *The Advocate*. And when he said that stuff about how I thought I was too good for the community, I just thought, *You are now clutching at straws! You are thinking that I've been humiliated, and people are still not turning against me, so what can you say now to get me in trouble?* Because to say that I'm some kind of snob when it comes to the gay community, trying to turn people against me by making out like I had some sort of prejudice against gay people—I'm sorry. Am I too good for the gay community? No. Am I too good for the likes of Boy George? Yes.

Do you have many gay friends?

No, the vast majority of my friends are straight. The people I grew up with are straight, and I spent the first half of my adult life doing all the same things as they did, really. I think my straight friends were a lot more worried about me than they ought to have been after the arrest because, well, they're straight. I don't have the gay friends who would automatically think, *Oh this has happened to a lot of us.* I didn't have that kind of support, which made me feel for the first time in my life that it was difficult that I didn't grow up among gay people.

You know Elton [John].

Oh, yeah, I know Elton. It's not like I don't have any gay friends. But my closest friends are straight—most of whom are still with me from a time before I was famous. It was difficult because I wanted to explain to them that the arrest wasn't the big deal they thought it was. The women especially don't understand it. I think it's difficult for gay women to understand gay men's sexuality, let alone for straight women.

Men—gay or straight—understand each other better.

Straight men don't find it easy to get quick casual sex with attractive women without paying for it. They normally have to do a lot of groundwork. They are different hunts, but they are still hunts. I've been there with my mates in clubs when we were younger, cruising for women. I know all the stupid games you have to play. I also know the lack of game playing that goes on between gay men. Men have that easy access to meaningless casual sex, which gives them a totally different thrill. I don't think you can explain that to women.

Dare I ask you about monogamy? I mean, remember the video you did for "I Want Your Sex," where you wrote the words EXPLORE MONOGAMY on a woman's back? That probably seems like a lifetime ago to you.

[*Laughing*] It wasn't that long ago. It was around '86 or '87 when I last saw you. And at the time, I believed in it. I still believe in monogamy as an ideal. I'm not saying that I'm perfectly comfortable with my sexuality in terms of my enjoyment of casual sex. And that's coming from someone who really would like to be monogamous—even though I've failed dismally. I don't know whether I'm capable of it anymore.

Well, what do you want?

I'm not good at self-deprivation. I think part of that comes from being spoiled, having been a celebrity for so long and actually being able to make most of my fantasies come true. It's not that I've given up on monogamy, but I've realized what an ideal it is—for most men especially and gay men in particular, where the availability is there and the social pressure is not. Gay men know each other's motivation.

And you didn't feel this with women?

My relationships with men showed me there is no second-guessing. If a man tries to pretend to you that he doesn't have the same urges as you, he's lying. If a woman tells you that, it could be. But the basis of a relationship between a man and a woman is the sense of the unknown. You're constantly trying to work out each other's boundaries simply because there are areas you just don't understand. That is the mystery of straight relationships. It's the downside and the upside.

Why?

Because on one hand, if you're an honest person, you find it very difficult to not say what you feel. So I find that the openness in gay male relationships is great for me in terms of really making things stronger, getting through the bullshit, having problems but working them out. There's very little misunderstanding between myself and my boyfriend.

How did he feel about the arrest?

He wasn't shocked when this happened. I knew I could call him from the police station and get him to come down and pay my bail.

Did it make your relationship stronger?

Yeah, it's definitely made us stronger. But the issue of

monogamy and casual sex had already come up voluntarily on my part. I wanted to be as open as possible with him. See, I can't bull-shit myself. In situations where sometimes men and women have to take a deep breath and cross their fingers—which kind of gets them through it—I can't do that with men. We know each other too well. I'm sure two women know each other as well. You know the way your sexuality works. I really never knew that in terms of my relationships with women. When I watch my straight friends, I see that mystery between them the whole time. That's what glues straight society together.

Do I sense any regrets about not being straight?

It's all a double-edged sword. I don't look at my earlier life or any of my friends and wish that I had been straight. And I don't really think I'm glad I'm gay. I just know that that's the way it is. There are pros and cons to each. I don't believe either would have made me a happier person. I am the person I am, and my sexuality is secondary to that. I don't believe life would have been easier if I had been straight; I just think life is different—but it's every bit as hard.

In terms of your relationship with Kenny, is it all right with you if he isn't monogamous as well?

I'm very pragmatic. I'm not an emotional hypocrite. Once I've acknowledged my own behavior, I have to be able to say it's OK for my partner.

So it's honesty that holds you together?

Absolutely. When I was younger, with every relationship I thought, *Oh, my God, this is the only one. If this one slips through my fingers, I'm going to be a sad and lonely old figure.* But I think having gone through bereavement and recovery and then meet-ing someone else taught me that you can go from that terrible low to that high again. I now know if I cannot have an honest rela-tionship with the person that I'm with, I need to move on to anoth-er relationship with someone who's capable of that or who can take that amount of honesty. Having spent the first half of my life in secrecy, I now find secrecy a very threatening thing. I'm terri-fied of secrets now. If there's something that I feel, I say it. It doesn't matter what happens. I always feel better because I feel we've come closer to the truth.

That's real intimacy.

Exactly. And because of that intimacy, when all this happened, I knew I had someone who would come get me.

Did you call him from jail?

Yes. Poor Kenny. I had to leave a message. He was out work-ing. Can you believe I was stuck in the cell for four hours with a blanket and a copy of the *National Enquirer?*

You must've thought, *Oh, no, this will be all about me next week!*

Yes, and it was! It was! I left Kenny a message that said, "Darling, I'm in big trouble. You're going to have to get me from the police station." He called me back and said, "What did you do, darling?" I said, "Use your imagination." And he said, "DUI?" I said, "Fuck—if only. Think again." He said, "Oh, no!" I said, "Please just come down and get me." But because of the honesty in the relationship, I wasn't terrified about calling him. My imme-diate thought was, *Thank God I have him.*

How long have you been with Kenny?

About 2½ years now.

[*Waving a photo of Kenny in the latest British tabloid*] Where do they get these, darling? [*Kenny, a handsome blond from Texas, enters the room, looks at the photo, laughs, and leaves.*]

It's a nice picture, though. Wonder where they got it.

And then there was a three-year period after Anselmo?

Yes. I was with Anselmo for two years. After that was a total nightmare. It was a difficult time to lose someone—after two years—because I was still really in love with him in such a roman-tic way. It was also difficult because I felt like I waited so long to find him. Not many people wait until they're 27 to actually have that experience. I literally had five or six months of pure joy before I found out he was ill. Then it was all fear—pure fear. I just wish I'd had a bit longer before I had that ripped away.

Do you remember the first time you heard the word *AIDS*?

You know, I was just thinking about that. It was when Andrew and I first did personal appearances, and we'd go to five or six clubs a night. We went to straight clubs and gay clubs. Andrew and I didn't realize how homoerotic our image was. We had leather jackets; we had these cuffed jeans. We just thought it was cool. Andrew was the stylist—ironic that it was the straight one that was doing the styling! We did a benefit when the pro-ducer for Sylvester died. He was one of the first music industry cases. I remember everyone saying, "It's like a cancer thing that started in New York, and people say only gay people die of it." When I remember conversations like that, it makes my blood run cold.

At what point did you think, *My God, this could happen to me!*

Almost immediately.

Did it change your behavior?

Immediately. AIDS helped along my self-discovery. The occa-sional times that I'd invite a man home, I was very careful. There was no way I was having sex without a condom, and there were only certain things I would do. Then it got to the stage where AIDS became common enough that I thought I could no longer with good conscience—condom or not—have sex with a woman if she didn't know that I was bisexual.

Oh, that's interesting.

What's really interesting is that it didn't stop the women. It actually made the women more involved. It was a challenge: *I wasn't really gay; they could change me.* I got that a lot. I had slept with quite a lot of women, especially at the end of my Wham! days, because I was still thinking that maybe I could still be straight. It would make life easier. But suddenly it turned into a time when bisexuality seemed to be the most dangerous form of sexuality—and I suppose it still is—so I felt like the bad guy. I couldn't have it both ways with AIDS around.

AIDS changed what bisexuality meant. It used to be a safer place to be.

And quite cool. You just had more options. But gay and straight people look at me with suspicion when I say, "I'm bisex-ual." They want me to be one way or another. I still have the impression when I'm talking to gay men about my earlier life that they want to believe it was bullshit, that I was always gay.

"Andrew and I didn't realize how homoerotic our image was. We had leather jackets; we had these cuffed jeans. We just thought it was cool. Andrew was the stylist—ironic that it was the straight one that was doing the styling!"

When you were younger and sleeping with men as well as women, did you tell anyone?

I nearly came out when I was 19. My two closest friends at the time were Andrew Ridgeley and his girlfriend, Shirley. I'd been friends with Andrew since I was 11 and friends with Shirley since I was 15. I had come back from a trip to Cyprus on my own, where I'd had a few experiences that, well, opened my eyes to certain things. I had decided I was really bisexual and told them. I told them that I wanted to tell my mom and dad.

How did they react?

It was more shocking to them than I'd expected. The pair of them talked me out of it. I don't mean it was their fault. They were very young as well. But they did make me think just long enough to back out of it, and I often wonder if things would've been very different. I might have slept around a lot then. And nobody knew what was going on in those years. So they might have saved my life in some strange way.

Did you resist coming out back then because of your career?

The only time I ever thought of it in career terms was, yes, when I was with Wham! and at the beginning of *Faith*. I thought, *It would be really difficult to be with a man right now*—because I hadn't made that commitment to be with anyone yet. But sure, there were times when I was thinking, *Is this just because of my career?* But actually, I would say from *Faith* on, I thought it would make no real difference outside of America. Here in America, on the other hand, I've had doors slammed in my face. I still do.

Are you going to write about any of this on your next full studio album?

I don't know. Going through two bereavements one after the other—I just can't write about pain again. Two days after I met Kenny, I found out my mother was sick. I was certain that she was going to die. Having been through that and having reached lower points than I'd ever experienced—and definitely didn't think I'd experience again quickly—I realize the value of the stuff that I do, which is not about my misery. It's about making joy. By the time I come around to doing my next album, hopefully it'll be a lot more upbeat than *Older* was. It has to be triumphant in a sense. I have to write a "Fuck off!" hit record. I think it's very important that when people are outed or out themselves that it's seen to be a positive thing for the future of their lives. Whatever kind of artistic statement I make in writing about this experience has to be a hit. It has to say, "It doesn't matter."

But losing control over your private life did matter to you, didn't it?

Oh, yes, but I'm lucky. I'm a strong person, and I could take it. I could've been the person they wanted me to be. I could've been as closeted as they thought. I could've cut my wrists!

In America we're engaged in a battle to legalize gay marriage. If you could marry your lover, would you?

I have feelings about marriage anyway. I don't understand marriage without children. I understand the need for the ceremony and the need for the legal protections that I think gay couples should have. I do believe that we should be entitled to exactly the same protections. But I don't think I would ever want it for myself.

Do you want to be a parent?

I wanted to when I was 22 or 23. I used to think I'd love to have kids. Looking back on it feels like it might have been a biological trick. Now I have no desire to have children. I see what an incredibly difficult task it is.

I'm surprised you didn't accidentally become a father.

Believe me, there are five or six women—some of whom have taken legal action—who've said that I fathered their children. None of them are telling the truth. They name their children after me; two gave them my full Greek name.

Suppose I had a retro hetero moment and slept with a woman and she became pregnant. I would have no option but to be responsible for the child. Then I'm sure having a child would be just like everything else in life—a complete balance of joy and misery. I know I'm missing good things, but I'm also missing the anxiety. I have an overdeveloped sense of responsibility, so as a parent, I think I would be verging on the neurotic.

But then again, if I had a child, I'd probably think, *It would be terrible if I'd never had children.*

What about Kenny?

No, he doesn't want children, but I know he'd be a fantastic parent. I'll probably get flak for this, but I feel it's much easier to imagine a lesbian couple making a great home for a child. Because of the nature of male relationships, I think that women are better suited to it. Women find it easier to be monogamous as well, which holds the stability of the relationship. I don't know any perfect families, and I don't believe in the textbook dream of a family anyway. If I'm really honest, I think a child would be getting a better chance at a stable family life between two women than even in a straight relationship. But I'm kind of ignorant about this stuff. I don't know enough lesbians. I know only three gay women.

What? You're kidding.

No, I admit it. But I do know enough about the female and male personality to know that if you pick a gay female couple, you have the advantage of not having the games played. You have the nurturing, which is—I don't care what anyone says—more prevalent in women. And you don't have the instability that comes from the sexual lifestyle that gay men have.

If the arrest hadn't happened, would you have eventually come out on your own?

I don't know. But I would've been outed. I knew this day would come. I knew I was going to be [the British tabloid] *The Sun*'s "gay singer" rather than "George Michael."

"Gay and Fat."

[*Laughing*] Yeah. "Gay, Fat..." Oh, "and Gray!" But the advantage is not having to watch what I say anymore or fearing that I'll give them what they want. It was a game with the press, and it wasn't worth the energy. I suppose because of my pride and hatred of the tabloid press, I was kidding myself about the energy it was taking. I thought because I was living my life openly and doing what I wanted with my boyfriend, I wasn't giving the press my energy. But just by allowing so much misconception, I was giving them a lot. I have done interviews in which I said everything but "I am gay." So the truly important thing about doing this interview with you is realizing I don't have to waste that energy anymore, ever again.

It's been over a year since your *Advocate* coming-out interview. What advice would you give to a sexy, talented male pop star who is in the closet?

I don't think that I could offer any solid advice, actually. I don't really know what I would do if I were given the opportunity to start over. I would advise any gay person that being out in the real sense (I mean out with those you love and respect: friends and family) can never happen too soon. On a professional level I would love to give you a PC answer, but I have to say that the truth in today's world is a little less simple than that—at least if you're a British celebrity who happens to be gay. In the U.K.—since my left hand outed me to an audience of millions on that fateful day in 1998—my personal life, or rather my imagined personal life, has rarely been out of the tabloid press.

I am apparently engaged in a ménage à trois with my boyfriend, Kenny, and Geri Halliwell (formerly of the Spice Girls), who will be carrying our child, of course. (No mention of whose sperm the poor thing is getting.) I want to "bed" Tom Cruise, which would be handy, especially since Geri has stolen Kenny from me. The fact is, I am a very private person and I hate to have my life written about with this puerile, gently homophobic snigger. I lived with Kenny very happily out to our loved ones for two years before all this crap started.

Ultimately, though, I suppose I would have to advise a young version of me that these days, celebrity and secrets don't go together. *The bastards will get you in the end, baby.* So don't give them that power. Be proud of who you are and deal with the shit. Oh, and stay away from public conveniences unless you *really* need to pee.

What do you think about the way gay and lesbian Americans are fighting for equal rights—as it compares to gays in England?

There are intrinsic differences between the two situations. First and most important, I think that America is a far more fearful society in general at this point in time, far more afraid of change—and that is holding American gays back in terms of political change. In Europe in general the '90s didn't see the horrific backlash against liberalism that the United States did, and we don't have the religious right to deal with, thank God! I think that many gay people in the States would be genuinely shocked at just how much more progressive Europeans are. The other major problem I think you have here is that your political system is actually too democratic. The fact that Americans vote on every bill and proposition can prolong bigotry indefinitely, especially where it is aimed at minority groups. I don't see how you can change that process at this stage.

For the Brits, it's a different story. The ludicrous stumbling block in our system is the House of Lords, an unelected group of hereditary peers—mostly too old and deaf to even hear any debate clearly—who are as backward-thinking as they come. But when push comes to shove (which it did recently over the age of consent for gay men), our *elected* politicians in the House of Commons have the power to overrule them and normally do when it's obvious that they don't have the support of the public. Gay Brit men of 16 now have the same rights as their female counterparts, and that is something I don't see happening soon in America.

You've often said that the most important way that you want to express yourself is through your music. Talk about your new CD.

I've only just begun the new record, so anything I say about it will probably be completely off the mark by the time it's done. But I can definitely say that I want to make a pop album—something more upbeat than my stuff was in the '90s. That is, as long as nobody else decides to die on me in the next year or so! Or arrest me! Although actually, I would have to say that getting arrested was quite inspirational in a way.

What I mean to say is that my songs are—and always have been—so attached to my day-to-day existence that there was no way I could have made an up-tempo album in the middle of the melodrama I've called my life for the past nine years. The strange thing about it was that even though my life was falling apart in many ways, my career went from strength to strength, even though I was not doing the touring or promotional work that I had done before.

In fact, I'm sure it would surprise most Americans—hell, it surprised me—to know that last year I was the best-selling male artist in the world outside of the States, courtesy of a long-overdue greatest-hits collection. Lots of the singles on it were never on the radio here, but obviously there were quite a few people who were enjoying my misery!

Why did you decide to perform at this awesome Equality Rocks show?

I'm doing it because you, Judy, asked me to. And because you nagged me incessantly!

Seriously, it's because it is quite clearly an inspirational event and because some of the information I have been reading in recent years, particularly with regard to "ex-gays" and "cure centers," just makes my blood boil. When you told me that we could address some of this onstage I was in for sure. I really don't think that much of society, especially in Europe, is aware of the horrific treatment of some gay teenagers here in the States. Never mind gay rights—how about plain old child abuse!

Also, I was very impressed with Garth Brooks's commitment to the show. He's upsetting some of his core audience for something that he believes in, and that is admirable. Let's be honest, it's people like Garth's audience that we are trying to reach. If we preach only to the converted, then the show is just a celebration—which is cool in itself of course, but it would be great if it were to become something more than that, something with influence.

Apart from all of that, it's a great way to say thank you to my American gay audience because they have continued to dance and sing to the music I make in a way that straight Americans haven't. And I am grateful to them for that. I am very happy that I have a loyal, if smaller, following here, and an event like Equality Rocks allows me to make contact with them. But wait a minute! You're not going to turn away straight women, are you? Look, I need all the help I can get!

George Michael

Melis

The story of Melissa Etheridge

and *The Advocate* is a long one by now. It started in 1993 with an interview she did with Barry Walters in which she ducked questions about her sexuality and refused to come out. The experience made her so ill that she decided she couldn't hide anymore and a year or so later I caught up with her in Amsterdam, where she and then-girlfriend Julie Cypher spilled almost every bean they had. Melissa had already officially come out during the Triangle Ball during President Clinton's inauguration, but this interview marked the first time she dropped her guard completely. In fact, I later learned that she and Julie were somewhat taken aback by both themselves and the magazine when they first saw their cover-story interview in print.

"Oh, I knew you were going to go for the 'dangerous lesbians' angle," Melissa confided to me a year later when we were in London for our second interview. "But we were surprised to see that everything we'd said was actually there in print. Julie had never done anything like that before with the press, and she's a more private person." *Then it was a good thing we didn't use the photo of Julie naked with Melissa from our Greg Gorman cover shoot*, I thought to myself. It was this *Advocate* cover shoot that later evolved into Gorman's famous nude poster of Etheridge and Cypher for the People for the Ethical Treatment of Animals' campaign "We'd rather go naked than wear fur."

Over the years Melissa has been a constant friend to me and to the magazine. When I first arrived at *The Advocate* in 1993, there were not a lot of lesbians working on the publication, nor were there many on its pages or covers. Yes, k.d. lang had come out in an *Advocate* interview the year before and Amanda Bearse did a cover story in fall '93 after having been outed by the tabloids. Later, Chastity Bono and Janis Ian also both did riveting cover-story interviews with us. But Melissa Etheridge was historic. Her courageous, forthcoming interviews helped the magazine begin to live up to its tagline "The National Gay *and Lesbian* Newsmagazine." Suddenly, women readers began to trust us. Suddenly, other lesbian celebrities in all fields said yes to *Advocate* interviews. Melissa's upbeat career story—basically that she had come out and done better than ever in album and ticket sales—made her a guiding light for other celebrities who were understandably concerned about losing fans if they spoke openly about their personal lives.

In addition to the many full-throated *Advocate* interviews Melissa has done over the years—including those with revelations about her life-changing journey into motherhood and eventual breakup from partner Julie Cypher—Melissa has also lent her presence to Advocate covers that cried out for a visible lesbian to represent important civil rights issues. Most notably was the cover shoot Melissa did with Julie, Mitchell Anderson, and his partner, Richie Arpeno, representing gay marriage and the battle against California's 2000 anti–gay-marriage initiative. For this cover shoot the stylist took out a white wedding dress and showed it to Melissa. Melissa in a dress? In a wedding dress? I thought she would balk or at least pull me aside to beg off for her. Instead she laughed and with remarkable open-mindedness, said, "Sure! Why not? Let's try it."

The sound of Melissa saying yes is usually the sound of the curtain going up on an ambitious and inspiring project. When *The Advocate* produced a special commemorative issue—not one of our regular biweekly newsmagazines—celebrating the Millennium March on Washington, we knew we wanted both a gay man and a lesbian celebrity for the cover. Once we had Melissa aboard, the challenge was to find a gay man of equal stature. After a series of brainstorming sessions, we landed on George Michael. While Melissa is likely to say yes, George is more apt to say no. And initially he did. After weeks of back-and-forth, somehow, some way, he agreed to do it. But I knew the real challenge would be the photo session itself. And for that task I would need Melissa's upbeat, warm, engulfing energy. Over the course of five hours she gave it to me, George, and the magazine without hesitation. When photographer Blake Little's camera began recording the historic event, our hearts stopped and started again. They were magnificent together. No two out gay pop stars of their level of success had ever been photographed like this before. And it could never have happened without Melissa—both in the photo and behind the scenes.

I believe Melissa's ability to say yes to the unknown has made her an exceptional star. While she has all the concerns any sane celebrity has about her personal and public life, she also has the ability to take risks without driving everyone around her insane in the process. Once she has agreed to do something, you don't have to worry that she will bail on you because someone with less courage has tried to convince her otherwise. Her words mean something. That's why the following two vintage Melissa Etheridge *Advocate* interviews remain such fascinating reading. When you speak from the heart about anything, the sentiment always remains true. People and circumstances may change—that's life. But if you are telling your truth, the essence of your spirit will remain consistent. Melissa is a testament to this.

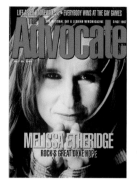

A bra hits Melissa Etheridge in the face. A pair of ladies' undies narrowly misses the neck of her guitar. "Stop it!" she tells a Rotterdam stadium full of 11,000 swooning, fainting Dutch rock fans. "Stop it. You're scaring me, and you're going to need

these things later when you go dancing."

Blatantly ignoring her, a young woman climbs on the shoulders of another woman and holds up a handmade sign that says, in English, LET'S GET IT ON! Clearly, Dorothy isn't in Kansas anymore—though she hasn't forgotten being there.

Born 33 years ago in Leavenworth, Kan., the electrifying Etheridge has been packing European sports arenas and massive concert venues like London's Royal Albert Hall as she prepares for her American headlining tour—as well as for several highly touted gigs with legendary '70s rockers the Eagles and a prestigious appearance at Woodstock '94, the 25th anniversary celebration. Etheridge's passionate and unpredictably sexual live shows coupled with four platinum albums, four Grammy nominations, and one win for her 1993 single "Ain't It Heavy" have catapulted her to the kind of worldwide popularity no female rocker has ever before achieved.

And with all this going for her, the tiny woman with the big, tattered, bluesy voice rolled the dice nearly two years ago (while celebrating President Clinton's inauguration at the Triangle Ball) and came out. "I always intended to do it," Etheridge says, "but I didn't know when or where. I just couldn't dodge it anymore. I felt like I was lying, and my music is so much about the truth."

Etheridge's personal growth is almost as fascinating as her blistering rise to stardom. She fell in love with her best girlfriend at 17, and the two carried on a secret love affair for years. Like a tornado out of Kansas, she soon fled to Boston's Berklee College of Music; the school didn't take, but the community did. "I met all these gay women," she recalls. "I wasn't alone. There were people just like me."

Returning to Leavenworth just long enough to come out to her father (Etheridge didn't become close to her mother until she was 24), she moved to Long Beach, Calif., where she began playing in local lesbian bars. In a fortuitous move that resulted in the securing of a manager at this early stage in her career, Etheridge passed a tape of her songs to a gay woman she'd met in the bars who played on a softball team with a straight woman married to manager William Leopold.

What followed was truly unprecedented in show business: After taking her on, Leopold (who managed the rock band Bread) refused to hide Etheridge's lesbianism. Instead of making her perform before straight rock audiences who didn't know her, Leopold brought executives from mainstream record labels to see his client where she was the most popular: lesbian bars. Several execs showed interest, but it was Island Records founder and CEO Chris Blackwell who walked into Long Beach's Que Sera bar in 1986 and signed her on the spot.

Although Etheridge was originally discovered in a lesbian setting, her appeal is definitely universal. Men and women—both gay and straight—respond to her intense talent and sexual charisma with unabashed enthusiasm. "Frankly, I'd consider it a compliment to be linked romantically with Melissa Etheridge," says actress and friend Laura Dern about the rock star's "honest and sensuous sexuality. She's got that lusty man/woman sound in her voice that I love and respond to on a raw level."

"I want to be the biggest, most sexual star ever," the rocker says. If Etheridge's record-breaking live shows are any indication, she's well on her way.

The following interview with Etheridge and her girlfriend, filmmaker Julie Cypher, took place in three locations: the American Hotel in Amsterdam, Etheridge's tour bus, and backstage at Rotterdam's Ahoy Stadium.

What was your biggest fear about coming out?

You think there's some big black hole you're going to fall into and that all of a sudden people who have loved you all your life aren't going to love you anymore. And I'm here to tell you that *that* does not happen. If it did change anyone's mind about me, then that's their problem—and they weren't there for me to begin with.

And this fear extends professionally as well?

Well, to put it in record business terms, my exact fear was that I had been embraced by rock radio—which was unheard-of for a woman of any sexual orientation. So just as a woman, I was already breaking ground. I was dealing with that and thinking, *OK, if I come out, how many stations are going to drop me?* It's another version of the same fear: being dropped, being abandoned.

But you had k.d. lang as a successful model for coming out.

Sure. But k.d., in my eyes, is a personality, an unusual chanteuse kind of androgynous something else. I have always been the working woman's singer. I come from the Midwest. Mine is heartland music. My audiences are very mixed. So I worried, *If I come out, will it make me strange?*

But don't you think people were already picking up something from your songs?

I write from a genderless place. I don't think I will ever write or sing "I love *her*." I like that my music reaches not just gay but straight fans—men and women both.

But wouldn't you like to write a song that expresses your love for Julie, where you would actually use her name?

There could be a song that I'd write about Julie saying how much she means to me. Maybe not the next album but maybe after that—when the dust kind of settles.

What dust?

The dust is still settling about my coming out.

What was the weirdest thing that happened after you came out?

Etheridge: Journalists! There were all these journalists who would come out to me. They're not out, but they felt like they could tell me.

Cypher: It's so sad because they're stuck in the closets of their little daily papers, and along comes Melissa talking openly about being gay.

Has your fan mail changed much since you came out?

Etheridge: I was getting a lot of lesbian mail anyway.

Do you get hate mail?

Etheridge: I've gotten letters from crazy people saying that I'm the devil and that they're going to shoot me—but that happened before I came out!

Have you had unstable people interested in you since coming out?

Etheridge: I've hired private policemen to watch over me if there's a crazy person in some town looking for me.

What part did Julie play in your coming out?

Etheridge: She was very, very supportive. We always knew that if I came out, she'd be coming out. See, she came from a straight…well, you know the story.

Well, I'd rather hear this story directly from you, Julie.

Cypher: Well, I was straight. I was married to Lou Diamond Phillips. I'm originally from Texas, and he and I met there. I'd known lesbians as friends in college, but I'd never met a woman that I was attracted to, so lesbianism had never occurred to me—until I met Melissa. Then it occurred very strongly.

You were working on her video when you met?

Cypher: I was working as an assistant director on her video "Bring Me Some Water." There was a very long two-year crazy period where we were both circling in our own relationships, trying to figure out what we were going to do. Then we came together.

What was that like for you with no other lesbian experiences?

Cypher: I think after growing up straight in Texas, when all of a sudden I found myself in a relationship with a woman, I didn't see any reason why there should be a difference. Why is my relationship with this woman any different from my relationship with a man? So when she was ready to do it publicly, I was completely ready to support her in that. I was already out to my family and in my professional arena. I was just waiting.

Do you now consider yourself a lesbian?

Cypher: I absolutely do.

Were you having difficulties with your marriage to Lou Diamond Phillips before Melissa entered the picture?

Cypher: The marriage was a troubled one. Lou and I were really young, and Hollywood's a big place when you've just come from Texas. We thought, *Well, we'll just get married, and we'll have each other no matter what.* And then our paths started spinning in different directions, and it was a long and cold separation and ultimately a divorce. But because we took so much time doing it, we're friends. He's remarried and actually lives down the street from our new house. He's also in my first feature film, *Teresa's Tattoo.*

Did he have a problem with your leaving him for a woman?

Cypher: It certainly wasn't something he expected, but I don't think it threw him for too much of a loop because he's a very open and loving person. When he met Melissa he realized what a wonderful person she is. He could see how the two of us clicked so well.

How long did the whole process—your and Melissa's leaving your relationships and finally getting together—take?

Etheridge: We met in '88, and we finally were officially together by January of '90.

Cypher: But I didn't get a divorce until '92.

Were you frightened to become involved with a woman who hadn't previously explored her gayness?

Etheridge: I wasn't so worried about her straightness. She's the perfect example of people being attracted to each other's souls—whether male or female. So I wasn't worried that I was just an "experiment." Of course, there were some different lifestyle things she had to adjust to.

Cypher: Like my first rock music festival. Whew! [*Laughs*] Believe me, it's harder to be in love with a musician than with a lesbian—that's the real bottom line.

What do you think you would do romantically if Melissa were no longer with you? Would you be with a man again?

Cypher: I doubt it. I would look for the person, for the soul, but I just feel that the female psyche is where I find my satisfaction with relationships.

Melissa, because k.d. came out first, did anybody ever say to you, "Oh, well, sure, now you're jumping on the bandwagon"?

Cypher: I don't think she was ever accused of jumping on the bandwagon because she admitted right off to jumping on the bandwagon.

Etheridge: I think k.d. was their first lesbian. I'm their "other" lesbian.

Cypher: She's the vice president of lesbians.

Etheridge: I'm the Al Gore of lesbians. k.d. is a friend of mine, and I remember talking to her when she was thinking about coming out. I said, "Go for it. It'll be great!" And she did. And I said to myself, *Hey, why don't I listen to what I'm saying?* Helping her come out helped me to come out.

The music trade magazine *Billboard* called you the "second Top 40 lesbian."

Etheridge: Who ever thought we'd live to see it? I really want to be a positive role model—I hate that expression—to Midwestern people. I'm not some crazy girl. I'm just like you.

Which is the scariest thing you can tell people.

Etheridge: I know. I could be anybody, even you. I don't look strange. I'm not avant-garde.

Did you ever date men?

Etheridge: I was 16 years old the last time I dated a man. I dated my first woman when I was 17.

So you were never in an intimate relationship with a man?

Etheridge: I had a few crushes but nothing I wanted to do anything about. I appreciate—

Cypher: Sting?

Etheridge: Oh, *there's* a crush! I opened a few shows for him.

Sting? Oh, well, we've all had that crush—jeez.

Etheridge: I know. I know. He'd brought me up to sing "Every Breath You Take." And it was his first encore, so he'd taken off his shirt. He's so beautiful. I just wanted to touch him.

Cypher: And you did.

Etheridge: Yes, I did, a couple of times. I appreciate beauty in all its forms—male and female, all energies. But as far as relationships go or really falling in love, I've been attracted only to women.

So when you think of yourself, do you think of your sexuality as a choice—do you think you were born that way? Was it an environmental thing or an interaction of everything?

Etheridge: I think I was born that way, and I think my environment made it even more possible for me to be who I am.

What was in your environment?

Etheridge: My relationship with my mother. It was strained as a child, and I think that adds to my attraction to women. It's about what I didn't get as a child—that female energy I crave. But I think I had to be born that way first.

Did you ever feel strange?

Etheridge: No, I've never felt strange. I felt that the world had to catch up with me. I still feel society and culture have a lot of catching up to do. Being lesbian is very normal and natural to me.

Do you know any closeted gay celebrities who are afraid to hang out with you now because you're out and someone might say that they're gay too?

Etheridge: Yes. We had that once.

Cypher: Guilt by association, yes. But we won't name them. We won't do that to anybody.

Etheridge: For one thing, I don't hang around with people like that. Julie, do you think it's OK for me to mention…?

Cypher: What?

Etheridge: Brad Pitt! He's been a good friend for years. He's just the most amazing person, and he's a huge fan of mine. He actually came to my London show last week, and we flew here to Amsterdam together. I had a night off, so the three of us went out. But I did have this one thought: I wondered if he ever wonders that by hanging out with us that it makes him look gay.

Cypher: That thought would never occur to him.

Etheridge: Yeah, he doesn't think like that. He's very pure, and he's very secure with who he is. Everybody is attracted to him—men and women.

Cypher: I think you have a little crush on him.

Etheridge: I want to be just like him. I want to attract all kinds of sexual energy to me—straight, gay, men, women.

Cypher: It's working, honey.

Etheridge: I went to see a Bette Midler concert with Laura Dern. [*To Cypher*] You were working. And I thought, *This is very cool. Laura and I just hangin'.*

Nobody tried to link the two of you romantically?

Etheridge: No, but I've been linked to Martina.

Cypher: Oh, Martina! Well, you know, all the famous lesbians sleep with her.

Etheridge: Because there's only six anyway.

Cypher: And we've pretty much hit every combination.

Etheridge: Actually, the only combination I've never seen is me and k.d.

Cypher: Are you sure?

Etheridge: I'm positive. I've never seen anywhere that k.d. and I have been together.

What have you seen?

Etheridge: I've read that Martina was going out with k.d., and then she dropped k.d. for me.

Cypher: Yeah. "The Canadian singer k.d. lang and the petite rocker Melissa. Insiders say that they go for long hikes in the mountains."

And how do you like stuff like that, Julie?

Cypher: It cracks me up. You know, they say, "There's Martina blowing kisses to Melissa in the stands." Well, I was there too. How did they know that those kisses weren't directed at me?

Etheridge: And Martina says she just wishes she was having half the fun they say she has.

Cypher: It's like whenever anyone comes out, they've automatically slept with Martina.

Melissa, your parents were the children of alcoholics. Why is that significant?

Etheridge: There comes a point in your adulthood when you separate yourself from your past and look at your parents as people. I looked at them, and I saw children of alcoholics—terrible alcoholics. They did not have a drinking problem, but they lived with that, and the emotional stigma was still passed down.

And do you feel it too?

Etheridge: I used to never drink at all. I never was addicted to drugs or alcohol. But I was very scared of it. I've now learned that moderation is the key to life.

Your father died recently. Did that change you?

Etheridge: Yes. I was very close to him, and I actually saw him die. It's an amazing experience. Suddenly I was parenting him. It's a cycle.

Did you discover anything about yourself as a result of his illness and dying?

Etheridge: I believe that his illness was brought on by his difficult childhood. He kept his anger about his alcoholic parents inside himself. His anger turned to cancer. The body can only hold that stress in for so long before it becomes something else.

And what has that to do with you?

Etheridge: I don't want that to happen to me. I want to resolve that anger inside me.

Cypher: Yeah, and sometimes it gets crazy because I'm stomping my foot going, "Doesn't that make you angry?" And Melissa's saying, "Well, it is unfortunate." I'm screaming "No, Melissa, it's not unfortunate. It's maddening!"

Etheridge: We balance each other out that way.

You've had a lot of girlfriends. Why is your relationship with Julie working?

Etheridge: I met Julie the second night of my first American tour. She's always known that although I may come and go physically, emotionally I'm always there. We have to be able to commu-

"I don't respond to groupies. I think that if I did respond to that, it would get out immediately, and I would have a big groupie situation on my hands. It's not something I want now. Ten years ago it might have been a whole different story."

nicate and relate to each other on the phone and have it really count. The relationship that I was having before I met Julie suffered from my sudden stardom. I had been physically there in the relationship for two years, and then suddenly I was gone out on the road. But it wasn't the right relationship anyway. Julie is the right relationship.

How do you both think you are handling the emotional part of your relationship?
Etheridge: Not very well.
Cypher: Oh, very well.
Etheridge: It's a lot of work. What's this "happily ever after" thing? They don't tell you that you have to work at it every day.

If you had to give up something...
Etheridge: I'd do anything for her. If I had to choose, the career would be the thing I'd give up. We've worked out the dynamics. She knows what the relationship means to me, and she comes out on the road whenever she can.

Do you both want children?
Etheridge and Cypher: Yes.

What are you going to do about it?
Cypher: What do you mean "do about it"? [*Laughs*] Which part? It's such an important thing.

Would both of you get pregnant?
Etheridge: Yes.
Cypher: By a donor that we both knew. You see, I'm adopted, and I didn't know where I came from until I was 24, so I feel that it's important for the child to know who its biological parents are. So there'll be two mommies and Uncle Fred or Daddy whoever.

When do you want to do this?
Cypher: I keep saying after I make two more movies.
Etheridge: It's tough for me. I always try to visualize my lifestyle professionally. Having a child would mean I would have to be ready to take a lot of time off—which I can't do now. I'd wait until there wasn't such a demand on my time.

What if that doesn't happen?
Etheridge: I know. It might just be Julie who gets pregnant.

So the ideal plan is that you would each have a child?
Etheridge: Yes. But she wants about seven.
Cypher: No, I want 20!

What about adopting?
Cypher: That's certainly an option, but I'd rather have the experience myself.

Why do you want to have children at all?
Etheridge: Because I think the world needs the children of gay parents.

To show people what?
Etheridge: I think one of the many fears that people have about homosexuality is around children. They think that we're horrible to children—that we shouldn't be teachers and parents, that there's some horror going on. I think that the more gay parents raise good, strong, compassionate people, the better the world will be.

Do you want boys or girls?
Cypher: It doesn't matter.

What if the child is gay?
Etheridge: I'll tell them it's hard but great! What else can we say?
Cypher: We'd be more concerned if they wanted to be musicians than if they were gay.
Etheridge: Hey! Watch it!
Cypher: No, it is harder to be a musician than it is to be gay.

Melissa, do you think that, as a woman in rock, you've been more readily embraced than other female rockers because you're a lesbian and therefore that supposedly makes you "tougher, harder, and rougher" in the minds of hard-core rock fans?
Etheridge: Wow! I actually had a discussion with a Dutch rock journalist, and he made that point. He was saying that rock and roll was a male energy. And I said, "Well, I'm female, and I'm in rock and roll totally." And he said, "Yes, but you're a lesbian"—meaning that it's still that yin-yang thing. So I guess that until a straight female rock artist makes it, it can't be proved that it's not male energy that drives rock. But I *am* a woman, period.

Why don't you have any women in your band?
Etheridge: I did. Last year I had a woman on keyboards for a good portion of the tour. I held auditions, I listened to women, and I chose the musicians who played my music the best—and the ones I could live with as people on the road. But I saw lots of women, and I felt like these guys played better.

Have lesbians ever given you trouble for not being more politically correct in your music and live performances?
Etheridge: I played the women's bars. And it was a very hard-edged crowd that came to see me. But when I played the music festivals where the other part of the women's community was, I remember doing a monologue once where I talked about being with a girl and having her leave me and what I went through—gaining 10 pounds and stuff like that. Well, after the concert I literally had to hold off all these women who were saying that the songs I sang were all about abuse and that the comment I had made about being 10 pounds overweight was terrible and that they were going to come and string me up. It was my first PC call,

you know. I realized, *Oh, there's so many things I have to be aware of.*

Cypher: Melissa's sexy stuff often collides with being PC. She really runs it down!

Etheridge: Yeah, I was left there saying "What? What did I do? It was always fun in the bars." Sometimes it's hard to be a lesbian.

How did you get chosen to open several of the Eagles' tour dates this summer?

Etheridge: It was good for them and good for me. I think I'm a new rock step. Even though they didn't need help selling tickets, I think they wanted to kind of marry themselves to some cool, some hipness.

Tell me something about groupies.

Etheridge: Oh, no!

Cypher: You mean fans?

In a way, but I'm talking about fans who offer sexual favors to rock stars. It happens all the time with heterosexual male rock stars.

Cypher: Like an entourage?

No, I'm talking about girls who come back to the bus and literally wait in line to sleep with the rock stars.

Cypher: Oh, my! That's gross. Melissa, has that ever happened to you?

Etheridge: Well, there are people waiting around the bus, and sometimes there is that energy. I have never chosen to go with it.

So are you saying that the women waiting for you after your shows are not offering you sex?

Cypher: She's not saying it's not being offered. She's saying she deflects it.

Etheridge: But is it being offered? Yes, it is. Sometimes the guys offer it too. I get a lot of notes saying "Please call me. I want you."

From women as well?

Cypher: Mostly women.

Etheridge: But I don't respond to any of it. I think that if I did respond to that, it would get out immediately, and I would have a big groupie situation on my hands. It's not something I want now. Ten years ago it might have been a whole different story.

I've certainly seen them throw their undies and bras at you when you're performing.

Etheridge: Yes, and last night during the gig in Amsterdam, there's a part of my show where I ask everyone in the audience to "get lower with me," and they all crouch down. Well, I looked up, and the women who had pushed to the front of the stage had taken off their clothes. They were all reaching out to me…naked!

Cypher: Last night?

Etheridge: [*Laughs*] Yes! But it's a very sexual show. And there's a lot of people who hang around the bus afterward wondering if it will go any further.

But I wonder if quick, hot sex between women would really work in the back of the bus.

Etheridge and Cypher: [*Pointing to their bed in the bus and laughing*] Yes, it does.

Cypher: Men like to fuck. Women like to have relationships.

Etheridge: Oh, come now!

Cypher: Well, women in their 30s anyway.

Etheridge: Yeah, right. I had a lot when I was younger. When I was playing in the bars, I was very promiscuous in my early 20s. It was all these one-nighters and that sort of thing.

Sex, drugs, and rock and roll?

Etheridge: Yes, sex was part of it in the beginning. I have since grown out of that. I have grown up.

What about safe sex? I assume you're both monogamous, right?

Etheridge: Yes, please assume that.

So noted. Have you both had HIV antibody tests?

Etheridge: I've had a couple of tests for insurance purposes. I think I got my first one four years ago.

When you and Julie got together, was it important for you to share that information with each other before you got sexually involved?

Etheridge: Yeah. We talked about it

Cypher: And she talked about her past. She'd come from multiple partners, and I'd come from a relationship with one guy.

Do you like the word *lesbian*?

Etheridge: I'm liking it more and more. I totally could not stand it before. I had less trouble accepting myself than I did that word. Sometimes I wish it had been any other island but Lesbos. We could have been called "Mauians" from the island of Maui.

Cypher: Lesbian sounds like *lizard*.

You've been quoted as saying you're the woman who wants to do it all. Are you going to act in a movie? Do you want to have a sitcom called *The Melissa Etheridge Comedy Hour*?

Etheridge: No, I'll skip television, but I would like to act in films. I want to play Janis Joplin.

I imagine that with Julie being a filmmaker, there could be some real opportunities for you.

Etheridge: Oh, I don't want to take advantage of—

Cypher: Sleeping with the director? I think you should. She'd do a good Joplin. She's the only person who should play it, but that could be 10 years away.

Why wait that long?

Cypher: There's a big battle being fought between Hollywood and the people who own the rights to Joplin's story.

Etheridge: I think it better be resolved pretty soon or else I'm gonna have to play a really old Joplin. She was only 27.

Is it difficult being a couple and having two entertainment careers to deal with?

Etheridge and Cypher: Yes.

Etheridge: Her career is definitely up and down. She gets rejections, and you know, I'm patting her, healing her, and then—oh, something happens that I didn't get. It's like, "OK, Julie, can I have some time now?" So, yes, it is hard because there are two very competitive, seriously creative people here. It's fucking hard.

Cypher: There was a period before I got my first movie made— *Teresa's Tattoo*—where it was so hard for me to be with Melissa because she was doing exactly what she wanted to do professionally. I was just hanging on, tagging along with no purpose in my life. Now that the film is finished and I have this sense of accomplishment, it's much easier for me to tag along, to be on the bus.

Etheridge: When she was making her first movie, I was making my last album, saying, "Where are you? You're usually in the studio listening to me." Suddenly I had to play wife; I had to feed the dog every day.

Cypher: She played a really good wife, though.

What do you think your image as a lesbian couple represents to other lesbians?

Cypher: Oh, God. We're not perceived as having problems at all. But we do have problems. We read in a *Rolling Stone* interview with Rose Troche, who directed *Go Fish*, that she said something like "Look at k.d. lang. Isn't she great? And then there's Melissa and her girlfriend. Aren't they cute? Aren't they nice? I think lesbians should be perceived as more dangerous."

Etheridge: We are dangerous!

Cypher: No, we're perceived as too wholesome and too cute.

Etheridge: So we were thinking maybe we should take you shoplifting or something just to prove that we're dangerous.

What would you dangerous lesbians like to see in a lesbian sex survey?

Etheridge: That's such a male concept. Like, "How do girls do it?"

Cypher: There are so many ways. We're quite resourceful.

Etheridge: We have so much variety in our sex, so it's always "What fruit do we pick tonight?" It's like our little lesbian secret. I think the sex that women have together is magical.

Are you pierced or tattooed anywhere?

Etheridge: No. Well, I've had my ears pierced.

Oh, dangerous one!

Cypher: We thought about tattoos. But we haven't yet.

Etheridge: Wait! Let's get dangerous here. I'm going to say, "Yes, I'm pierced and tattooed, but I'm not telling you where."

Cypher: Yes, let's answer everything dangerously.

Etheridge: OK. Yes, I do have groupies. In fact, we both see them. We bring them on the bus with us and take them from town to town.

If you had to live without love or sex, which would you choose not to have?

Cypher: Oh, please! So few women can distinguish between the two.

Etheridge: Well, I'm going to say love because—

Cypher: You'd rather live without love?

Etheridge: No! I mean…oh, without?

Cypher: Well, we could have sex and then pretend we don't love each other.

No, Julie, you're not allowed to lie or negotiate.

Etheridge: Then it would have to be sex that we'd live without. What a horrible choice.

Cypher: We could probably still masturbate to have sex, right?

She's still negotiating. Never mind. Have you ever been verbally assaulted for being gay?

Etheridge: I've played in gay bars, and people would throw eggs in the windows.

Cypher: Really?

Etheridge: Yeah, I've been walking down the street with another woman, and someone yelled "Fags!" I was like, "Hello? At least get it right, guys."

Have you ever paid for sex, or have you ever been paid for sex?

Etheridge: No, just paid for writing about it.

Have you ever done anything that you thought might be really unsafe?

Cypher: I thought it was unsafe of Melissa to go shopping by herself in New Orleans.

Etheridge: I'm not afraid of heights, but just two days ago I played Albert Hall in London, and the building manager took us up to the roof. There was this chain-link fence you can stand on and look down into the middle of the Royal Albert Hall. Julie said, "Yeah, cool." But I held on to the edge going "A-a-ah."

But someone else would have been horrified to perform in Albert Hall.

Cypher: Exactly. I had to go onstage once and do a guitar change for Melissa. I wanted to feel the kind of shit that she likes to play with every night onstage. Oh, my God! It freaked me out.

Would you say that coming out is enriching—in spirituality, in love, in purpose, in career, in finances?

Etheridge: Yes, it certainly is. And it has been for me. *Yes I Am,* the album that came out after I did, is my most successful album so far; my work has been more successful than it ever was before—my tours, everything. On a spiritual level I believe that confronting the fear of coming out loosened up and freed all other aspects in my life. I just think that when you do that for yourself, when you stand up and say "This is what I am," then good things come to you. I believe that, and I am totally an example of that.

I read that you bought a $1.3 million house.

Cypher: Oh, that's a fucking lie.

Really? Let me read this article to you. It says you bought a "Hollywood Hills home for $1.3 million, which was owned by Edward R. Pressman, who coproduced *Hoffa* and Brandon Lee's *The Crow*. It's a four-bedroom, 3,000 square-foot hacienda-style house originally built in 1933."

Cypher: Do I get to stay? That shit was released by Pressman's publicist because *The Crow* was coming out and he wanted publicity. We didn't want anyone to know where we lived. Also *The Crow* is an object of consternation with us because Brandon Lee was a friend. Brandon's fiancée does not like it either. By the way, the price of the house isn't even right.

What was the price?

Cypher: Less than that.

What kind of car do you drive?

Etheridge: I just gave up my incredible Jaguar XJS because my lease was up, and—

Cypher: I hated it.

Etheridge: It was my dream car. I drove it 140 miles an hour. We also have a Jeep Grand Cherokee.

Cypher: We have three cars left. I have my original '69 VW Bug, which Melissa hates, and we have a '64 Ford Falcon convertible, which we're trying to sell. Oh! Maybe we should try to sell it in *The Advocate.*

Etheridge: We could lie and say we had sex in in it. [*Pauses*] Wait a minute. We did have sex in it.

Cypher: Dangerous sex!

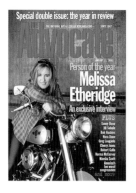

Special double issue: the year in review

"Yes, I know why you made me *The Advocate*'s Person of the Year," says Melissa Etheridge, sitting in the back of her tour bus as it rushes her from one promotional stop to another on the rain-drenched streets of London. "I'm sort of a gay success story, a

very inspirational one. What happened to me is exactly the opposite of what closeted people fear: They think they'll lose everything if they come out. This did not happen to me at all. In fact, everything came back tenfold."

What's more, Etheridge is still counting. Since her now-historic coming-out during President Clinton's inauguration celebration, the Grammy-winning singer has watched herself sell 5 million copies of her 1993 album, *Yes I Am,* duet with Bruce Springsteen on her VH1 special, *Unplugged,* play before thousands at Woodstock '94, grace the cover of *Rolling Stone* magazine, meet the president and—with her lover of seven years, Julie Cypher—become half of a sensuous poster couple for lesbians. What's more, she says these are only a few of the wondrous events she never saw coming when she spontaneously stood up and spoke the simple words "All my life I've been proud to be a lesbian" at the Triangle Ball in Washington, D.C., three years ago.

Person of the Year—and the emphasis here is on the word person—is the perfect award for the likable Etheridge. While her heartland rock music is predictably popular with the masses (her fifth album, *Your Little Secret,* debuted at number 6 on the *Billboard* charts in late 1995), it is Etheridge's exhilarating humanness that ultimately sets her apart. Whether she's worrying over a fan's misunderstanding something she's said or making sure that a band member gets just the right homeopathic treatment for the onset of a cold, Etheridge really is a nice person. Even after the high-velocity, pressure-infused year she just wrapped, her well-behaved Kansas roots prevail. "Well, you get what you give," she says simply, referring to something her late father taught her. What's truly revolutionary is that she still lives by his lessons.

"It's great to see a strong woman in charge of her career," says singer-songwriter Joan Armatrading, whose own career was visibly boosted when Etheridge recorded her song "The Weakness in Me" in 1995. Clearly inspired by the out lesbian rocker's unstoppable rise to stardom, Armatrading concedes, "Melissa knows what she's doing!"

Another friend agrees. "Melissa's career completely took off when she came out," says tennis champ Martina Navratilova. "And you can't say it was a coincidence. I think she's better at doing what she does because she's so out. It's such a freeing experience, not only to be out but to be vocal about it. You can hear it in her voice when she sings."

Many have heard the call to freedom in Etheridge's raucous vocals. From the lesbian bars in Long Beach, Calif., where she was signed in 1986, to the last rows of Madison Square Garden and the Royal Albert Hall, her leather lungs have roped in fans as diverse as actress Juliette Lewis ("Melissa sings like we all dream of singing") and Janis Ian ("The first time I saw Melissa perform at the Bluebird Cafe, I said, 'I have just seen the first female stadium act.' ")—to say nothing of Sting, Brad Pitt, and of course, Springsteen.

"Melissa's one of the leading women in rock because she exudes such pure, unadulterated honesty," says David Geffen, whose various record labels have handled such mighty rock acts as Aerosmith, Nirvana, and Guns N' Roses. "She's a first-class rocker with a huge heart. She's as honest about her personal life as she is about her music. How can you not relate to sincerity?"

For Etheridge, honesty really is her guide. "I believe when you're truthful and you put that out to others, there's a spiritual karma that rewards you," she says. "You clean yourself out to make room for other things."

Are you amazed at how the world embraced you this past year?

I've been learning all along this journey that the things we fear are so much bigger in our heads than in reality. Yeah, there's a noisy conservative far right, but they're not a majority. The majority of people—because I've been around the world and seen it—are good people who are not bringing down hellfire and damnation on anyone for loving someone. Besides, I think I'm really very nonthreatening.

Women in rock aren't exactly nonthreatening.

I'm not Courtney Love. I'm not spouting controversial things. I don't dress different. I'm not piercing myself anywhere—all those things that are considered on the edge. I have blondish-brown hair; I'm 34; I could be the girl next door.

The gay girl next door!

Yes. The people who have always felt that they didn't know anyone gay all look at me and think, *Well, I could know someone who is gay; she looks like 10 people on my block.*

k.d. is out too, but she hasn't walked hand in hand with somebody into the Grammy awards.

But I'm in a solid relationship and feel secure in it. I'm no longer in that single, sort-of predator stage. It's very much "This is who I am. This is who I'm with. This is our life, and this is how it is."

Why hasn't your success been more comforting to people who are considering coming out? As you know from your celebrity friends, your success has not brought them out of the closet.

Coming out is such a personal thing. So much personal baggage and issues go on behind it. Maybe if I hadn't had such a good experience with my family, perhaps I would not have had as much confidence when it came to coming out to the world.

So it's really about earlier coming-out experiences?

Yes. Some of my friends won't talk about their personal lives—at all. There are questions that they have about their lives; they

Melissa Etheridge

might be in tumultuous relationships that aren't working out. Turning the media light on a personal life is frightening!

You would know.

Yes, it's a huge light. If you are thinking, *I don't know if this person really loves me or if we're going to stay together,* or if you're wondering, *Am I happy?* you don't want to shine that light on such a fragile situation.

So you probably wouldn't have come out if you had not been with Julie?

Oh, I might have anyway. But I've had good coming-out experiences.

How did being out help you to enjoy this triumphant year?

I could really be 100% there for my success. I wasn't closeted, and I didn't feel like there was stuff that wasn't being acknowledged. I didn't have to constantly worry and think, *Well, but if they knew this other stuff about me, then it wouldn't have happened.*

Was there a low point this year?

Yeah, a little loss of personal freedom—a very small price to pay.

You go outside and people mob you?

Yeah, and it's changed from being just the people who love my music to being people who want my autograph because I'm someone famous. All of a sudden you feel very detached. I have had to really pull back.

How do you stay in contact with your fans?

I went online last August. I had the anonymity of doing it from the studio where I was finishing my album. It's a nice way to communicate with fans without crossing personal boundary lines that I now need to set up for myself physically.

How did you prove it was you?

I did two things: I had one of the people online give me a phone number, and I called her, and she said, "Oh, my God, it is you!" because she recognized my voice. The second thing I did was tell them that I was going to be *The Advocate*'s Person of the Year, and I told them I would put something about being online in the interview with *The Advocate* so that they could think back and realize that it really was me.

Let me ask you about the PETA ad that you and Julie did and the controversy that followed. What happened?

Julie is the vegetarian in the family; I am no longer a vegetarian. Julie's an animal lover and quite vocal and heartfelt about it. I wear leather, I eat meat—chicken and fish—but I do have compassion for animals in the fur trade and how they are treated. PETA contacted Julie and said, "We're doing a series of photographs of couples. We think you two are a great couple, and we want to put you in this campaign."

So it started with Julie?

Yes, Julie came to me and said, "I would like to do this." I said, "Well, I will do it if they understand that I wear leather and I eat meat." They assured me that Kim Basinger did a PETA photo and she's not a vegetarian and that there were other models who'd done it who wear leather. So I agreed. Once we got into taking the pictures, Julie said, "Gee, I thought we were going to have a sign

in front of us or something." She didn't realize that we were going to be totally nude. But a couple of glasses of wine, and we were OK with it.

Then the ad came out and...?

There was such serious controversy because there are so many gray areas. I was contacted by people looking for cures for AIDS who were saying, "I can't believe you helped PETA, because they don't support animal testing." I got impassioned letters about this from people in the fur trade, saying, "You don't know what you're talking about." I got letters like I'd never received before.

You—the person who never gets attacked?

It was my mistake. I was simply protesting cruelty to animals in the fur trade. The ad read, "I'd rather go naked than wear fur." I have never worn fur, and I never would wear fur. But the issue isn't that clear; it bleeds into all sorts of things. So I've made a decision not to do any more visible work for PETA. Julie will do what she feels she needs to do, and I will support her in that.

The animal-testing crisis seems to turn on the question, *What do we test possible cures on?*

Exactly! My father died of cancer, and I've lost too many friends to AIDS. So I do believe in animals losing their lives to eradicate cancer and AIDS from our lives; I believe in that.

You told *Rolling Stone* that you and Julie plan to get married. Do you?

What I said and what was written were two different things. My point was: I want to be legally recognized as married. I want all the benefits that a legal marriage has. I get crazy when so many heterosexuals take it for granted yet it's still something that Julie and I cannot have. There are situations that people don't even think about: my huge tax situation, for example. I've got to spend so much in accounting fees every year to solve it. Believe me, the first state that legalizes same-sex marriages, I'm there, Julie's there, and we're getting married. We're first in line.

I know you and Julie plan to be parents in the near future. Do you think that being a parent will make you more cautious and protective of your personal life?

Yes, because I talk to famous couples who have children, and I can see how very protective they've become. The celebrity issue is one thing when you're an adult and you understand it. But to be a child and have people run at you and take your picture when you have no idea why—I think that would be a situation I'd feel very protective about.

But you're still going to do it?

Yes, but it's a very private matter. I'm not going to say how, who, when, or where—not while this tape recorder is on. It's just not going to happen. I have let the world in on so much of my private life, so this is the one area that's going to remain private. Although at some point people are going to know.

Because one of you will be pregnant?

Yes. It's going to be obvious when it happens. But we need to be in total control of it.

That's going to be hard.

Yeah, there's going to be a lot of serious focus on it when it happens. People who have been going "Fine, fine, they're gay, that's great" are suddenly going to be going "Wait a minute—they're raising children?"

Here's a touchy subject for you…

[*Laughing*] Oh? How unlike you!

The *Los Angeles Times* reviewed one of your 1995 concerts by questioning whether you were ever going to reveal yourself in your music. The reviewer said, "Springsteen had his *Nebraska*, can Etheridge give us her *Kansas*?" What do you think he meant by that, and is *Your Little Secret* giving him what he wanted?

That kind of reviewer always wants to know where you're going; they never trust where you are right now. They're like a parent you can never satisfy. They always say, "That's great, but can you do this?"

Is *Your Little Secret* a departure?

There are pieces of *Your Little Secret* that go deeper into me, into my past, and into the things I'm made of. Songs like "Nowhere to Go," "Shriner's Park," and "I Could Have Been You" pull out parts of me that I have not examined before. No, I didn't sit in my room and record it on a four-track TEAC tape recorder like Bruce did with *Nebraska,* but maybe someday I will.

Naturally, I listened very carefully through *Your Little Secret* to hear if you sang a love song to Julie or if you used the words "she" or "her." You didn't.

True, but without being gender-specific in my songs, I think I'm becoming more sensual. Whereas before I might have shied away from using feminine descriptions, I feel freer in my writing—even though I'm not saying "I love her."

Why not?

I don't want to cut anybody out. I don't want to alienate anyone.

Melissa, I hear the words you say, but I still sense you long to address a woman in a love song.

[*Sighs*] Yeah, I would love to pretend that I'm the kind of artist who writes and writes and doesn't give a damn about anybody else. But it's obvious that I'm not a Dylan type, who's all involved with his art and the listeners feel like they're just looking in on him when they hear his songs.

Obviously you are afraid that some of your listeners will stop listening to you if you write a love song that's about another woman. Isn't it possible that these listeners have been waiting all along to hear from you about this?

Sure. There are enough straight people that know about Julie and me that if I wrote a song called "Julie," they would totally understand.

So?

OK, I realize that. It's not that it's never going to happen; it may very well happen. It probably will happen. I just haven't done it yet.

Are you afraid?

After years of doing it one way, it's going to be awkward for me to do it the way you're talking about. I will have to do an album just for me. Then if anyone wants to look in on it, they can. But, yes, it will probably be a big release. It will probably be very freeing. [*Groans*] Oh, you're right.

Well, it's not as if you haven't been addressing this issue at all. Isn't "I Could Have Been You" about being gay?

Yes. That is the basis for the song. It's about confronting someone who lives with that sort of intolerance. In a way, though, it could also be about racial intolerance.

But you're not black.

I know. I know. But you could stick religion in there or anything. I was just writing from my experience.

And you're gay. Please don't say, "Oh, no, no. It's about being a vegetarian."

[*Laughing*] Well, it could be.

[*Laughing*] Yes, indeed, it could. OK, you told me in the past that if you were a major romantic lead in film or television—rather than a rock singer—you would think twice about coming out. Do you still feel that way?

No. I would change my answer. I think if a person's work is good, that's ultimately all that matters. Obviously, had my album not been very good, I would not be where I am today after coming out. There would have been a little flash instead of this great leap. If someone comes out and then makes a bad movie, it's just not going to work. I don't believe there is going to be any problem if the work is good.

Do you think the public will believe a lesbian actress kissing a man on-screen?

Absolutely. If an actress can go inside herself and pull up that part that's in love with a man at that moment, then she has done her job. She has done it well, and it will be believed.

And if she's a closeted lesbian actress, do you think people will pick up on that fact when they see her on-screen?

Yes, I do, because her sexuality is all locked up. But I tell you, once you free it up, all of a sudden you are open to so many feelings. I stood there onstage with Bruce Springsteen, looked at him, and thought, *This man is just gorgeous!*

What was the reaction to the interview you did with Janis Ian for us last spring?

People loved it. It was tough being the interviewer.

Finally, some respect.

[*Laughing*] No, I mean because I didn't want to ask her things that are difficult to answer. I know how it is.

Are you still interested in film acting?

Oh, yeah. I have an agent, and I'm reading scripts.

You said that one of your goals was to help out your hometown of Leavenworth, Kan. They contacted you after your father died, but you were still grieving. Has that changed?

Oh, yeah! I went to my hometown. They had Melissa Etheridge Day. I went into my old music store, and my old guitar teacher was still there!

Did going home like that stir up things that you wrote about?

I remembered the young girl with such huge dreams. I remembered what I was like and what was driving me, and it was painful. It allowed that part of me to come back up, and I wrote from it.

Melissa Etheridge

Were you able to see the roots of your nice-girl personality back there?

[*Laughing*] Oh, yeah. A lot of that came from my dad. When he first saw me perform, he said, "You should always thank your audience."

For a big star, you are very caretaking of other people. Everybody notices this.

How many stars have you seen come and go away quickly because they have nasty attitudes? My dad taught me differently. I could see him treat other people in a kind way, and when I tried it, it worked.

I heard that you called your new album *Your Little Secret* because a gay fan hassled you for having gotten so big and commercial. She said, "I can see you're not our little secret anymore."

To me, that just says that it's not about my music. It's about being into unknown music. I hope that people will allow me to grow and make the music that is in me, no matter how many people are listening to it.

If people are overidentifying with you and you suddenly go off in unexpected directions, it's scary for them.

Oh, I know! Some people didn't like the way I looked on my third album: a little too blond, a little too pretty. What's up with that? I was feeling blond and pretty!

That must have made you angry. Is expressing your anger still your biggest personal struggle?

Oh, yeah. I was not shown as a child how to be angry. My parents kept their anger in, so I never grew up with examples of how to do that. I always thought, *Well, that must mean that if I get angry, the world ends.* I got in trouble for saying in my last *Advocate* cover story that I believed that my father kept his anger in and that it led to his cancer.

People wrote to you about that?

Yeah, I got a letter saying that people were tired of hearing people blame cancer on the victim. It is my belief, that's all. Julie still doesn't believe that I have ever gotten really angry around her because it seems like nothing to her. But to me it's scary, walls-falling-down horrible.

Do you think any of your rage is released in your music?

Absolutely. I started doing music as a child, so I can put my feelings into words much better in a song than I can in speaking to someone. So, yes, I get onstage, and I scream the scream. I am released every night.

Do you ever worry, *If I get healthy, I'll have nothing to write about?*

In my opinion, pain never goes away. There is so much light and dark inside of me that I do not fear I will become too happy to write. I might not write, "There is someone sleeping with the person I love." That's obviously not as big a part of my life anymore as I go into my seventh year in my relationship with Julie.

When *The Advocate* cover story you and Julie did in 1994 came out, I heard you thought it was too sexy.

No, I knew the angle was always going to be about a sexy lesbian couple—"dangerous lesbians." Yes, I expected the sexy stuff.

Traveling the world last year, did you realize how important it was to have been a part of something that showed a sexy lesbian couple to the world?

Oh, yeah! I am still signing the magazine! They save them and wait for me to come to their towns.

I've heard people object to the sexiness you and Julie showed both in *The Advocate* story and in the PETA ad. They felt it would be misused by straight men—the old "Ooh, two girls together!" But what's the answer? To hide lesbian sexuality from the world?

No! It is like the age-old argument about pornography in general. We have to say, "Yes, this is sexual too." That's why a lot of feminists actually embrace pornography, because in that way you free the whole machine.

Have you ever heard the expression "lesbian bed death"?

Yes. [*Pauses, then uprorious laughter*] It is untrue. It's a mean myth! Where did that awful idea come from?

That awful idea comes from the theory that when lovers get to know each other well, they become like best friends or relatives and they stop desiring each other.

Oh, no, this is not my experience! Why, just last night...! We're learning things all the time. It is like an adventure. After seven years it's better than ever. Look, I know that, sexually, you have dynamics in a relationship. There will be times when I am in more of a crisis professionally or maybe I'm dealing with something with my family—anything where you have to close down. You can't really open up physically. But just as that comes, it goes away, and on with the healthy sexual relationship!

Has your relationship with your fans changed because you're a part of a solid couple?

Yes, but I think that change is a part of my whole maturing. I think what I was looking for in my 20s is different from what I'm looking for in my 30s. Yes, there was a difference when I was available—meaning emotionally and physically—when I was looking, searching. This lasted only for about a year into my first record, because I started realizing that it wasn't very healthy; one can't spread oneself so thin. I'm glad I'm not still there. Now I am discovering the joys of believing in one person and not trying to gather it all from a host of others. I don't think it takes anything away from the fans. I put out as much energy onstage as I ever did. It's just that that's as far as it goes.

Melissa, your manager said that ever since I wrote the words "A bra hits Melissa Etheridge in the face" at the beginning of your last cover story, the bras have been flying hard and wild at your shows.

Yes, it's crazy. You did that to me.

Well, what *do* you want thrown at you?

My band was suggesting maybe diamonds! Or what about annuities? It's just that the bra thing is hard on me. During one show I watched this woman take her bra off right in front of me. I kept shaking my head, screaming, "Don't do that! Don't do that!" The security guard was no help. He moved so that she could throw it at me. Now they're actually bringing extra bras to my shows; they are not just wearing them. I guess soon they'll be selling bra launchers for the people in the back rows.

Generes

Back when Ellen DeGeneres

first began popping up on late-night talk shows doing stand-up comedy, I knew two things: She was funny, and she was gay. I don't know how I knew she was gay. I have no gaydar. But laughing I'm good at, and there was and is something thrilling about her humor. She has a point of view that is different, insightful, odd, and hilarious. When I heard that she was launching her own television series in 1994, *These Friends of Mine*, I immediately forced myself into her publicist's Los Angeles office. For some insane reason I thought she would have no problem advising Ellen to do an interview with *The Advocate*.

An assistant to the publicist smiled wearily at me, held up that week's *TV Guide* with Ellen on the cover, and said, "She's not ready to do anything like that. This is a big deal! This is prime-time television. This is network TV. She can't do anything like *this*," she concluded, replacing the *TV Guide* in her hand with the current *Advocate*. I left the publicist's office in distress. Suddenly the distance between a rising celebrity in "big-time" entertainment and The National Gay & Lesbian Newsmagazine seemed insurmountable.

As the years went by nothing much changed in the stance taken by the people representing Ellen. We were told off the record that as long as she was doing network television and feature films, it was simply too big a risk for her to sit around talking about her personal life. And since she was too ethical to sit around lying about her private life, there would be no talking to Ellen. Naturally, other gay publications wrote about her, but she never participated in the stories. Early on I made the decision that *The Advocate* would not write about Ellen until we actually had her for an interview. I felt we needed to distinguish ourselves from the herd just in case it mattered to Ellen at some future date when she was ready to talk. Fortunately, Ellen's own ambivalence about being in the closet began to eat away at her time line. Unfortunately, when a series of "spottings" (Ellen seen cuddling some girl in a lesbian bar in New York City, for example) was followed by a leak that her sitcom character was going to come out—it was deemed crucial that *The Advocate* cover the mounting hysteria surrounding Ellen. After all, we are a newsmagazine and this was rapidly becoming a huge news event. Reluctantly, we found ways to write about Ellen's "situation." But it made both the magazine staff and Ellen quite agitated.

Because Ellen had asked Chastity Bono (then the media director for GLAAD) to advise her in handling the coming-out episode, and because Chastity had done her coming-out interview with *The Advocate* [see page 70] and was now a good friend, the magazine was not caught off-guard when the show aired nor when Ellen did her own coming-out interview with *Time* magazine. Once the media blitz swung into full force and Anne Heche jumped into the mix by falling in love with Ellen, the lid blew off journalism as we knew it. Even I was being hauled onto *Oprah, Geraldo,* and *Leeza* to pontificate about Ellen, gays, coming out, and nature versus nurture. It all seemed pretty loony, considering I still hadn't met the woman who had set off such a monumental and historic discussion.

Opportunities to meet and talk arose and disappeared. There was often some crucial miscommunication that left either Ellen or the magazine bewildered and upset. But there were always gestures being made, apology letters being sent, and hopeful signals that one day it would happen. I would run into Ellen at functions and introduce myself. We would stare awkwardly at each other, never knowing how to change our situation. After one of these occasions, Ellen's casting director invited me to "sell *Advocates*" in the background of a Lilith-type fair during an episode of *Ellen*. It was a sign, a gesture. We offered to do a cover story with Ellen and her mother, Betty, for the release of Betty's first book, *Love, Ellen*. Everything was a "go" until a miscommunication concerning what chapter we wanted to excerpt and why we wanted to excerpt it sent another golden opportunity careening away from us. Fortunately, an *Advocate*-sponsored party for a reading Betty gave of her book in Los Angeles offered up the chance for Ellen and me to sit and hash out all the screwups. After a couple of heated hours together, we agreed to do an interview around the time of *If These Walls Could Talk 2*, which she executive-produced for HBO. A few of months later an unintentionally unflattering caricature of Ellen, Anne, and Sharon Stone for an *Advocate* fall preview issue nearly crashed the interview again. Luckily, by then Ellen and I had established some pretty solid communication skills. By that time we had hit enough bumps in the road that we had learned how to get over them by talking.

And so this long and winding road to our March 14, 2000, *Advocate* interview was not traveled in vain. We had come to trust each other enough to communicate. The interview itself is proof of that. It may have taken six years to get there, but when Ellen finally sat down with the gay press for the first time, it was as remarkable as we'd always hoped it would be. After that, Advocate Books published her mother's second book, *Just a Mom*, and had to deal hands-on with Ellen and Anne's divorce because of the way it affected everything from the book cover to Betty's book tour. Although many personal and professional changes have taken place in Ellen's world since this interview, the essence of how she deals with herself and the things and people she values most in life remain the same. She is a very special woman. After you read her words, I believe you will get to know a lot about Ellen DeGeneres. Even Ellen said she learned a thing or two about herself when she read the interview.

Because she's never addressed this readership before, I, like most people, knew Ellen DeGeneres only through the media. And what a tall tower of media babble it was. When the stand-up and sit-com comedian decided to free both herself and

her TV character from the burdens of the closet in the 1997 Emmy-winning "Puppy Episode" of *Ellen,* her heartfelt decision seemed to stop the world in its orbit. For DeGeneres it was simple: She couldn't stand it anymore. It was making her sick to live and create with only half her engines running. For the rest of society, apparently, it was much more complicated—yep, she was gay all right, but now everyone had an opinion about it.

"People kept saying how sick of all the media about me they were," the reluctant activist says in the privacy of her Los Angeles home. "But what people got so 'sick of' was all the press on press on press. It was never me talking. It was everyone else going at it."

What followed—the cover of *Time,* falling in love with Anne Heche, rising to the top of everyone's "in" lists, falling off them and into the depths of despair when the tide turned, striking out, folding her tent, finding a retreat from Hollywood, coming back—is history, inaccurate as it may or may not be. The truth is, no one knows what really happened—or, at least, not from DeGeneres's perspective.

So as she prepares to enjoy her first HBO executive-produced drama, *If These Walls Could Talk 2;* as she takes her first stand-up routine in eight years on the road (a tour that will culminate with an HBO special); and as she films her new television pilot for CBS about a variety show host ("I know, I know, the question on everyone's mind is, 'Am I gay on the series?' Well, I'm me, so yes, I'm gay, but it's not about my personal life."), the 42-year-old actress finally puts aside all distractions and does the one thing she's never done before...

This is the first time you've spoken to the gay press?
Yes.

Then we need to go back in time and catch up. When you originally came out you talked to *Time* magazine and *Primetime Live.* Unlike other gay stars—Greg Louganis, for example, who also did mainstream media when he came out but included the gay press— you did not. Can you talk about why you wouldn't? You know I tried very hard to get you to talk to *The Advocate.* I had heard that you were mad at us because we "pushed you too much."
Well, that's certainly not true. I was never mad. I did only three things. I was planning on doing two: the Diane Sawyer interview and *Time.* That's it.

And then you did *Oprah*?
I did *Oprah* because Oprah was in my coming-out episode. Oprah wanted me on her show. And of course I wasn't going to say no. Also, the other reason I didn't do the gay press is that there were people in my camp that were advising me, telling me, "Let's not just target a gay audience. This is bigger than that," which, of course, is true.

But talking with the mainstream is not the same as talking with, for lack of a better phrase, your "family," people who have gone through what you are struggling with.
Yeah. And that's the whole point. I think I was still scared and feeling, *Oh, do I want to just completely position myself as a gay person now?* As much as I was labeling myself, I was afraid. And yes, I knew your questions would be different.

We actually heard that *The Advocate* was "too gay" for you to do.
Well, certainly you know those words would never come out of my mouth—to say that something is "too gay." It was a lot of people advising me, saying "This is not a political statement. This is just you doing something for the show and personally for you." And then it did turn into a political thing. I became an activist, which I didn't intend on doing. I really was just doing something I thought would be creative and also freeing for me.

Well, as you know by now, the personal *is* political. Telling who we are is revolutionary.
Yeah.

When the whole thing happened with Chastity Bono being misquoted as saying your show was "too gay"—
I want you to know that we've worked all that out. We've talked it through.

Yes, I heard that, and I'm very glad. So what do you think people meant when they were saying that your show was too gay?
That was my question! What are they talking about? Is a show too straight? In my opinion there *are* some that are too straight [*chuckling*]—for me, anyway.

Is that what they meant by "too gay"? There was not enough room for heterosexuals to see their lives?
Maybe it was. I mean, my show was certainly a world that I identified with. And a lot of people I know identified with it. But, like you said, maybe it was too gay for somebody because [anything] gay at all is "too gay." I just substitute "gay" with "uncomfortable."

But weren't you prepared for a backlash? You are a pioneer. And when you're a pioneer, you're taking a risk, and when you're taking a risk, you're going to get hurt. What was so unexpected?
All of it! All of it! First of all, I didn't understand how big it was. When news of my character leaked out on talk radio and everybody was going nuts, I was just shocked that it was such big news. It was all everybody was talking about!

Except you.
I couldn't talk about it! I couldn't at all say anything. We hadn't

been given the go-ahead. I just had to hide. And then when the show aired and got such high ratings, when it turned into parties everywhere, it seemed like it was going to be great because the reviews were great. I was happy with it. And I didn't want to come back on the air.

Right! I remember that.

Because I didn't really know where to go with it. So I was fighting them, saying "Let me go, let's end on a high note, let me out of this." And Michael Eisner wouldn't let me. He said, "You have to come back." And I said, "I don't know where to go with this. I can't go back in the closet. We're going to have to deal with this." And I was afraid they wouldn't let me deal with it.

We had 45 million viewers for the coming-out show. It dropped to something like 15 million for the following show because it wasn't advertised. Then we came back next season and there was no advertisement for the premiere.

And you didn't even want to go back.

Right. Now I'm coming back, and they're not behind it. I heard stories that affiliates were threatening ABC, saying "Take this show off the air." And, of course, ABC had already bought it. So they just didn't advertise it—so they could just throw their hands up and tell people, "Look, we're not trying to help it! We're not doing anything. We have to air it because we already paid for it."

People said that the show wasn't funny. I laughed. And I loved the episode with Emma Thompson. Didn't she get an Emmy for it?

Yes, and it was considered one of the funniest ever. But all of a sudden it was too much for everyone. It was "OK, shut up." They didn't like the show. Yeah, it was a lot to take on. And I was aware of that. But, again, I'm really proud of it. I'm sorry that it ended the way it did, but I'm thrilled that we got to do it.

What about the "you're going too fast" criticisms?

Maybe I didn't go slow enough. I don't know. It was frustrating for me to go really slowly and take as long as I did for [the character] Laurie and I to go to bed together. I mean, I thought we *were* going slow. And then there were shows that had nothing to do with my character being gay.

Which didn't really work either because we were all waiting for you to get back to being gay.

Sure. Look, I was 40 years old, and I deserved to be a sexual being. Suddenly, it wasn't about Ellen getting her toe stuck in the blinds. They had to deal with a grown-up. And that's a different kind of funny. But it was amazing lessons for me to learn. And I should've just trusted that the path that I was on was the path that I was meant to be on. I was going through a birth. In fact, I'm thinking of calling my stand-up special "Born Again."

Going back to the gay press and the irony of *The Advocate* also being considered too gay, what do you think of the gay press after going through all this?

Well, for example, another national gay magazine, not *The Advocate,* at the end of either 1997 or 1998 had this horrible picture of me with the words, "A poll was taken and it found that many Americans know Ellen but few like her." And I remember looking at it and thinking, *Why, in a gay magazine, do you need to put that at the top of your chart?* Today, I am in a place of total forgiveness and compassion for how everyone feels. But at the time, when I was

going through such major grieving over losing my show, this kind of thing was so mean. Whatever publication I picked up was never celebrating the positive stand I took—it was always talking about the failed ratings and that the show was too gay.

You must have been afraid to read anything or turn on the TV.

Yes, after a certain amount of time I was saying, "OK: Straight people hate me. Gay people hate me. Even gay publications aren't trying to spin it around." I do believe that this community needs to support one another. If we were as organized as the extreme right, we'd be very powerful.

You and Anne did the *Los Angeles Times Magazine* together. It seemed to make people very angry. Were you happy with how you came off in that article?

Yes. Our work situation had changed for us. People may have thought it seemed like it was complaining on our parts—because people looked at us like poor little rich girls who have all this money and are celebrities and yet are complaining about not getting more work. It wasn't about that. It was about the shift in people's attitudes and the loss of work. It hurts any person if you want to do something and you don't get the opportunity to do it anymore.

And it was such a huge fall for you.

Exactly. I experienced both sides of it, because when I came out everything was great. I was "entertainer of the year," and I was one of the "10 most fascinating people." And it was a whole year of celebrating Ellen. And then it went to the complete opposite end. Suddenly I become this person that everybody was saying "Oh, I hate her. Oh, I love her." And I heard about all of it. It just got to be where I couldn't watch TV without somebody saying something mean. I was the punch line of every joke, like Monica Lewinsky.

What a ride!

Yes, I got to experience: Who am I when no one likes me? Who am I when I don't have a show? Who am I when nobody's laughing at me? And I found out that I'm still OK. So that's a blessing.

But you decided to retreat?

Yeah. My first idea was, "OK, Hollywood doesn't like me, so I'll leave." The one thing that I didn't want to do was get hard. I think for a while, instead, I got depressed. Then it turned into anger. I was so angry. And I just wanted to say, "Don't you all understand me? What did I do wrong?"

Did you do anything wrong?

Maybe I did a lot of things wrong, but I didn't know how to do it. I didn't have a booklet. I didn't open it to page 1 of *Coming Out: Here's How to Do It.* I just did what I thought I should do.

So you were human.

Yeah. I went ahead and showed you exactly who I am. And that's what hurt. It was like "Oh, God. They're seeing who I am, and they don't like who I am!"

And, of course, the world was also dealing with you falling in love with Anne and being so out there with it.

Yes, it was a new picture in people's minds, and they didn't know how to process it. People had never seen me with somebody before. They had never seen me at a premiere holding hands with my last girlfriend. Just like you hear that Brad [Pitt] and Jennifer

[Aniston] are together, but you don't see the courtship and the dating. Well, we didn't mean to show all that. We didn't mean to become *The Real World* of lesbian dating.

Since your coming-out became one of the biggest events in gay history, whose coming-out encouraged you?

Well, k.d. and Melissa both came out before I did. Martina…but not as much as k.d. and Melissa, because I was friends with them at the time. We used to talk about coming out all the time. I really think it would be such a great documentary to do. I'd love for us to get together again because those were great times when we all used to hang out every Sunday at Julie and Melissa's house in the swimming pool and sitting in the Jacuzzi, playing guitar and making up songs. But then we all got busy. Melissa and k.d wanted me to come out, but they never pressured me in any way.

I hear you're going to the Millennium March in D.C. this spring. Is that because you couldn't go in '93?

I remember crying, wishing I could be a part of the march on Washington in 1993. I thought, *This is a huge group of people that I belong to. And I can't do that because I'm not out!* That was a powerful thing, to watch the march and to not be able to be there—it impacted me and just tortured me more. I wanted to be able to be out. My friends were out! And I kept justifying why I couldn't—because music is different from television. If you sell 6 million albums, you're a huge star. If you have 6 million viewers on television, you're canceled.

I'd like to talk about some of the things revealed in your mother's first book, *Love, Ellen.* There's a scene in which your father calls out to you after you had your leg cut open and says, "You're OK, Ellen. Just get up and walk!" Naturally his actions, based on his Christian Science beliefs, were full of denial. Would you say that denial was a big part of your family?

Yeah. I've struggled with being raised in a family that didn't talk about anything at all. My father always said, "Just be nice and make sure everybody likes you." My father is a very fearful person. He's a wonderful person, a kind person, but he's never been a risk taker at all.

So how did you ever manage to pull off coming out?

I have done everything I could to break out of that. To go as far as I have is just amazing coming from that family. I knew I didn't want to end up like that. I don't want to be scared of anything. And this last year and a half I got the beautiful blessing of facing just about every one of my fears—including the fire that almost took our home. All I would have had left was my mother and my girlfriend and my animals—and that was enough for me. I realized when we were grabbing things that nothing else was important.

That's a big change.

I was raised to believe that celebrity is important. Money is important. I was taught that if somebody has money, then they're very important. And if they're a celebrity, wow, that's really important! And so of course I became a celebrity. And of course I wanted to make a lot of money. All those things seemed to be what would make me happy. Then I learned after having money and becoming a celebrity that it's not what makes you happy. It doesn't matter if you have the whole world loving you or hating you. And knowing this has enriched my relationship with Anne.

Which was under attack from the beginning.

Yes, they tried everything that could tear us apart. Even rumors of her having an affair with Vince Vaughn.

Right, what was that about?

She had done a movie [*Return to Paradise*] with Vince, and they had such great chemistry. So, of course, they said she was having an affair with him! And I thought, *What a mean thing!* It was really offensive to me—like I'd be that stupid not to know she's having an affair. And Anne was saying, "Well, it's offensive to me too." So we were arguing over who it was more offensive to. She was saying, "What does that make me look like! What kind of a person am I to have an affair?" And I'd say, "Yeah, but what kind of a person am I that I'm going to stay with you?"

Sounds awful.

But it just made us realize what is important to us, and we have such a strong foundation now, nothing can rock us. We went to couples therapy and dealt with a lot of stuff that we were going through. And our therapist said, "I'm amazed that y'all have made it this long and that you're still together. You should be proud of yourselves."

It's good to hear it wasn't all heaven and that you had to work at it.

Of course. And there were personal attacks too. One magazine put us in their category of "Women We Love." I had just been in their last issue. And then, when Anne and I got together, they put her in "Women We Love," and they put me in "And a Few We Don't." They would pit us against each other.

How have your relationships with closeted actors changed since coming out?

I don't have relationships with them. I did. At functions they avoid being next to me. It's very interesting. I used to be very mad. I used to think, *Here you have this opportunity to help a lot of people. It's not going to be as hard for the next person to do it.* It really was my intention that this would be like "C'mon! Line up! Everybody!" And it was interesting to see that not one person did.

And I think that there were people in this industry that were trying to make an example of us, like "Don't you dare think of doing this because look what happened to them." It's really a shame because there is power in numbers. If you have a whole lot of people that come out, they can't boycott everybody.

And I used to be very angry, but now I'm not angry. I feel sorry for them because I know the pain. You can say "It's nobody's business," but the only reason you say that is because you're scared that you're going to lose money. But it's not my place to judge. You know, we need a lot of help here. But my truth is my truth. And it doesn't mean it's everyone's truth.

Certainly you felt healthier after coming out?

Of course, but just coming out doesn't make you get rid of the shame that's been there for years. I think a lot of my passion over coming out was me fighting and saying "I'm OK! I'm OK! How dare you say I'm not OK!" I just had to say it over and over until I really believed it.

And then Anne comes along *without* all this old closeted lesbian baggage and shows you how pure and simple love should be.

Oh, yes, but that's what Anne has finally realized and has got to

"Maybe I did a lot of things wrong, but I didn't know how to do it. I didn't have a booklet. I didn't open it to page 1 of *Coming Out: Here's How to Do It.* I just did what I thought I should do. Yeah, I went ahead and showed you exactly who I am."

this place of saying, "Oh, God. No wonder people hated me on *Oprah*. This is a really hard thing, and people struggle with this. And I'm just coming on the show and going, 'Oh! I just saw Ellen across the room and fell in love.' Wow, I would've hated me too!" But honestly, I was doubting her too when I met her because I thought, *You can't possibly be for real; you don't know what you're getting into.*

Exactly. You had to make sure she wasn't on some happy little detour from heterosexuality.

That certainly could've been [the case]. And I would think that if you're a betting person, you're going to bet that this is not going to last. I told her, "I'm not interested in having an affair or a fling. I appreciate your interest. And thank you. But no." And she kept saying, "I'm not playing games." And her career was just taking off, so I said, "I think I should get out of your life." And she said to me, "Don't ever say that to me again." Anne is a remarkable human being. She's the most evolved person I've ever met. She is my little Buddha.

Ellen, I need to throw something else unpleasant at you...
Oh, sure, Judy. Please! [*Laughs*]

Your girlfriend Kat died in a car accident in 1980. You actually drove by the accident but didn't know it was her. Then you went on to use your pain over that experience in your breakthrough stand-up monologue, "Phone Call to God." What was it like having to perform that monologue from the closet, knowing it was about the death of a woman you loved—yet having to refer to her as "your friend"?

[*Sighs*] I had seen her right before the accident too. The most horrible part of it was, she was cheating on me and we were living together. I moved out to teach her a lesson, thinking that I'd go back. So I was staying with someone else at the time. My brother's band was performing that night, and I saw her at the club. It was really loud, and she kept saying, "When are you going to come home?" And I kept acting like I couldn't hear her, like the music was too loud. She left first, and then I left. We drove past the accident she was in.

You didn't know, so you didn't stop?

It had just happened, and the car was split in two. The sirens were behind us. We slowed down and said, "Jesus! Look at that!" And we kept going. And the next morning at 6 A.M. her sister came to the house where I was staying and said, "Kat died last night." When she told me where, I realized that I was there.

Oh, Ellen...

And she said she was alive for three hours and she didn't have ID on her so they couldn't call. And I was like, "She was alive. I could've been there." My mind was so full of so many things: *If I had just gone home with her that night. If I wouldn't have been such an asshole.*

How did you deal with this?

I moved out of our house and was in this tiny, tiny basement apartment and it was infested with fleas. And I just kept thinking, *Why are fleas here and this beautiful girl is gone? I don't understand this.* So I just started writing what it would be like to call and ask God why fleas are here. And it just came out in comedy in 10 minutes, and I thought, *I'm doing this on* The Tonight Show, *and Johnny Carson is going to call me over, and I'm going to be the first woman in the history of the show to be called over on the first appearance.* And I was. So I think about her a lot. I used to think about her when I would do that monologue. I'd think, *Wow. Where did that come from?*

A good way to handle all that pain.

Yeah. Great comedy is born from tragedy. It was a pretty devastating event in my life because I felt tremendously guilty. I really thought I could've done something. But it was a horrible accident, and there was no way she was going to make it. I don't know what she would have looked like, and it would have stayed with me forever. So I wasn't supposed to see her. And she was supposed to go. It was her time to go.

Was this your first death?

Yes. I was 20 years old, and it was my first taste of knowing that somebody could be gone like that—like you could be talking to them and then by the next day you will never see them again. And I started thinking how she was a cute girl. She was a bartender at a gay bar. She was very popular. She used to look at herself and check out her ass in the mirror and fix her hair. She was very vain and very confident and I thought, *None of that matters anymore. It doesn't matter about her hair. It doesn't matter about how great her ass was. It doesn't matter about how many girls flirted with her. It doesn't matter.* And it made me start living a different way and realize what's important.

Your mother has written about her second husband and how he sexually molested you. I wondered how you felt about having that disclosed.

Mother asked me if she could put that in the book. She wouldn't have done that without me. The reason we thought it was important to reveal was to show her journey and what women go through and how they'll justify anything to stay married, to have a husband— even go so far as to not believe their own child. As if your child would make something like that up.

She didn't believe you?

Yeah. I didn't tell her right away because she had just had a mastectomy. And I didn't want to hit her with this news too.

When I read how you protected her, I was extremely moved by your actions. As a young adult, how did this sexual abuse play into your feelings about men and trust and all of that stuff?

If you look at pictures of me when I'm 11 years old, wearing a tie when I'm playing, clearly I was gay. It had nothing to do with a bad experience with a man.

Were there any concerns on your part that having this revealed would lead to *Oh, great—one more odd thing about me.*

Yeah. I really didn't want to have to talk about it, but at the same time, the statistics are that one in three women have been molested in some way, and that's a pretty high statistic. And there should be more people talking about it; it shouldn't be a shameful thing. It never is your fault. So I don't mind talking about it. He did horrible things to me and was a bad man. I should have told Mother right away, but I thought on top of her just having a mastectomy, she doesn't need to hear that her husband tried to rape her daughter. So I just didn't tell her, and I should have.

And that's the lesson hopefully someone gets from the book: Don't ever stay silent when something like this happens. It doesn't matter who it is; you shouldn't be scared. Because of course they try to intimidate you and say "Nobody will believe you." But you should always—always—tell somebody. That's the important message.

How did growing up in the South influence you? Do you still think of yourself as a Southerner?

I do, and people make fun of me when I say "y'all."

You don't say that!

Yeah, I do. That's part of my vocabulary. But yeah, I'm proud to be from New Orleans. I love that city. And I don't know how it influenced me other than learning a lot about drinking at an early age.

You must know about alcohol there. There's to-go cups and there's drive-through margarita places. It's, like, the most dangerous city in the world. It's crazy that everybody drinks so much there.

Did you know any gay people?

I think there were two gay bars there. But I didn't really know anyone gay.

Did you know you were gay?

No, I didn't know I was gay. I realized it when I moved out of New Orleans and was in a very small town. I can't really talk about this because it was such a small town, they'll know who my gay experience was with. Then I went back to New Orleans thinking, *Oh, it was just that experience.* Thinking, *It was just her.* And then I met a group of girls. One girl was bisexual, and I had an experience with her. I was still dating guys, and I remember thinking, *OK, this was just her* again.

And then I got into a relationship with this girl, and we went into a gay bar. It was my first experience. I was 18 years old, and it was the weirdest thing in the world to walk in and see a whole bunch of girls all dancing together. And I was uncomfortable. But it didn't take long for that to wear off. Then I lived in gay bars. Not the healthiest experience, which is what's really sad. It's the only place where we could go then.

Of course, now there's lots more places. But when you're a young girl in a small town...

Were you telling yourself that you were bisexual?

I was still trying to date guys, and then I just gave up on guys. I wasn't really labeling myself at all at first, and then I think I'd decided I was gay. I realized I was definitely gay. I kept having bad experiences with girls, so I tried dating guys again. Then I thought, *I'm running out of genders. Where am I going to go next?* I was with a really sweet guy. I had sex with only two guys. I tried to have sex with him and just didn't enjoy it. I mean, just kissing a girl was so exciting to me, and kissing a guy was just so blah. Now all the guys are going to hate me.

Guys reading this, I love you.

In the segment of *If These Walls Could Talk 2* that Anne wrote and directed, called "Miss Conception," it felt like Sharon Stone was playing Anne, or at least that Anne was expressing herself through that character. Do you two want to get pregnant and be parents?

We hadn't gone through the process of trying to get pregnant the way Sharon and I do in the film, but it was a daily conversation between us. We did a lot of research on the sperm bank, the donors, and what you have to go through. So while she was writing it we were actually looking into it. We were really trying to have a baby at the time she was writing it. Right afterward we decided not to have a baby. And so we've gone back and forth, and at this point we're at the stage of not—but that changes every day. Tomorrow you may find out that we're pregnant.

Would you want to be a mother?

Well, that's the question. I think that we love our lives so much and of course that would change it. I mean, this is so nice now: to have our time and be able to be spontaneous, to stay in bed all day. [Having a child is] a responsibility for the rest of my life. It's not just a cute little baby that I could put in Gap clothes. It's also going to be a teenager that's going to want to pierce its nose. And so much as I think I'm liberal, I think I'd be very conservative as a parent. And the whole potty training thing scares me! I like the fact that with a cat you have a litter box. And I don't know if that's appropriate for a child—to just have a litter box.

Well, as Anne's HBO piece shows, it's not all that easy to get pregnant, anyway.

If we could get pregnant, we'd get pregnant now. Anne was just offered a documentary project in China that was about panda bears, which would have been fun. But she would have been in China, and she said, "You know, if I go to China, I'm going to come home with a baby."

I thought you were going to say she'd come home with a panda bear.

I would've come home with a panda bear; *she'd* come home with a baby! Anne wants to have the baby because she wants to have that experience. I really want to adopt a baby because there are so many children in this world and we're overpopulated. Of course, most of the babies that need homes are African-American babies, and people always want a white baby. Meanwhile, Chinese girls are just thrown out into the streets. But I don't even know enough about my own culture. I think Columbus came over and he killed Indians, and here we are! So I don't know what to tell an African-American baby; I don't know what to tell a Chinese baby. I know that we can't rely on our schools to teach our babies because our schools aren't doing such a good job. And…oh, no, now I'm going to get letters from teachers!

You teachers who are reading this are good!

What are your spiritual beliefs?

I was raised Christian Science, which is like "mind over matter." I think there is something to that. But I have a problem with a lot of the rules. I don't believe the god that I believe in is judgmental. I think whatever works for you is right. Heaven or hell is what you create right this minute where you are. You have a choice to live in joy or not. And that's my belief. If I'm wrong, then I'm wrong, but I'm not hurting anybody.

Were you able to hold on to this? Did it sustain you during all the hard times?

Not at all. [*Laughs*] When I met Anne I was in this beautiful place of just knowing that whatever we create in our minds, we create in reality. Yet I slipped into the darkest, darkest place. But I had to go that far down. I had to slip into that place to confront all of these fears because I was still trying to hold on to approval and all the things that I'm trying to let go of—pride, ego. But now I'm there, and hopefully I won't slip so far down again.

OK, Ellen, *Advocate* readers are a very special kind of audience and you've never addressed them before, so is there anything special you wish to say?

Well, instead of focusing on what we've talked about before, about the people who weren't supportive, I'd really much rather thank the people that were so supportive. I have received so many letters from around the world. I'm in a really healthy place right now, but the only thing that kept me going during those darker times were the letters from people saying "Thank you so much" and explaining how I impacted their lives. I always say that even if it was one person, my coming out was an important thing for me to do in my life. It's more important than any ratings I'll ever have on television or any good review—just that I saved a life.

I'm really glad you're saying this.

It got kind of scary because people would say, "You know, if you never do anything again in your whole life, you've done enough." [*Laughs*] I've heard that so many times, and it's supposed to be a compliment. And I guess it is a compliment, but I feel like I have so much more to do. I mean, I just accidentally did something that people look at as a very courageous, brave thing. And it wasn't. It was just something that I did, and it accidentally helped a lot of people. But I'm not a brave person. I'm learning to be. I think I've become a brave person through the journey and the slide down.

The slide down?

I will be the first to admit I slid down. And I think I participated in that. And I have to take responsibility for the bad things, the negative things, the mistakes I've made. I can't change them, but I take responsibility for them. And I just want to apologize to anyone I've rubbed the wrong way. Sorry for making my mistakes in public. And so I really want to let go of anything negative that happened and just say "Thank you so much for the support" to the people who have stayed with me.

And for the people who haven't, please come back [*laughs*] and give me a chance to be funny again, which is what I want to do—to really get back to my art. Not avoid who I am as a gay person, but really just get back to doing what I do and what brought me here in the first place. And hopefully people will find it in their hearts to say, "Oh, OK. I didn't get it for a while. But maybe I would've made the same mistakes. I don't know." So I just want to thank the people who supported me.

Catherine D

eneuve

It was 1995, and we were having a last-minute cover crisis at *The Advocate*. A cover crisis for us usually means something that we're about to go into production with has fallen out and we have nothing else in the issue that is as appealing to put on the cover. Worse yet, because we are a biweekly magazine, we have only 10 working days to fix the nightmare. "Well, we've never gone to press without a cover yet," I remember then-editor Gerry Kroll saying hopefully. "Is there nothing from the arts?" He looked at me, the senior arts-and-entertainment editor at the time.

I did know of one slim possibility. The French diva Catherine Deneuve was coming to America the following week to promote the rerelease of her 1967 shocker, *Belle de Jour*. The bad news was Deneuve had never spoken to the gay press. The good news was that her publicist was a friend. So naturally I called her in a semihysterical state.

"Well, she's totally booked," my PR friend sighed, "but I could try to get you into a roundtable with her and other journalists that we've flown in for the junket." My heart sank. How could I possibly ask Deneuve anything gay or intimate with a dozen other people all hurling their own agendas at her. But, of course, this was a crisis, so I said yes. In the meantime, figuring I wouldn't have much of her in the article, I began making phone calls to everyone and anyone who could possibly shed light on Deneuve's allure for lesbians. I was desperately seeking lesbian angles—something other than the 1987 film in which she starred and ignited the Sapphic fires, *The Hunger*. I even called the editor in chief of *Deneuve*, a lesbian magazine located in San Francisco. She told me her magazine was not named after Catherine Deneuve but after an old girlfriend of hers. Clearly, I wasn't coming up with much. Still, I beat the bushes, following my own strong feeling that there had to be a reason why this luscious legend who lit up the screen with so many memorable woman-to-woman celluloid images—including her erotic mother-daughter dance in the Oscar-nominated *Indochine*—was such an intense object of lesbian affection.

When I arrived at the Four Seasons Hotel in Beverly Hills, my publicist friend met me at the door. "I have some good news for you, but you'll have to be able to stay all day," she said. "Catherine will speak with you alone after the roundtable." I couldn't believe it. This meant there would be opportunities for relevant *Advocate* questions.

Although the roundtable—with Deneuve at the head, wearing sunglasses, smiling, and correcting all the statements being offered up to her as questions—was interesting, I was right to have worried that it would never have been enough for an *Advocate* cover story. Deneuve is a seasoned pro, fully capable of batting back any idiotic question she doesn't like or would rather not answer. So I left the suite and returned to another room where journalists ate little cakes, drank hot coffee, and gossiped about La Deneuve. I looked for my friend, who told me that I'd have to hang out for several hours. (When I saw the film *Notting Hill* years later, with the journalists swarming around Julia Roberts, I saw my life passing before me.)

Finally, at the end of the day, I was beckoned into the elevator to go to Deneuve's private suite. My friend waited until the elevator door closed and then dropped a bomb: "Judy, whatever you do, don't mention *Deneuve* magazine!" "What!" I wailed, "But that's my way of talking to her about her lesbian fan base here." "Judy," she snapped sharply to stop my objections, "I'm not kidding you. You can bring it up if you want to. I won't be there in the room with you. But I promise you, if you do, your interview will be over. She will walk out." I agreed and thanked her. Naturally, I was puzzled and frustrated.

The subsequent interview with Deneuve was groundbreaking for the magazine. I have been fortunate enough to have had the opportunity to talk with a lot of fabulous people, but Deneuve was the first one to possess that illusive "power" it is said that some stars have. It wasn't just about her (considerable!) sex appeal. It was bigger than that. You could feel it breathe in the room.

Although there was the occasional language barrier, Deneuve was up for all of it. We talked about closeted actors; her own relationships with women; Susan Sarandon; Cher and her daughter, Chastity; the sexual side of the characters she's played; the gay woman she was about to portray; and how she may have accidentally kicked off "lesbian chic" with *The Hunger*. Then, suddenly, when our time was almost up and I was about to turn my tape recorder off, Deneuve looked up at me nervously. She leaned forward, pointed a finger at me, and asked if I knew of the magazine *Deneuve*?

I swear, I thought it was a trick question. This was the one thing I was not supposed to bring up, and there she was bringing it up! I didn't say a thing at first. Then after an awkward moment I choked out the word yes. "Well, of course you do!" she announced with great Parisian flare and then launched into a long explanation of why she was suing the magazine for using her name. She felt she was a commodity. Her name could sell perfume. Her name could sell a lot of things. She had never given them permission to use her name, and now they were trying to take the magazine to France. She wouldn't have it, and she hoped people—especially lesbians—would understand why she was taking this action. After all, if a magazine decided to call itself *Streisand* or *Cher* or *Madonna*, lawyers for those stars would swoop down on them in a heartbeat.

At this point my friend—her publicist—poked her head into the room to let us know time was up. When she heard Deneuve talking heatedly about *Deneuve* magazine, she glared at me. Only later, when I explained how it had all come about, did we laugh with relief. Over the years, this *Advocate* interview has become a part of Deneuve's incandescent lore, helping to cement her strong hold on women as well as men. Numerous Deneuve fan Web sites have asked to reproduce it in many languages and have conducted some pretty racy chat-room chatter all around it.

And we, by the way, had one of our best-selling cover stories ever.

"People don't know very much about me. They do not know what really goes on in my private life," says 51-year-old French film sensation Catherine Deneuve as she sits in her pink Saint Laurent suit in one of several suites she's taken over at the

Four Seasons Hotel in Los Angeles. "Most people still believe I am the person I have played on-screen—whatever person they have liked the most. I enjoy that."

For many women, lesbians in particular, the career of the elegant and enigmatic Catherine Deneuve did not take off with Jacques Demy's 1964 French musical, *The Umbrellas of Cherbourg*. Nor did it begin with Roman Polanski's pathological 1965 classic, *Repulsion*, nor with Luis Buñuel's *Belle de Jour*—the shocking 1967 film Miramax is rereleasing this summer that Deneuve has come to America to celebrate. It didn't even begin with her 1980 award-winning performance in François Truffaut's *The Last Metro*. None of these legendary films that so skillfully exploited the icy fire of Deneuve's inscrutable presence—nor any that came between or after—marked the beginning.

Instead, that cataclysmic event, which has now become part of lesbian lore, began when a luminous Deneuve, playing an aristocratic vampire in Tony Scott's 1983 film, *The Hunger*, swooped down on an innocent and utterly bedazzled Susan Sarandon and for eight hot minutes devoured her with explicit sex and unprecedented, everlasting sensual enthusiasm. Then she bit her, and the rest is history.

"The lesbian vampire has a long and honorable past," says *Allure* magazine chief writer Lindsy Van Gelder, who authored one of the first articles on lesbian chic in 1992—called "Lipstick Lesbians"—for the *Los Angeles Times Magazine*. "The idea of a beautiful, predatory, undead glamour-puss has been going on for some time, but it is surprising how many lesbians I've interviewed mention *The Hunger* and *that* actress!"

That actress was born Catherine Dorléac on October 22, 1943, in Paris. The daughter of a veteran stage and screen actor and the younger sister of Françoise Dorléac—a vivacious and popular actress killed in a car accident in 1967—Deneuve took her mother's maiden name and made her screen debut at 13. After a series of small parts, the 16-year-old ingenue met French film director Roger Vadim, who became her mentor and lover. It is significant that Deneuve replaced Vadim's first wife, sex-kitten actress Brigitte Bardot, in his life and on-screen, offering a new image to cinemagoers. For while Bardot's appeal was the promise of availability, Deneuve's most certainly is not.

"Catherine is unattainable and represents everyone's existential dilemma—wanting what we can't have," says lesbian author and psychologist JoAnn Loulan. "There is this feeling, and not just among lesbians, that if we could attain something we can't have, then our lives would be smooth and easy, then we would be turned-on all the time, and then we could even have great sex with Catherine Deneuve."

Indeed, Deneuve's remote femme-fatale persona has always served her well. In the '70s her frosty elegance brought her to the attention of Chanel, who had Richard Avedon photograph her

draped over a bottle of perfume. That incredibly successful campaign eventually led to the launch of her own fragrance line, Deneuve. "I realize that I am better known for those advertisements in this country than I am as an actress," she muses.

Au contraire.

Liberated and independent in her private life, Deneuve has been married only once—to British photographer David Bailey. That brief interlude notwithstanding, she has declared, "Marriage is obsolete and a trap." Instead, she bore children by both Vadim (son Christian, 32) and Italian actor Marcello Mastroianni (daughter Chiara, 22) and refused to marry either of them.

Still, a liberated heterosexual lifestyle isn't necessarily a focus of fascination for lesbians. But perhaps the secrecy that veils Deneuve's private life combined with the fearlessly sensual lesbian love scene she did in *The Hunger*—in which she was the seducer, the corrupter, and the powerful one—does matter. "Ever since that movie, it has been very erotic and provocative for people to wonder about my feelings for women," she says simply.

But for many, watching *The Hunger* caused more than wondering about Deneuve. For some, it caused some wondering about themselves. "I remember the first time I saw *The Hunger*," says Guinevere Turner, cowriter and star of *Go Fish*. "I was 16, straight, and over at my boyfriend's house. I had no idea a sex scene between two women was going to come on. I was so blown away. I remember thinking, *That's so sexy! I hope someday I get to be gay so that I can do something like that.*"

Comedian Suzanne Westenhoefer had a similar revelation. "I watched the movie with a platonic gay girlfriend of mine," she says. "We had known each other since we were 18 and had never been attracted to each other. After the love scene was over, we started looking at each other very seriously. We couldn't help ourselves because it was so incredibly erotic."

Completely aware of the lesbian firestorm she set off 12 years ago with *The Hunger*, Deneuve is remarkably, though not unexpectedly, cool about the attention. Instead of being opposed to taking on another film role in which she makes love to a woman, La Deneuve has already done so. "I have just finish filming André Techine's newest film, *Child of the Night*, in which I play a philosophy teacher having a relationship with my female student," she says without apprehension.

Have you ever talked to the gay press before?

Well, in Paris one time I did something for their ACT UP movement to raise money for AIDS. But I did not do an interview. This is the first time I have spoken with the gay press.

For a beautiful actress to have the devotion of men—gay or straight—is not a new phenomenon. *You* have distinguished your-

self by having not only the men but the women—gay and straight—as well. Why do you think that is?

I don't really know. I think that in some of the films I've done, I've kind of deceived some people—maybe gay or lesbian—to feel much closer to me than to some other actresses. Of course, it is true that I have been involved in some films other actresses would not have done.

Do you like women in general?

Yes, I like women. I feel very close to women. I have been very supportive of women's issues. I signed the French abortion paper in 1972 and took a position about abortion at a difficult time. I am very sad that once again abortion is becoming very suspect. I find that incredible. I think all these things have helped to make women have an image of me that is different from other actresses.

Do you think your role in *Belle de Jour*—where you are living a double life, being a whore during the day without your husband's knowing—resonates with some gays and lesbians who hide parts of their lives from the world?

Yes, I can see that. People are very fascinated with that aspect of the film. They assume it is my way also. I am a very private person, so I think that sort of helps to maintain this image of me living a secret double life.

In *Belle de Jour* the brothel madame, played by Genevieve Page, obviously has a thing for you. You actually grab her and try to kiss her at one point. Did this cause any lesbian interest in you when the film came out in 1967?

No. That didn't start until after I did *The Hunger*. I think it was because the love scene between the women was so beautiful in *The Hunger*. I think Tony Scott, the director, made such a visually beautiful film, especially at the time, because it was a vampire story. I love vampire stories. That's why I did the movie. Women especially were taken with that movie—even more so when it came out on video. They always ask me to sign the cassette box of that video.

Susan Sarandon did an interview with *The Advocate* in 1991, and she said the press kept asking her if she had to get drunk to go to bed with you. She told them that was ridiculous: *Why would anybody have to get drunk to sleep with Catherine Deneuve?*

[*Laughs*] Oh, yes, I feel the same about her. The relationship I had with Susan Sarandon was very good, and I think something came out of it onto the screen. You can tell. There was something very natural between us. She is a very warm lady. It was a very long shoot, and neither of us was in our own countries, so we spent a lot of time together. Afterward, we saw each other and wrote to each other. We have a bond. I have a picture of her children in my home. She is always in my mind and heart. Also I think the scene we did was very sophisticated and good-looking. I think it was a very idealistic image of women together, a very good thing to have on film for homosexuality.

It's interesting that lesbians watching *The Hunger* did not—at least at the time—grab on to Sarandon the way they did to you.

I do not know why, but it is true.

You didn't even play a lesbian. You played a vampire.

Yes, but even at the time, when the film was first released, I could tell in interviews that the women did not see it that way. I could feel it in the questions. They were not thinking of me as a vampire. I had become a symbol for lesbians.

Have you ever heard of the phrase *lesbian chic*?

No. Oh, do you mean gay women who go with men as well as with women?

[*Laughs*] Well, no, but who knows? That could become chic too. I'm sure every lesbian would give you a slightly different definition, but it refers to a trend that started in the '80s, when some lesbians consciously took back some of the things usually associated with straight women. Things like fashion, makeup, femininity in general.

Oh, yes, now I know what you mean.

Do you think you might have accidentally helped to create an early picture of lesbian chic in lesbians' minds because you are very beautiful and feminine and you did an erotic love scene with another woman?

It is true that before *The Hunger* the film image of a lesbian was always very masculine. She would have to dress like a man. If there was going to be a woman who liked a woman, then she had to look like a man. *The Hunger* had a very strong image of beautiful women, so perhaps it is true. Suddenly, there was a woman looking like a woman and liking women. Yes, I showed you can be beautiful and be a lesbian. Maybe I did that.

When an actress plays the owner of a rubber plantation, the way you did in *Indochine*, no one asks her if she really owns a rubber plantation. But when an actress plays a seduction scene with another woman, the way you did in *The Hunger*, everyone wants to know if she is a lesbian.

Isn't that true! I think anything that has to do with sexuality makes people very interested. When you are working on the sexual side of a character, things become very complicated. When you have to touch and kiss someone in a film, it is not any longer something that belongs to the character. It belongs to you, because it is a continuation of your physical self, your desire. Some people fall in love with their costars and feel things that they never thought they would feel for them because they are touching. I may know an actor for years, and then we'll do a film together with a love scene, and I am astonished. It's not necessarily a sexual thing that happens to you, but it has to do with the fact that you touch and kiss and can be physically taken by someone—because we don't touch each other like that in real life, unless, of course, we really are lovers.

So people questioned your sexuality after *The Hunger*?

Yes, there were many questions. In the film I just finished for André Techine, *Child of the Night*—he also directed *Wild Reeds*—I play a teacher who is in love with her pupil, a girl.

I'm glad to hear this because I was wondering whether you would ever dare to play another romantic role with a woman after *The Hunger*.

Well, you are the first person I'm telling this to. And I do have concerns about talking about it because if I say that I am doing this movie where I play a teacher, there are not many questions. If I say I will be playing a love scene with another woman where there is kissing and touching, then suddenly it isn't about the film. It is personal to me. It's not anymore the role but the actress. It is all about me touching another woman.

[*Laughs*] **Still, you're doing it again.**

[*Laughs*] Oh, yes! I do yet another role with a woman, and the questions will come. Well, it is normal, really, sex being so important. It is still a big question mark about me. It is something people will talk about forever—and not just because of *The Hunger*. That's why I think *Belle de Jour* is such an important film for me. You can look at it today and still find it relating to the fantasies of women and men—but mostly women.

You've said that you are concerned that women might have a problem with *Belle de Jour* in the '90s because of the prostitution.

Yes, because prostitution is something that happens to you because of troubles you had when you were young. In reality no woman would choose to do that just for pleasure.

There's a split-second scene with your character as a child, and it seemed as if she was being molested. Is that true?

Yes, that is why it is not a choice for her. All women who do extreme things like kill or have sexual obsessions or who are prostitutes have trouble with their fathers. Even if a woman is abused a very long time ago, it comes out in her life in a negative way. Some women get into relationships where they are physically hurt. Women are talking more about this because a long time ago they didn't dare.

Do you think this private side you've maintained has helped to create interest in you from lesbians too?

Oh, yes. And women know that I like women. I have very, very close women friends, and so people often say of me that I like only women. It is something that appeals to people. Me being an actress, not being married but having children, means I have this whole other side, this secret, private life. People still wonder. And the less I tell them, the more the wonder grows.

People actually think you are gay? I mean, I know lesbians *hope* you are, but do they actually think you are?

Oh, yes. If I go out with a man three times, they don't immediately say that he is my lover. But if they see me in a private situation or going on a holiday with a woman, they say, "Oh, yes, I think she is!"

They ask you if you are a lesbian?

No, they don't dare ask me that to my face. Never in France because the press is different from the way the press is here. But sometimes I can feel it.

But you have a very public heterosexual life.

But I *don't* really let people see it.

You say you are very close with women. Where do you draw the line? Have you had moments of knowing what it would be like to be in love with another woman?

The word *love* means many things to me.

Have you ever had a physical romance with a woman?

I cannot imagine having a physical relationship with a woman. I have not done that. But I really love women. I have a very strong relationship with a woman that I have known for a long time. I knew her for some time before I knew that she was a lesbian, but that never changed anything about my relationship with her.

Do you know what the word *closeted* means?

To close?

Oh, that's interesting. Well, sort of. It's when people know they are gay, but they don't want other people to know…

Oh, yes, yes. I understand, but in my opinion they should not be pushed. I know here in America you are very strong about publicly pushing women to openly say that they are gay, but I don't agree. I think that is wrong. I think it is very shocking.

But the other side of this is that there is strength in numbers. People have no idea how many people in this world are gay.

Yes, that's very true.

If a woman is gay and she does wonderful work in the world, something that other people would admire, she could be a role model for young gays and lesbians who are desperate for people to admire. The suicide rate among gay teens is high.

I didn't know that. I thought it was much easier today to be open.

It is, but still there are relatively few role models for young people.

Yes, it is very hard. We are in a society that is ruled by men, and the image that people have of a woman is that she is married and has children. It is a problem for gays; I do know that. I have a lot—no, no, not a lot—but a few very good homosexual friends. I know one intellectual who told me he cannot officially tell people while his mother is still alive.

That is very sad.

Yes, but why should you force—

No, not force…

No, not force, but push someone to be officially recognized as being homosexual? I think that when you have a public life, you still have the right to have a private life. And some people have been talked about before they have decided they are ready themselves. They have been pushed before they are ready to…to go out?

Come out.

Yes, come out. To me that is not right.

If a friend of yours came to you—and she was a closeted romantic-lead film actress—and told you that she was considering coming out, how would you advise her?

I would tell her that she would have to choose carefully whether to reveal something that is still, in our profession, difficult to be—without having a lot of trouble. You see, it is still a man's profession in France. Even if there are a lot of women in films, there are few who are lesbians—that people know about.

Yes, that's the point. No one knows about them if they don't come out.

I think she would have to choose carefully because she would have to fight for it, for her career. If you are an actress and people know you are a lesbian, many people in the audience would not be able to forget—when they watch you—that you like women even though maybe you are kissing a man in the film. The filmmakers would say, "No, we cannot have her play the lover of this man. The public would not believe what they see." This is why it is good for the public not to know very much about your private life. You should be able to have a big range to be believed in many different roles.

But we know other things about actors and actresses that don't stop us from believing them on-screen. If we see Clint Eastwood and Meryl Streep kissing, we don't say, "Oh, I can't watch that! I know they are really in relationships with other people."

But that is different because people expect to see a man kissing a woman. It is what people believe. If they know that an actor really likes only men, they will not believe him making love to a woman in a film.

People believed you making love to a woman in *The Hunger*.

Yes, but they do not know that much about me. People don't think I am a vampire, but people don't know what goes on in my private life.

So what would you advise your friend? Not to come out?

[*Pauses*] No, but I would tell her it is going to be a problem: *Are you ready to fight for your career? You are going to have to be very open about it and very committed. You are going to have more troubles getting the parts you want than someone who is not gay, so you are going to have to fight a lot of people who are very conventional.*

You would support her in this fight?

Yes. I would say, "I'm sure you can do it, but you are going to have to fight hard for it."

There is a persistent rumor that you used a body double in the sex scenes with Susan Sarandon in *The Hunger*. Is that true?

There was a body double, yes. We both used body doubles. It is true. I confirm this.

Really? Thousands of lesbians just read that and wept.

Not the whole bed scene, no, but there were some images with body doubles.

Have you ever witnessed any homophobia on the set of a film you worked on?

[*Pauses*] What is homophobia?

It's a fear of homosexuals that usually leads to some kind of discrimination against them.

Yes, I've seen it. People do this sometimes without even knowing it, you know. There is an incredible, conventional attitude that people have about homosexuals to the point where you have to say something to someone. But then sometimes if you do, if you get into a discussion about this attitude, it makes it worse. People get more upset.

So you don't say anything?

What? Oh, no, they would never say this in front of me! But I've heard about it; people tell me things. But no, no one ever is...

Homophobic.

Yes, homophobic around me. Because to tell you the truth, I am not shy. I have a big mouth. I would not stand for someone to humiliate a homosexual man or woman in front of me—ever. It is

something I cannot stand. I am a Libra, and I cannot stand anything that is unfair.

[*Pauses, then nervously*] I want to ask you something. Have you ever heard of the lesbian magazine *Deneuve*?

[*Long awkward pause*] Yes.

[*Loudly*] Yes, of course you have! Well, I am suing them.

You're suing *Deneuve* magazine?

Yes, in France. They are trying to bring the magazine to France now, and it is not fair. They are using my name, and my name is a commodity. You cannot do that.

Well, it's strange that you're telling me this, because I called the editor in chief of *Deneuve* for background information on her magazine before this interview. And she told me that the magazine isn't named after you. She said it was named after her first girlfriend.

Yes, yes, I know they say that. They say that it is some friend or lover of something, but that does not matter. Everyone thinks it is me. Didn't you?

Yes, I did. In fact, I was shocked when she told me otherwise. I even asked her if she thought people buying *Deneuve* knew it wasn't named after Catherine Deneuve, and she said, "No one thinks *Deneuve* is named after Catherine Deneuve."

That is ridiculous! No one thinks it is anybody but me.

But this is going to be very tricky for you because it will look like the big guy going after the little guy.

Yes, I know, and it is a lesbian magazine, so lesbians will think I am suing them. It's not true. It does not matter what the product is—whether it is perfume or a magazine. My name is a commodity, and you cannot put it on something without my permission. It is not fair. I hope people will understand the real issue here.

I hope so too. Many gay men and women have had loved ones lost to AIDS and breast cancer. You had a tragic loss early in your adult life when your sister was killed in a car accident. I realize this was a long time ago for you, and you've never talked about it. Still, a grieving process is a grieving process. How did you manage to deal with this loss?

Yes, I don't talk of this, but I will tell you something: It was terrible. I was very young, and she died violently, so it was quite awful for me. Now, I have lost friends to AIDS, and I have been again living through those painful sensations. What is very different for me today is that there are other people to grieve with. There are so many friends who have also lost people to AIDS and, yes, cancer, that we can share this.

When my sister was killed, I didn't have people to share my pain with, so I kept it inside. I was young, and I was working on a film and had only one or two days to mourn. But it was a bad thing, being alone with this pain. Years later it caught up to me. It took over my life. It was a very difficult time for me.So I would like to say that even though this epidemic is a terrible thing, something good has come out of it. It has taught people how to grieve with each other. People are learning to share this long process. That is incredibly important. I wish I had known about sharing pain when I lost my sister. I am very, very grateful to know how to do this much better now.

Steve K

metko

As I write this introduction,

there are still no out television anchormen other than E! Entertainment's Steve Kmetko. No wonder he was a nervous wreck while making the decision to do his *Advocate* cover story interview. It took him years. And for better or worse, we can remember most of the courtship. Sure, Steve was dropping the usual hints that a gay celebrity often leaves around as he works himself up to the big moment (showing up in gay clubs, ambivalent appearances in gay or gay-friendly publications, etc.), but it took a cataclysmic event to finally make it happen. It took the brave, open life of someone Steve had never met. In fact, it took much more than his life—it took his death. It took the senseless death of gay Wyoming college student Matthew Shepard to make Steve Kmetko call it quits and finally out himself with style, honesty, and courage.

I still remember Steve talking to me during a preinterview meeting at Musso & Frank's, a legendary restaurant in Hollywood. "An innocent young kid being murdered and left to die like that in the middle of this country—for being gay! This is still going on?" he fumed over his dinner. "What am I afraid of, then? My career being hurt?" His blue eyes flashed anger at the thought of something so ridiculous. "Look, I've handled things a certain way most of my life. But it isn't making sense to me anymore." He folded his napkin carefully, still thinking about what he was going to do. "Let me call you tomorrow," he said, in a tone of voice that did not signal wavering. "There are some people in my private life that I want to talk to, to let them know what I am considering. I also need to inform people at E! Television. But I promise you I will call you. I will give you a definite answer, one way or the other."

Sometimes preliminary meetings like this one go nowhere. Or perhaps they go somewhere, but not to an interview. Coming out is such an intensely individual experience, such a profound awakening, that no two journeys are the same. Laying the groundwork and foundation can take years. It must be tailored to fit and deal with every single thing that has shaped a person's life up until the moment he or she comes out. There is no formula because we are all so different. Additionally, for a variety of reasons, some people never do it.

It was clear to me that up until he changed his mind, Steve thought coming out wasn't anything he really needed to do. Then one young man's death made him realize that his own visibility as a successful, professional, attractive gay man might make a difference in the lives of young gays and lesbians desperately seeking role models and reasons to live and believe in their own futures.

The next day *The Advocate*'s senior arts and entertainment editor at the time, Alan Frutkin, came into my office with a big smile. "Steve just called. He wants to do the interview. But he wants you to do it. He says you talked him into this, so now you've got to do the interview with him." It didn't feel like much of a punishment. I was delighted.

Months after the interview came out, I bumped into Steve at a Los Angeles film premiere. Since I never know how someone is ultimately going to feel about seeing his "gay" life sprawled across the pages of The National Gay & Lesbian Newsmagazine, I hesitated for a moment. Steve turned, saw me, and smiled. We hugged spontaneously, and I stood back to watch him effortlessly pull movie stars off the red carpet to interview them on camera. He looked happy, confident, and handsome.

"So…?" I asked. He knew what I was after. "Yes," he laughed, "it was a good thing. In fact, it was no big deal at all, except to me. It meant a great deal to me." I assured him it also meant a great deal to the thousands of readers who bought and read his candid, heartfelt interview.

Steve Kmetko stands at the door of his airy, rustic Silver Lake home. His dog, Frankie, is in his arms. He often is. "He even travels with me," the good-looking TV anchorman says, smiling cautiously. Kmetko can't quite believe he's actually inviting

someone into his home to grill him about his personal and professional life. Although he has dropped the occasional sound bites about himself, this interview marks Kmetko's first shot at connecting all the dots. It is also the first time the 18-year veteran of broadcasting—who arrived at E! Entertainment Television by way of *CBS This Morning, Studio 22, The Rock & Roll Evening News,* and WAVE-TV in Louisville, Ky.—has ever discussed his romantic relationship with Olympic gold-medal winner Greg Louganis. "He's a lot more relaxed about talking and having the facts revealed than I am," Kmetko says of Louganis. "He's just the most remarkable person."

And Kmetko would know. At one time or another he has talked to every luminary in Tinseltown. And yet despite his often self-effacing remarks ("Did I just have another blond moment?"), the 46-year-old interviewer is embarked on a very nonpublic journey toward self-discovery. "People talk about coming out, but I just don't think there is such a thing," he says. "I think it's a process that takes many, many years and takes many forms for different people. Today, thank God, for a younger generation of gay people, it's much easier than it was—and is—for me."

What does it feel like for you—a professional interviewer—to be interviewed?

I'm so accustomed to being on the other side. When I read things I've said in print, all it is is black-and-white words. I feel like the meaning is not as clear as I'd like it to be.

Let's try to be clear then. Did you always know you were gay?

No. I had suspicions. After all, I liked Judy Garland an awful lot and Edith Piaf and all the gay icons. But instead I got married because I thought that was the right thing to do.

The right thing...?

With my Baptist upbringing there was and still is some residual shame because they say that this is "an abomination."

Where are you from?

I was born in Cleveland, and my family moved to Chicago when I was 6. I was also the fifth of five children, and by the time I was 10 all my siblings had moved out of the house. I was pretty much a latchkey kid. I didn't have anyone to discuss my fears with. I think a lot of gay people early on feel that they must be defective. I didn't want to confront those things, and there were very few people to confront them with.

So you had no physical experiences with homosexuality?

I had a few physical encounters. I just thought it was a phase!

"Please, God, let it be a phase"?

Please, dear God, don't let my wrists go limp today. Amen.

Tell me about your marriage.

I was married for three years, but it was almost instantaneous that it just didn't feel right. It was like, "I've done something wrong!"

Did you two talk about it?

Actually, my wife told me I was gay. I would not approach the subject at all. I was taught you didn't talk about things—you put them in God's hands. You prayed about them.

So your wife confronted you?

Yes, and I had to agree with her. It was a very difficult split because I cared a great deal about her and I knew I hurt her terribly.

So obviously you were in the closet as a young reporter?

Oh, yes. I can remember having to cover some minister in Michigan while doing a story about homosexuality, and it was so hard because this minister was looking me in the eyes, saying, "You know, the world wasn't begun with Adam and Steve." And I was nodding, "Uh-huh," trying not to have an ick attack, worrying, *Is my face giving something away?*

There have been times that being gay held you back in broadcast journalism?

Yes. I was supposed to be promoted to the primary anchor position in Grand Rapids, Mich., and the general manager got wind of the fact that I'm gay and called me up to his office. I answered every one of his questions as honestly as I could—and I'm talking real honesty, not Bill Clinton honesty. At the end of the conversation, he said, "You might as well start looking for a new job because you're not going any further here." And that was a jolt and, I thought, a good reason to be closeted.

What did you do then?

I started looking for a job right away because I didn't want to live or work in that environment. I wound up in Louisville, Ky., where "it" was not an issue—which was very funny because, having been raised in the northern Midwest and having lived in Wisconsin, Michigan, Ohio, and Illinois, I thought, Kentucky is, well, the South! But "it" was never an issue in Louisville.

Did they know?

Yes.

What was your job at the station?

I was just a general-assignment reporter and weekend anchor. I was there for less than two years—before I wound up here in Los Angeles. But everybody there knew my spouse, Kurt, and was

"Actually, my wife told me I was gay. I would not approach the subject at all. I was taught you didn't talk about things—you put them in God's hands. You prayed about them."

friends with him. Kurt and I were together for 17 years, and we're still very close. Without his support through the years, I don't know what would have happened to me.

This is the man you were with right up until Greg?

Yes. Kurt and I came to the realization that when we both moved in together, we were very young. Over the years we developed tastes that were not exactly compatible, and we developed other interests. There was never any animosity. We just came to an agreement that we might have other areas of life that we needed to explore and that might be better explored without each other. When he moved out he bought a place just about a mile away from here. And we talk regularly.

Sounds like good communication.

Now, yes—we probably talk more openly with each other than we did when we were together. Kurt and I differed. I'm very much the homebody, and he's much more socially oriented. So he felt

in many ways that life was passing him by. And I felt I wasn't getting enough of him.

But you live alone now, right?

Yes, and I have never lived alone before. I went straight from my parents to my wife to my first boyfriend to Kurt. And it's only now that I'm living alone for the first time in my life, so I'm having to do a lot of my growing up now in my mid 40s.

Is that what Greg wants?

I think Greg would have liked it had I moved in with him three years ago, but I think this is a very important time for me. And I've discussed that with Greg and said, "I'm not ready; I need some time to learn how to look after myself."

Greg has talked about his being HIV-positive and your being HIV-negative. How has that affected your relationship?

It hasn't at all. If you love someone, you love them. It doesn't matter if they have an illness. What kind of person would I be if that mattered to me? Besides, Greg takes such good care of himself. He is so strong. When we go on a bike ride, I absolutely cannot keep up with him!

Whenever you talk about Greg, you seem to be almost in awe of him.

I think I am amazed at him, to see how people react to him in terms of being a hero. He's mythical to them.

Does that get in the way of your relationship?

Sometimes it does. Fans have literally reached over me to hand Greg their phone numbers when we're out in public. I've had people step on me to get to him. So yeah, sometimes that can be a little devaluing.

Are you and Greg comfortable being called a couple?

I think it's safer to say we see each other steadily. We vacation together; we spend a good deal of time together. After living with someone for 17 years, in all honesty, I don't think I'm completely past that yet. Any relationship is a lot of give and take. People don't understand that. I think they sometimes look at that as conflict. I don't know if I'm ready to give and take as husband and husband. I'm not at that place.

Greg's got a nice house in Malibu that I go to on weekends, or he comes here to the city. I thrive in this kind of urban environment; I love living in the city like this—and in an ethnically diverse neighborhood. But we have a good time together. Sure, we don't always see eye to eye. He's not always good at communicating; neither am I.

Sounds like a relationship that's still unfolding.

You know, I think of Rod Jackson and Bob Paris or even Ellen [DeGeneres] and Anne [Heche], and I wonder, in retrospect, if they think, *Oh, God, I wish we hadn't been quite so public.* Because then you have to live with that private piece of information in other people's minds: "Oh, look at them! I thought they were the perfect couple!"

But there are so few "great couple" models for gay people, period.

But is it a good idea to talk about it? See, the kind of background I come from is so different. Let me give you an example of what this upbringing can lead to: Every year my sister Becky used to take a vacation from her husband and two children and would come out to visit me here in California. In 1990 she came to visit, and I had just moved into this house. She went swimming in the pool alone and had an asthma attack and drowned. I came home from work and found her in the pool.

My parents, several months after that, came out to visit; they always stay with me. I was trying to have a conversation with my mother about how this had emotionally impacted me. My mom's response was, "Honey, just try not to think about it."

See, you don't talk about it. You don't sit down and work it through. Well, this may work for my parents, but it doesn't work for me. I think they're wonderful people, and they do wonderful things for others, but I can't live like that.

So this interview is a huge step.

Yes, actually sitting down and talking about something! I've been working with a shrink on that for 10 years now. And I still have trouble.

Why are you doing this?

It's like what Nathan Lane said in explaining why he was doing the cover of *The Advocate*. It's about what happened to Matthew Shepard. I think—as someone who has a fairly high profile and someone whom people have seen on TV for more than 20 years now—by making this simple statement, maybe people will think twice about other gay people they encounter. Hopefully they'll look at me and say, "Well, he's succeeded, and he's got a pretty good life, and he's not out to hurt anybody."

Can you give us examples of how you find yourself coming out at work?

Yes, it did seep into an interview I did with Susan Sarandon for *Stepmom*. I told her I'm a sucker for tearjerkers and had to sneak out of the theater before the lights came up so nobody would see me crying. And she said they were starting a campaign that it was OK for men to cry. I said, "Well, I kind of know that." And then she said, "I've got news for you. Chicks dig men who cry, men who are sensitive. If you can let a woman see that…" So I said, "But I'm gay." And then she said, "Oh, well, chicks like that too."

Did you keep that in the interview?

Yes, we just went on with the conversation. It aired. I couldn't sit there and let her tell me how chicks would like me more because I cried when in reality I don't date chicks—to use her word. I couldn't be false in that way.

When you're interviewing celebrities who are gay but still in the closet, what do you do? Do you go near "it"?

"It" is not something I would bring up in an interview unless "it" had appeared somewhere else first.

Is there anything, professionally, that you haven't done that you want to do?

I suppose if an acting job came along, I might be interested in that. In all honesty, I tell everyone that I have the best job there is. I have a very short day, they send me all over the world, they provide clothes for me, they send me first- or business-class wherever I go.

What about *Dateline* or *20/20*? Are those jobs interesting to you?

No, I don't think so. I'm a big fish in a little pond at E!

Do you think it's still difficult to come out in broadcasting?

If only Stone Phillips would come out!

If only he were gay. Do people confuse the two of you?

Are you kidding? Please! Yeah, right! No, but somebody on the Internet wrote that they thought I was the illegitimate child of John Tesh and some other guy.

Do you think there will come a point in the industry when coming out in broadcasting will be easy?

I hope so. We'll find out if I ever get another job [*laughs*].

Especially when news anchors are thought of as such great authorities. If Walter Cronkite tells the world, "This is how it really is," and he's talking about being gay, will that be OK with viewers?

[*Laughing*] Maybe, but I don't think it would be OK with his wife, Betsy.

"I can remember having to cover some minister in Michigan while doing a story about homosexuality, and it was so hard because this minister was looking me in the eyes, saying, 'You know, the world wasn't begun with Adam and Steve.' And I was nodding, 'Uh-huh,' trying not to have an ick attack, worrying, *Is my face giving something away?*"

Emma
Thompson

ma

It was an incredibly hot July day

in 1995 when I first met Emma Thompson. She had just completed two films, *Carrington* and *Sense and Sensibility*, for which she was being run through the interview mill at the swanky Hyde Park Hotel in London. Usually when the sun comes out in England, well, you know the expression about mad dogs and Englishmen in the noonday sun. They take to the parks and streets, soaking up every fogless ray.

This, however, was a really hot afternoon, and no one was prepared—especially those desperately trying to fix the hotel's air conditioner. As I looked around for an open window to stand near, a blur of anxiety and excitement rushed by me. Emma was wild. She had been sitting in front of hot TV lights for a BBC special and had gotten horribly overheated. Flushed and panting, she blew into her hotel suite, where I was waiting, like a windmill. Immediately my fears of meeting a stodgy British Oscar-winning thespian with no humor or passion went out the window. Emma was sexy, contemporary, hilarious, and fearless. Tearing her blouse free from her blue jeans and kicking her shoes across the stately suite, she wailed, "Shit, damn, it's hellish, absolutely hellish!" I laughed, and she slid to a halt to take me in. Smiling, she ran her hand through her hair dramatically and pleaded, "What are we going to do?" I was about to suggest ice cubes when she snapped her fingers, grinned, and said, "Let's order hot tea." I thought she was kidding, of course, until the most elaborate platter of steaming hot water and tea leaves arrived. Emma—still tearing off articles of clothing and reappearing in new ones—sat down to serve us. "Hot beverages can help you with the heat," she said. Completely disarmed by now, I would have believed anything she said. As it turned out, she was right about the hot tea—and a lot of other things too.

About a month after I returned to Los Angeles, we were having an *Advocate* staff meeting when one of the editors announced that I'd better have a look at a report on Reuters (a wire news service) that was covering Emma's sudden breakup with her actor-director husband, Kenneth Branagh. The report implied (incorrectly, we later found out from Branagh himself) that Emma and Kenneth's marriage had come apart because he had become terribly upset over things she had said about her sexuality in her *Advocate* interview. Naturally, this was insane. However, what I did realize was how much must have been going on in Emma's head and heart during our interview. There was a freedom and openness coming from her, a vulnerability and clarity that usually accompanies great changes in a person's life—and certainly the fracturing of such a highly regarded marriage would qualify. No wonder she was so thoughtful, so fascinated with the conversation, so forthcoming about herself.

Years later it was no surprise to me when someone working on the *Ellen* show called to have me send over a copy of my interview with Emma Thompson. Emma was going to make a guest appearance on the sitcom as...a closeted lesbian. It was also not surprising when that episode went on to win an Emmy award. Spirited, funny, and sexy, Emma was a riot. Her open attitude about her own sexuality and life gave her the freedom she needed to make the episode both hilarious and important.

She's also a terrific sport. At the end of our interview in London, I had decided to surprise an *Advocate* editor (who was mad for Emma) by asking the actress to record an outgoing voice message for him. As I stuttered out my request, her face lit up with glee. "You're kidding! No one's ever asked me that before. What fun!" She was, in fact, so excited about the idea, she insisted on doing one for me as well. Breaking up in the middle of it several times, she finally pulled herself together by chanting "Focus, Emma, focus!" To the delight of my friends and family, for months anyone calling my home phone was greeted with, "This is Academy Award–winner Emma Thompson. Judy and I are not home. Please leave a message, and one of us will get back to you as soon as possible."

Over the years I have learned that when straight actors talk to *The Advocate*, we've got to be careful. Sometimes they're doing it only to court gay readers, say all the right gay-friendly things, and win a few new fans. In Emma's case it's the real thing. She is incredibly consistent in her life and her work. For example, she delivered a breathtaking performance in the HBO production of Pulitzer Prize–winning lesbian playwright Margaret Edson's *Wit*. She played Vivian, a woman dying of stage 4 ovarian cancer. Emma also cowrote the screenplay. The title, *Wit*, refers to the ways in which very bright people can use language and wit to keep their feelings away. That Emma was attracted to playing and writing this role is completely logical to me. Here is an excerpt from our interview:

"I think that I have always been beguiled by people who can use words, which is very confusing, because people who can use words don't necessarily know how to live life. In fact, people who use words best use words to keep life at bay. It's a great temptation, and it's something I probably suffer from, because I want to explain all the time and I want to analyze all the time instead of saying, 'Yeah, but what do I need? Where are my feelings?'"

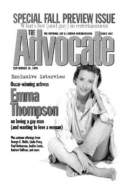

"Someone from the press tried to talk to me while we were making *Carrington*, and I just couldn't do it," four-time Oscar nominee and two-time winner Emma Thompson says passionately. "I was too into my character. I couldn't get out and be Emma."

Exactly where the lines are drawn between Thompson and Dora Carrington—the unconventional '30s English painter she portrays in *Carrington*, which opens November 10—is up for grabs. During the course of this interview, which took place in London at the Hyde Park Hotel, the 36-year-old actress came to the realization that there may be "more of Carrington in me than I've been admitting to myself. I always thought she was so different. It's a bit unnerving."

Equally unnerving is to expect to interview a somewhat austere actress with a stiff-upper-lip public image rooted firmly in Cambridge thespian aristocracy, Merchant-Ivory adaptations, and Shakespearean grandeur—only to encounter a free-spirited, barefoot, and blue-jeans-clad renegade who wishes she could get out from under words and wouldn't mind having a thing with a woman someday. Maybe it's an early midlife crisis? "Actually, I'm always looking for adventure," she says, her clear blue eyes shining.

"Emma's candor and openness are very much like Carrington's," says the film's scriptwriter and director, Christopher Hampton, who won an Oscar for his screenplay *Dangerous Liaisons*. "I don't know what the role is making her rethink in her own personal life, but like Carrington, Emma seems to have one skin less than everybody else."

Born in London in 1959, Thompson is the daughter of director Eric Thompson and actress Phyllida Law. After early forays into acting at Cambridge University with the comedy troupe Footlights (which included longtime gay friend and actor Stephen Fry), Thompson won a British Academy Award for her performances in two 1987 BBC series, *Tutti Frutti* and *Fortunes of War*. It was during the shooting of *Fortunes of War* that Thompson met and fell in love with her costar, Kenneth Branagh. He cast her in his 1989 Oscar-winning adaptation of *Henry V*, and the two were married soon after.

Thriving in the safe environment of her off- and on-screen relationship with Branagh, Thompson went on to costar with and be directed by her husband in *Dead Again* (1991), *Peter's Friends* (1992), and *Much Ado About Nothing* (1993). But it was her Oscar-winning performance in Ismail Merchant and James Ivory's *Howards End* (1992) that once and for all staked out Thompson's own special screen terrain.

Although more awards and Oscar nominations followed, with *The Remains of the Day* and *In the Name of the Father* (both from 1993), for those who missed much of Thompson's earlier comedic BBC and stage work, her slapstick stint opposite Arnold Schwarzenegger in *Junior* (1994) came as something of a surprise. Still, nothing she's done to date is likely to prepare audiences for the extraordinary departure her performance in *Carrington* represents.

"I don't think I've ever done anything that has meant more to me," Thompson says of the androgynous Carrington. The film tells the true love story of the courageous female painter and the celebrated Bloomsbury writer Lytton Strachey—a gay man portrayed by Jonathan Pryce, who won the 1995 Cannes Film Festival's Best

Actor Award for his performance. Daring to explore the differences between love and desire, the film has had such an impact on Thompson that she's begun "to question all sorts of things in my life."

"Emma is an activist, so nothing she does would be surprising," says Julie Christie, one of the original free spirits to reel out of London and on to international fame in the mid '60s. "She's not afraid to stand for—or stand up for—things that challenge conventional thinking. That's something I value very highly."

Currently putting the final touches on *Sense and Sensibility*, which she costars in with Hugh Grant and adapted herself from Jane Austen's novel, the unexpectedly contemporary Thompson bursts into her hotel suite with a big grin and a friendly commotion.

Have you ever spoken to the gay press before?
[*Circling the room, looking for something*] Not knowingly.

Emma, are you ever going to sit?
Oh, yes, of course. I'll sit here. [*Flapping the shirttails of her blouse to cool herself down*] I have just been doing telly interviews, and it got so fucking hot. My shirt is sticking to my back. Do you mind me smoking while we talk?

No, no... [*Watches Thompson pull out papers and roll a cigarette*] You roll your own?
Yeah. They go out a lot, and there are no chemicals in them, but they're still not good for you. [*Gets up to look for matches, then brings in her floppy purse and begins dumping things out of it*] Good, I've got a lighter. My handbag is so full of shit. OK.

In your career, you've worked with several gay directors. Is there something in the sensibility of a gay director that connects with you differently than a straight director?
Yeah, I think so. But it's a generalization, because one of the most feminine directors I have ever worked with is Ang Lee [who directed *The Wedding Banquet* and *Sense and Sensibility*]. With Ang, it's an Eastern thing. But, yeah, there is something different. My uncle was gay and my godfathers; I was brought up in a very gay environment.

Really?
When I was young, the fact of their homosexuality was not hidden. It was so much a part of my life that when I went out, as it were, from the family environment into the world and discovered that homosexuality was not generally acceptable, I was deeply shocked.

So your introduction to homosexuality was quite different...
My experience is the opposite of most people's—which is that they leave their homes and encounter homosexuality as something

new and different. I was surrounded by gay people. It has never been odd.

Your gay uncle and gay godfathers actually raised you?

My uncle certainly did, and my godfathers, yeah, absolutely had a lot to do with my upbringing and my attitudes toward life. I was really lucky.

What about gay women?

I lived with two gay women at college, which was wonderful.

In both *Peter's Friends* and *Carrington* you play a woman in love with a gay man. Has that ever happened to you?

No. I have never actually fallen in love with somebody who is gay. However, I have the honor of being the only woman I have ever known to pick up a gay guy in a gay club. I'm so proud of that!

Did you know he was gay?

Oh, yeah! He was just gorgeous. I'm just not used to thinking about the difference. What I think is more interesting is people who are asexual. I think that most people really are bisexual, but asexual people are very interesting.

You wonder if that is a real state or a frightened, withdrawn side of some other sexuality.

I know. I like people who are sexual because I am a very sexual being. I have always been driven in that way. That's why I have gone for men who are very heterosexual, who have a very strong response to women.

That's quite different from Carrington's character.

What is so interesting about Carrington and Lytton is that they do contain so much of the masculine and the feminine, only the opposite in each other. Carrington didn't like being female at the beginning. I think that was because she didn't want to be penetrated in any way—not morally, physically, or spiritually.

And a gay man would leave her this space?

Yes, she didn't want to be judged and she didn't want anything to get inside. One of the things that attracted her to a homosexual—and I think it attracts a lot of women to homosexual men—is that he didn't judge her.

Gay men don't judge you physically?

They don't judge you full-stop, actually. There is a great link between homosexuals and women, because women are also not part of the patriarchy that makes the rules and says what is right and wrong.

You see a bond?

Yes, but that might be changing. When I talk to my gay male friends, they say there is a new conflict between gay men and women. As the gay structure has gained weight and momentum, that creates a conflict. I think it will be very interesting to see what happens to a relationship that started off as the unspoken, mutual understanding of not being part of the superstructure.

Everyone assumes that there's a huge bond between gay men and gay women, which there is, but unfortunately, until AIDS gay men didn't always wish to include gay women. When AIDS hit the gay male community, they often turned to gay women for help. It can be seen as one upside to this awful disease.

And it's very important to look at the positive sides to AIDS. I know AIDS has produced so many changes, not only in the gay world but also in the straight world, where people have had to think about very, very deep-rooted taboos. Matters of life and death always break these kinds of things down. AIDS has started to break down a lot of taboos, particularly between gay children and their heterosexual parents. They have to deal with homosexuality, and in dealing with it, they learn about it. Then they are able to communicate their learning to others around them.

Do you know that you have a dedicated following in gay men?

I have no sense of an audience or a group of people, any group of people, being aware of me. But I mean, that's thrilling.

You have no awareness?

Well, yes, of course I know I have an effect on people. I suppose, in some ways, I have always tried to be the sort of woman I'd want to be. [*Laughing*] Do you know what I mean? I had a great role model in my mother, who was always against a kind of manipulative femininity. I too fought against that—even looking feminine.

Are you a feminist?

When I was young, I was very angry about the woman's position and society's attitude toward gay people. It just spurred me on to be berserk, and I wanted to get away from all those stereotypical women.

I know you've said that you get irritated with people talking about your marriage. I don't know if you were speaking particularly about here in England, where they call you "King Ken and Queen Em." So I don't want to put you off with this question—

No, no, not at all, not at all.

Well, wait, you might be put off. Are you aware of the fact that there are rumors that you and Kenneth are a marriage of convenience?

[*Puts her hands over her mouth to muffle laughter*] Oh, no! I've never heard that one. That's marvelous!

Yes, we actually heard a rumor that your husband fell in love with his male exercise trainer for *Frankenstein*.
Emma, are you going to leave the room?

[*Rocking back and forth in her chair*] No, it's wonderful! Just the thought of my husband with Josh is just very, very amusing. I'll pass that on to them. They'll both love that. They'll *adore* that!

Did Kenneth just sign to do *The Normal Heart*?

That's another rumor. I have heard him talking about it, but at the moment I know he's not. He's doing *Hamlet* next year, so he's stuck in Shakespeare.

There are so many layers of sexuality going on in *Carrington*. Also there's clearly a lack of monogamy, and yet there's a devotion that's even bigger than monogamy. Does this ring true for you and the way you lead your own life?

Oh, yeah, absolutely. I think the film asks so many questions—questions that have always been asked by the gay community. Masculine gay promiscuity has always been a tremendous fear for people who want to believe in the ideal of romantic love. That it is possible to have all kinds of erotic experiences without necessarily having that romantic relationship is very, very threatening to people.

But not to you?

I think it is something that human beings *have* to start accepting and exploring, because it is powerfully a part of our nature. Then, of course, you get into the question of female sexuality, which has never really been understood. And because we live in a Christian patriarchy, the whole notion of women having a kind of free sexuality is threatening simply because of inheritance.

What do you mean?

Meaning a man does not wish to pass all his wealth on to a child who is not his. And he may be doing that if his wife is allowed her independent sex life. This question of possessing other human beings has to be looked into. If we persist in this notion that somehow people have to belong to us, we are not going to get very far in any kind of development of our self-understanding. A lot of people find this thinking threatening because it asks exactly these questions: How do you live? Do you live full-stop? And do you understand that if you do live full-stop, you will suffer, because this will cause impermanence, and impermanence will bring loss and grief—and yet life is constant impermanence.

It was surprising to me that there were no women in Carrington's life, that she never explored women sexually.

She did! Carrington had several female lovers later on in her life. We didn't bring them to the screen. We couldn't.

Why?

First of all, we had only two hours in which to examine 17 years, and the main love story, upon which we had to hook everything, was the Lytton-Carrington love story. We had at least four more love stories going on with all the different men that come into their lives and relate to one or the other of them—or in some cases both of them—sexually. I think to introduce more lovers, particularly female ones, complicates the story to such an extent that people would have gone away thinking, *Well, fuck 'em all!* But I would love to have done that—*love* to have done that.

We have heard that you are going to do the film version of Radclyffe Hall's 1928 lesbian novel *The Well of Loneliness*.

I want to do it, yeah.

The book is very stereotypical compared to our thinking about lesbians today. Would it be updated?

I would think it would have to be in some ways because it suggests that the main character, Stephen, is a lesbian because she's been brought up to be a boy with a boy's name. You *couldn't* make that the premise. I think that's a problem for whoever writes the screenplay. Actually, I hope that in a few years' time I'll get a gay role in a romantic comedy.

In the beginning of *Carrington*, you are mistaken for a boy. Your hair is cut shortish, and you're dressed somewhat butch.

Definitely!

A lot of lesbians have been told they don't want to really be women when they dress like this. Did you feel any loss of femininity dressed this way?

Oh, no! I felt lots of freedom, complete freedom. But when I

went to university, I shaved my head, wore little wrap glasses and butch overalls, because I didn't want to be trapped in femininity. I felt it as a trap. I don't think it is necessarily; I love seeing gorgeous women dressing themselves up as gorgeous women. I like looking at them.

But you don't want to dress that way?

It's not something that I feel comfortable with because it draws a particular kind of attention that I've never wanted and that I'm really not interested in. I've never, ever wanted that extreme femininity. Carrington's persona was incredibly liberating to me, even though it was also frightening because it posed so many questions.

You have said that Carrington's character is so different from yours. I'm not getting that from you at all.

I know, I know! I don't know whether that's true. I think maybe I'm just kind of kidding myself. Why did I end up playing her?

So that you could play out some part of yourself?

Yes, I think so. I've got this very articulate image of myself—and I think that's especially to do with Cambridge and with learning how to speak and how to really express myself. One of the major differences between me and Carrington is that I use words all the time to color everything. And Carrington was a visual creature. For her it was a wave of feeling—nothing to do with words.

And that's not you?

I think that I have always been beguiled by people who can use words, which is very confusing, because people who can use words don't necessarily know how to live life. [*Laughs uproariously*]

Exactly.

In fact, people who use words best use words to keep life at bay. It's a great temptation, and it's something I probably suffer from, because I want to explain all the time and I want to analyze all the time instead of saying, "Yeah, but what do I need? Where are my feelings?"

What about when you do a physical love scene with another actor, something that is beyond words, that only involves your body? Have you ever been taken away by that?

I think that part of the eroticism of doing a sex scene is that there *are* boundaries, but within those boundaries you can do whatever you want. If you want to be that vulnerable and that open, you can even make love.

Do you like doing sex scenes?

I haven't done very many nude scenes or sexually explicit scenes in my career because a lot of the characters I've played have been living in times when you don't show that. But I found all the sexuality in *Carrington* incredibly moving to do. It was naked in every way because I was using my body. *Carrington* was definitely a very sexual experience. It was very releasing.

What did it release in you?

The fact is, once you are at it hammer and tongs, as it were, the delicate thread of sexual tension is broken. I find that very satisfying. Look, we're talking about sex, and sex is its own master, its own mystery, its own life force. It's beyond us. Yet we're always trying to get the "animal" back in the cage, you know?

"Carrington had several female lovers later on in her life. We didn't bring them to screen. I think to introduce more lovers, particularly female ones, complicates the story. But I would have loved to have done that—*loved* to have done that."

What you're saying is particularly important for gays because the "animal" that runs through our lives scares homophobic people big-time. They really want it caged.

Oh, God, yes! But sex is the most powerful force in the world. So forget it. If we could only accept our own ambiguities and the variation of our souls and our desires, we would be so much happier.

You don't have children. Do you imagine you will someday?

I never wanted children, but it doesn't worry me one way or the other. I think if I got pregnant, I'd be very excited because I would think, *Oh! A new era, a new phase, a new life. Wow!* Anything that has ever happened to me that is different, I have welcomed. That's what excites me, something that is unexpected or different or that I don't know how to do.

There are a lot of fears about gay parenting. How do you feel about gays and lesbians raising children?

I think the more different kinds of parenting that we examine, the better. I've got two male gay friends and two female gay friends who have children, and to me there is no difference. I don't understand why people would think gay parenting is threatening. It's only threatening to what they perceive as some sort of inculcation. They think that if you are brought up by two male parents or two female parents, you are bound to look for a different kind of partnership. (A) That doesn't matter anyway, and (B) I just don't think it's true. I think people will go their own way, whatever.

You think that being gay is biological?

Oh, yeah, absolutely. There is no question in my mind that it is entirely natural; therefore, it must be biological. Whatever any human being does is natural because a human being has done it. We like to call it unnatural because we like to demonize: good-bad, right-wrong. That way we can fit in. I don't even like using the word "natural," because it implies that there is an unnatural. That's not the case. But don't you think people are very frightened of their sexuality? I think a lot of people are very, very frightened of it.

Were you ever?

Never. I was incredibly lucky because as a very sexual teenager, I was allowed to have a sex life. When I was 15, my mother took me to see one of the first proponents of birth control, who was 80 at the time. There was this 80-year-old woman telling me, "I give out birth control to allow human beings to enjoy each other sexually." Even at that age, it was a revolutionary notion. I was so lucky—but even luckier that I wasn't judged by my parents for having a very active sex life from a very early age and really enjoying it.

Was there ever any time—from your 15-year-old sexuality to today—that you felt sexuality for another woman?

[*Long pause*] No, not really. I've never met anybody who made me feel that way. But I have absolutely no problem whatsoever imagining it. And it wouldn't be something that would be difficult to play onstage or in a film at all. It would be a tiny shift in perspective, actually.

Would you be surprised if you felt sexuality for another woman, if that ever really happens to you in your own life?

No, I have always *longed* for it to happen to me. I've longed for it to happen to me because it would be a really wonderful experience. And it probably will happen to me one day.

Perhaps if you do *The Well of Loneliness* or anything in which you play a woman who is in love with another woman, then you will—

Yes, I think that's when I will experience it, because it doesn't frighten me, so I'll allow myself to experience those feelings—which is why I would really like to play a lesbian.

If you do *The Well of Loneliness* or something else where you play gay, what actress would you like to be in love with?

[*Pulling her hair and laughing*] Oh, God, well, lots of women, because I love women so much. I think that because of my masculinity—I've got a lot of masculinity—I would probably put myself with somebody very feminine, overtly feminine like Michelle Pfeiffer. Actually, I find Michelle fantastically attractive. I'm always kind of rushing up to her and kissing her on the mouth because she's so delicious. She's so-o-o delicious. But oh, God, it could be any number of women, actually. I would go for somebody that I could really communicate with.

Do you ever get love letters from women?

No, I never have.

Well, you will now!

[*Laughing*] I sure will! A lot of women do write to me. I think more women write to me than men. Young women write to me a lot because I represent something that is really strong for them.

You did a diary for *Premiere* magazine on the making of *Junior*. Would you considering doing that for *The Advocate* if you do *The Well of Loneliness*?

Oh, absolutely! That would be great! If I do *The Well of Loneliness* or anything that you're interested in, I would love to!

Chastity

Bono

I remember sitting with my girlfriend

and two friends on the island of Catalina, off the coast of Los Angeles, in January 1990. As we ate breakfast we gawked shamelessly over the January 2, 1990, issue of the *Star* tabloid with its bawdy cover headline CHER SHATTERED AS DAUGHTER CHASTITY TELLS HER: I'M GAY. There was something secretly pleasing about the information despite the source and scandalous presentation. An Academy Award–winning actress and a California Republican representative had a lesbian daughter.

Since the phenomenon known as coming out had yet to really take hold in the American media (k.d. lang, Melissa Etheridge, Greg Louganis, Ellen DeGeneres, etc., were all still in the closet), the way the world usually got to know a famous gay or lesbian person was by outing. Rock Hudson, for example, never publically admitted that he was gay. He was outed by AIDS in the late '80s. And now, suddenly, America was dealing with our lives again. Chastity Bono was gay, and the rest of our day on the island somehow seemed brighter.

Little did I know that this merciless outing was one of the darkest hours in the life of the daughter of Sonny and Cher. Years later I would learn what Chastity was going through while we were gossiping and devouring her story. "I'm glad you were having fun," she once told me sarcastically. "I was not!" Instead she was trying to keep her fragile life from blowing apart. Her mother was frantic for her. Her father was worried. Her band, Ceremony, was trying to land a record contract. Her secret relationship with one of the band members was coming apart. A woman she was in love with was dying. All she could do was lie and deny. "It was so utterly painful—everything," she told me. "I was trapped."

During my first year at *The Advocate*, the magazine tried many times to get Chastity to do an interview. I focused on her band's record label, Geffen. I had a friend there, and she knew exactly what I wanted. One day when I called pressing for a contact number, my friend closed the door to her office and told me two things: (1) Geffen had dropped Chastity's band from the label and (2) Chastity's home phone number. "Good luck!" she concluded.

I sat at my desk looking at the phone number. *How can I call Chastity Bono out of the blue?* I wondered. Surely that would freak her out. The mere thought of it freaked me out! I waited a few days, worked up the courage, and dialed. I got her answering machine and left a message with my weekend phone number. I asked her for an interview. I never expected to hear from her.

My home phone rang on a Saturday morning, and it was Chastity. "Look, I'm a dyke," she said clearly. "I don't deny it. I'm proud of it. I would like to come out—believe me, I really would. But this isn't a good time. My life is a mess. I need to get myself together, figure out what I'm doing and where I'm going. Then I'll do an interview." I couldn't believe she was blurting all this out to me; she was so honest, so straightforward. I asked her to have lunch with me, and she accepted.

When I walked into the dining room of the Hollywood Roosevelt Hotel the following Monday to meet her, a very telling thing happened. The maître d' came up to me and with a knowing tone of voice asked, "Are you looking for Cher's daughter?" I told him I was and let him lead me to Chastity's table. "Did you tell him you are Cher's daughter?" I asked her, surprised that she would identify herself that way. She rolled her eyes, shook her head no, and looked pained. "That's the way it always goes," she muttered. "People may recognize me as Chastity, but what they think and say is 'Cher.' Every public thing I do affects my mom, and everything she does affects me. That's one of the reasons why I can't just come out. I have to prepare her as well as my father—who is now in Congress. I don't necessarily have to do what they want, but they deserve to be well-prepared."

Over the next year, I had many lunches with Chastity at the Roosevelt Hotel. God knows what other people thought we were doing; few would have guessed that we were going through the long, arduous process of clearing the way for an interview. Over half a dozen salads, I learned more and more about her life so far—her struggle for individuality, her professional yearnings, her untapped creativity, her complicated but loving relationship with her famous parents, her grieving for lost love, and her quest for the right life partner. She would bring to the table her concerns—some of them voiced by her family and friends, some of them her own worst fears. We got to know and trust each other. One day she said to me, "I love what you guys do at *The Advocate*. I wish I could do that kind of work, connect my life to the movement in some way." It was a particularly surprising remark because of how bitter Chastity's own experiences with the gay movement had been thus far. The tabloids were not the only media to out her. The gay press came after her as well, leaving her frightened and understandably paranoid. It was significant to her that *The Advocate* had not done this. She had also become a fan of the magazine now that I was bringing copies to her on a regular basis. She was full of questions, suggestions, and enthusiasm. She saw a door opening for her, and she began pushing at it.

"But how could you write for *The Advocate*…from the closet?" I asked her. "We wouldn't feel right about it. I don't think you would either."

One thing I've learned about Chastity over the years is that she is a doggedly honest person. As with her mother, you generally get "the bloody truth" from her, whether or not you expect it or like it. It didn't take very long before Chastity's desire to be free and clear of the shame and hiding she'd experienced most of her life—combined with a possible creative writing road beckoning in the distance—led her to pick a day, place, and time for the following interview.

"There was no k.d. lang. There was no Melissa Etheridge. There was no Janis Ian. No one was out then," says Chastity Bono, remembering the January 2, 1990, issue of *Star* that outed her as a lesbian years before lang, Etheridge, or Ian challenged

public opinion by coming out themselves in *The Advocate.*

"I was the first famous lesbian to be outed. I'm not talking about rumors or innuendos—I mean outing. Because my parents were so famous," says Bono, who was first carted out onto *The Sonny and Cher Comedy Hour* when she was 2, "my life was considered public domain. Being outed was the most destructive, terrifying thing anyone could imagine. I panicked. We all panicked."

Bono's tabloid outing with its sensational headline—CHER SHATTERED AS DAUGHTER CHASTITY TELLS HER: I'M GAY—launched the only child of Academy Award–winner Cher and Rep. Sonny Bono (R-Calif.) into a life of hiding, lying, shame, confusion, and rage. With her rock band, Ceremony, on the verge of being signed by Geffen Records, the 20-year-old singer-songwriter followed the advice of all those around her and denied everything.

Among those giving her advice was Cher, who is well-schooled in the damaging effects of tabloid journalism. With no examples at that time of successful out performers in the music business, Cher—who knew of her daughter's lesbianism before the outing—encouraged Chastity to hide or destroy any photos she had of herself and her girlfriend, warning that the tabloids would find and print them. Both family members and business advisers worried that confirmation of the young singer's homosexuality would instantly kill her career. They told Bono that when she and her lover, a fellow musician, left the home they shared, they should leave by separate entrances. Even so, the tabloids stalked her, as did the gay press. Her life was being ambushed by all sides.

When Ceremony's album [*Hang Out Your Poetry*] was finally ready for release in September 1993, a meeting was called at Geffen Records to decide how Bono should handles questions from the press about her lesbianism. Surrounded by chairman David Geffen, several label executives, two or three promotion people, and Cher, Bono listened while well-meaning professionals tried to figure out what she should do with her life. By then Cher had changed her mind: She wanted her daughter to come out. "She told me, 'You're a writer. How can you write real feelings and live the way you want to if you hide who you really are?'" Bono recalls.

But by then the constant barrage of tabloid outings and criticism from gay journalists had taken its toll. Overwhelmed by the stormy breakup of her five-year relationship with her lover and the subsequent consummation of an affair with an older woman she'd loved since she was a child, Bono retreated into the closet.

Chances of inching that closet door open were further dashed when her new lover, Joan, was diagnosed with cancer. Bono found herself running back and forth, taking care of her dying girlfriend and publicizing her new album. "I just couldn't come out then," she says. "I wanted to, but I just couldn't."

Again the tabloids attacked: CHER WIPES AWAY THE TEARS AS HER DAUGHTER MOURNS GAY LOVER'S DEATH, a 1994 *National Enquirer* headline read. And again Bono went into hiding.

"It was painful for me to see her having to deal with this, to live in fear of being discovered, feeling that it would do such personal harm to her," Bono's father says from his Washington, D.C., office. "But I knew the minute she crossed the threshold on it, she'd be OK. I wanted her to take a position and not withhold something, because if you go through your life hiding, it's a constant nightmare."

For Cher, the situation forced her to do something she normally never does—lie. "I remember I had to go on some show after the tabloid outing," Cher said in an interview for this article, "and someone put the question to me. It's a very difficult thing to have to lie point-blank. It was a maternal instinct kind of thing: You do stuff for your kids that you wouldn't do for anybody else. What she's doing today—taking the initiative—makes me very proud of her."

Geffen is equally supportive: "I've known Chas since she was 3. She's had a difficult time growing up, but I think she's very talented in a variety of ways, and I'm rooting for her."

So what finally caused Bono—who made a guest appearance in lesbian writer-producer Lauran Hoffman's 1994 film *Bar Girls*—to take control over her life? What caused her, after a year of off-the-record meetings with *The Advocate,* to understand that the constant din of gossip dogging her for nearly six years could be silenced only by her own candid words telling her own remarkable story? The 26-year-old Bono explains it best herself: "I was never very courageous about this kind of thing. But I think my story may mean a lot to others who are struggling to come out. Today, being in the closet is in my way. I have things to do, and I have to be out to do them."

When did you first realize you might be gay?

As a kid I thought that I was a little boy. My dad kind of pushed me in that direction. He really wanted a son, and I was kind of naturally inclined to that. I hated wearing dresses. I remember a point on *The Sonny and Cher Comedy Hour* where they used to put me in these little outfits that matched my mom's, and I said, "I'm not wearing any more dresses. You have to put me in pants."

You were 2?

No, I was probably 5. I especially liked it when they put me in clothes that matched my father's.

As a little kid I had crushes on girls. I remember talking to my dad about this girl. One of the roadies was going out with her, and I said something like "I have a crush on her too." I was teeny.

My dad encouraged me to play football. He used to say that he wanted me to be the first female quarterback in the NFL. Some of my fondest memories are of watching football with him on Sunday, and then at halftime we'd go out and throw around this little Nerf football I had. I always had crushes on women who were friends of the family—older women that I remember liking, wanting to impress, wanting to be around.

When was it you first heard the word *gay*?

After I saw the movie *Personal Best*. I had just turned 13, and I remember watching the love scene and thinking, *Oh, my God, it all makes sense. That's me.*

What did you feel?

Actually, the way I dealt with it—I mean, you can't go to a gay bar at 13 or 14—was to start writing a screenplay called *Jumpshot* about a women's professional basketball team. It was terrible, but it was a love story between two women on the team, and it was my way of expressing my feelings.

What about your parents? Did you tell them?

My mother was playing a lesbian in *Silkwood* at the time, and I remember reading over and over the scene where they're out on the swing talking together. I had a big crush on Meryl [Streep]. It's hard not to.

Your mom had no idea you were gay when she was doing *Silkwood*?

I was so young. I don't think she thought of me as having any sexuality one way or the other.

Too bad. She could have come to you for advice on how to play a lesbian.

I think she probably would have. Whenever my lover, Joan, used to see that film, she would comment on this scene where my mom is carrying Diana Scarwid's luggage into the house. Joan used to say, "That is exactly you, running in the house. She must have studied your walk."

So even though you were full of feelings about the fact that your mom was playing a lesbian, you didn't attempt to communicate any of them to her?

Fuck, no! I was scared shitless of telling her, and I also didn't think anybody would really take me seriously at that point because, you know, you always hear, "Adolescent girls go through that. It's a phase."

Why were you afraid to tell her?

I was afraid of disappointing her. They're your parents—you love them, and you want them to think that everything you do is great, and here's this thing that's not really accepted. It was just my own fear of not living up to her expectations. I knew she wasn't homophobic—there were always a lot of gay people around—but it's different when it's your own child.

Do you remember the first lesbians you ever noticed?

I think they were Joan and Scotty. Scotty was a friend of my mother for years. She's an older woman. She's kind of like my godmother. Joan and Scotty used to be a couple. My mom lost contact with them for years and years. I don't think my dad was too happy about my mom hanging out with them.

Why?

I'm not sure. But they lost contact. Then one day during the late '70s, my mom was going out with this guy, and he was talking about his neighbors, Scotty and Joan. My mom said, "Wait—what are the odds of there being another Scotty and Joan living together?" So she went over to their house and knocked on their door, and it was Scotty and Joan! They came back into our lives, and that was the first time that I remember meeting them and knowing they were lesbians.

When were you first attracted to Joan?

One night—this was in the '70s—I was watching the tape of Mom's Vegas show, and Joan walked in. Now, I'd seen Joan a million times, but I'd never paid attention to her. She walked in, and I looked at her, and it was like, *ba-boom, ba-boom*. I followed her around for the rest of the night like a little puppy dog. It's weird how you can see somebody all the time, and then one day you *see* them, and everything changes.

How old was Joan then?

She was my mom's age, late 30s.

Did Joan have any idea what was going on with you?

She kind of figured that I had a crush on her. We became very close friends. I was always kind of flirty.

I heard she was your baby-sitter.

That's a total rumor.

Did you ever date men?

Twice. The only time I ever slept with a man, I was 16. I did it because I was sick of everybody saying, "How do you know you're gay if you've never slept with a man?" So I slept with a man so I could say, "Well, I did it, so now I know."

Did you like him?

He was a marine, which is the most hysterical thing. I get shit from every woman I've ever been with: "The guy you fucked was a *marine*? I went on one other date with a guy after that, in Palm Springs. I was totally in love with this girl at school, but she was not comfortable with the whole lesbian thing.

I met this guy who was the son of one of the people who worked in my dad's restaurant. He was an arts student—good-looking, bohemian, long hair, gentle. I thought, *Well, if I could be attracted to a guy, this would probably be the kind of guy, because he's not rough and rugged.* We went to see some movie, and I thought about this girl from high school the whole time. It put me in a really bad mood, and I just wanted to go home. I thought, *You know what? I gave it another shot, and it's just not happening.*

How did the relationship with Joan evolve?

It was one of those things that would flare up and die down. When I was 18, we kissed. I was in L.A. for the summer, and we went to this party. At the time she was dating two different women, and they were at the party too. Joan wasn't paying attention to either of them. She was flirting with me. But again, this wasn't uncharacteristic of our relationship.

Did she know you were gay?

Yes, at this point we had talked about it. When I first kissed a girl, I told Joan. She was one of the few people I really could talk with about being gay. She was always my mother's friend. But I spent much more time with her than my mother did.

Did your mom resent that?

She didn't understand it. Actually, Mom took me to a shrink at one point because she was worried about my being gay. I was spending all this time with Joan and Scotty. Of course, I knew I was gay at that point, but I didn't tell her, and I didn't tell the shrink because I knew that would be a bad idea.

You were sitting there, lying to your shrink?

Yep, I did that twice. I was in a relationship with this girl in high school, and we spent the summer at Mom's house, and Mom kind of sensed that something was up and dragged me to the shrink again. [*Laughs*] And I lied again.

What finally changed?

Mom walked in on me with a girl.

Oh, drama! Was this after she'd sent you to the shrink twice?

Yes. Mom and I were staying at Tom Cruise's house, and he had two lofts. Mom slept in one, and I slept in the one with a kitchen. Mom came in to get something to drink, and this girl and I were on the pullout sofa bed making out. Instead of rolling away from each other and pretending that we were just sitting there talking, we both jumped up like dorks. Mom walked in, saw us jump up, and went right back out.

She never confronted me about it, but the girl with me told her, "Oh, we fell asleep, and you scared us." My mom's always hated her because she knew something was up.

OK, back to Joan.

We were at a party. I had just gotten my driver's license, so I wasn't a very good driver yet, and I was drunk.

Were you doing a lot of drinking at that time?

I wouldn't classify myself as an alcoholic by any stretch. I could take it or leave it. My family is super straitlaced when it comes to drugs and alcohol. It's hysterical: My mother has this image of everyone thinking she's totally wild. Not true at all. Even about sex she's very conservative. My mom was never promiscuous. I would tease her because she would sleep in bed with somebody for a month and they would not touch each other.

So you were drunk at the party.

Yes, and the party happened to be a few blocks away from Joan's house, so she said, "I'll drive you back to my house, and you'll spend the night." Her girlfriend Suzanne was her date that evening. Joan and I got in my car and started making out. The next thing we knew, there were these headlights on us, and it was Suzanne.

More drama!

Dyke drama! She totally busted us. I was trying to calm Suzanne down. Luckily, she wasn't pissed at me. She figured Joan had seduced me, but Joan wouldn't talk to either one of us because she freaked out. So I ended up spending the night at Suzanne's because I was still drunk and felt I couldn't stay at Joan's because she was being so weird. Just what I wanted to do: sleep over at a girl's house after I'd just gotten nailed making out with her girlfriend!

So you and Joan got off to a good start.

Actually, yes. For the next week, Joan and I dated each other. We fooled around a little, but we never slept together. I started really having an affair with Joan right after I started making my record—which was bad because I was involved with somebody else who was making the record with me.

At the same time?

Yes, I was falling for Joan and sneaking around. If I had come clean and said, "Yes, I am seeing Joan," the person involved with the record would have pulled out. And we had worked so long. It wasn't like it happened overnight. We started [putting together the band] Ceremony in the summer of '88, and this was probably already '90 or '91 when we were making the record. I was going, "I can't fuck it up now!"

Did Geffen's relationship with your mother have anything to do with your being signed to his label?

No, it was not a favor at all. I think people in the record industry thought, *Here's a recognizable name, so that's an added plus,* but my record cost more than any other band starting out, ever. It cost over half a million dollars, so that was no favor.

Geffen—along with Gregg Allman, Gene Simmons, and Val Kilmer—was once your mother's lover. Do you remember him?

Well, I really didn't like Geffen because he was the first serious person Mom dated after my dad. Actually, Geffen tells the funniest story: Apparently, I walked in on him in the bathtub when he was naked, and I made some comment about my dad's dick being bigger than his. He told me this story when Ceremony was on his label.

So you were afraid of blowing Ceremony's record because of your affair with Joan.

Yes, and my lover at that time was my first serious relationship. It was kind of an abusive relationship in the sense that she was very emotionally abusive. She was very self-centered, very self-involved, very dominating. I was really afraid of her as well. So trying to break up with her during [making] the record, I thought, *This is not going to work.*

What did you do?

Finally, when the record was over, the relationship ended. It was every bad dyke-drama cliché. All my stuff got broken, destroyed, and thrown at me. Finally, I moved in with Joan.

Was that before or after the tabloid outing?

The outing happened back in New York, right after I got signed to the development deal with Geffen in December 1989. When it came out I was like, "Oh, my God, my career is going to be over before it even gets started."

Talk about the tabloid outing.

I got a call from my mom's publicist. She'd gotten an advance copy of the *Star* and read it to me. My first reaction was, "Can't we stop it? Isn't there something we can do?" She said, "No, it's done. They're running with it." My mom was completely freaked out. She had warned me, "This could happen—be careful." And here it happened. Before that I used to go out to bars, and I would go out to gay pride events and stuff like that.

Cher worried you could be outed?

Yeah. She always told me, "Be careful. If this ever got out, I don't know if you could handle it." But I didn't think it would happen because it had really never happened before. You didn't have that shit before me.

At least your mom knew you were gay by then.

Yeah, but my mom was not happy about it being in the tabloids

"I was the first famous lesbian to be outed. I'm not talking about rumors or innuendos—I mean outing. Because my parents were famous, my life was considered public domain. It was the most destructive, terrifying thing anyone could imagine."

and said, "Your career is over! We have to do something." The tabloid article had said that she didn't want to talk to me, so Mom told me, "We have to be seen together a lot because I don't want people thinking that what they wrote is true." She was going to London, and she wanted me to go with her, but I couldn't—which was a good thing, because the tabloids there were even worse.

They were outing you in London?
Sure, because my mother's huge in England. It was one tabloid story after another for the longest time. I was a fucking wreck. It was a nightmare. They were trying to get pictures of my girlfriend and me together. We hid pictures of us at my girlfriend's house—which was not a smart thing to do because during our breakup she threatened to blackmail me with them. After that everybody got more and more paranoid, and they started sending me out on dates.

Who's "they"?
Publicists, my mother, the record company, everybody. Then there was this really big fuckup because there was this premiere that Mom's publicist wanted me to go to, and she set me up to go with a flamboyantly gay man who worked in her office. I said, "They're never going to believe this!" The dyke and the fag—it's the classic thing. So I ended up going with my guitar player. Well, I guess the guy I was supposed to go with originally was pissed off,

and he shot his mouth off, and it got to that guy, Michelangelo—whatever the fuck his name is—Signorile.

He painted the Sistine Chapel, I believe. Go ahead.
So he wrote this article in *OutWeek*. It's a great article, actually, and he was right on the money, but it really pissed me off at the time. Then the publicist had me do an article with the *Enquirer* that said I wasn't gay. So that was totally embarrassing, stooping to the level of giving an interview to the *Enquirer.*

And lying?
Yeah, I lied. But at that point I didn't feel bad about lying because I was just so pissed off that it even happened, that they were invading my privacy that badly. I lived in total fear with my shades drawn. I was being followed and hounded. No, I really didn't have any guilt about lying.

How did you feel about the gay community at the time of the tabloid outings?
I was pissed. I hated the gay community. I was beyond angry because I found out that it was a gay man who leaked the original story. They were getting quotes from people in the gay community saying, "Oh, I saw her at this club." This gay bar called the Cubbyhole had its bathroom wallpapered with my tabloids. They were selling T-shirts of me at Gay Pride.

What about the idea that celebrities are fair game?
Most people who are stars wanted first to be artists, and in our society we raise famous artists to the level of stars. Because you have a particular talent at something and are making a living at it, why does that give the media unfair advantages over you that they wouldn't have over an ordinary person? I learned a lot about what the press could legally do when I was outed, because they couldn't say the name of the girl I was with. They blacked out her face because she was not public domain. I was. I was the daughter of Sonny and Cher.

Is that why they outed you?
Yes, my mother is a huge tabloid seller. People knew I was gay, and they printed it to sell papers. I think after that everybody kind of jumped on the bandwagon, and they were outing Richard Chamberlain and John Travolta and Kristy McNichol. At one point they were going to pay $25,000 for a picture of me and my girlfriend—not a sexual picture, just a picture of us walking down the street or something.

You should have given them one!
I know: "Here! Give me the cash!" It got so ridiculous: I was doing this gig, and the tabloids ended up writing that my girlfriend and I were singing "I Got You Babe" to each other onstage!

So you decided to lie to the press. You came to Los Angeles, finished the record, and moved your affections more openly to Joan.
Right.

What did Joan think you should do?
Joan always thought that I should come out and thought that I was being totally ridiculous. That's why she would love what I'm doing with *The Advocate.*

At your cover photo shoot for this issue, you said, "I really wish Joan could see this."

She would have loved it. She probably would have wanted to get in the picture with me.

When did Joan get ill?

In July '93. She had already been diagnosed with non-Hodgkin's lymphoma once before, in '89.

You knew that?

Yes, but it wasn't very bad at the time; she lived with it for years. She never felt sick until that July, when she got really sick.

When you were finally living with Joan, was there any friction with your mom because of their old friendship?

No, she was really cool. I told her, "I'm seeing Joan," and she started laughing. She said, "Well, I think this is going to be a very good life experience for you."

You have to understand: Mom hated my girlfriend before Joan. At one point she wouldn't let her in the house. Later Mom told me, "I couldn't understand why she treated you the way she did, and your taking it was just too difficult for me to watch." My dad felt the same about her. He never forbade her to come in his house—that's not his style—but he didn't like her. Nobody liked her. She treated me like shit. I was basically her glorified slave. I remember one of the first times I was ever with Joan, she got up out of bed and went to the kitchen and said, "Do you want anything?" and I about fell on the floor. I couldn't believe that somebody was actually asking me if they could get me something.

What did you discover about yourself during Joan's illness?

Lots of people, when bad things happen, disappear, or they don't rise to the occasion. I now know that I'm the kind of person who, when the chips are down, is there. Joan said that to me countless times: "I wouldn't be able to do this without you." I thought, *I really hope my cosmic role in this whole thing is to help her die gracefully and in the least painful way that she can.*

Here was this woman that I had loved for years who had loved me. Our relationship turned romantic and sexual, and looking back on it now, I think that's why it happened: because she was going to get sick, and she needed somebody who had the time and the love and the patience to take care of her and to help her through and get on to the next place. I literally took care of her that whole time. The nurses used to tease me: "We won't have to come in while you're here."

They knew you were her lover?

Some did, but one nurse said to the doctor, "You know, Joan's daughter really looks like Chastity Bono."

You said your mom was great with you during this time.

Yeah, she was very supportive, very there. Joan had gone through a stem-cell transplant, and the doctors thought she was in remission. But she got pneumonia and died. I really wasn't prepared. I thought she was going to be OK. So after the funeral I fell apart—I mean really apart, where I just thought, *I don't know what I'm going to do. I don't know how I'm going to get through this next minute, let alone what I'm going to do with my life.*

Did you feel suicidal?

I was very close to getting into heavy drugs. There were a lot of prescription drugs around, and I was very depressed. I was doing some prescription drugs when Joan was sick. There were pain pills

around, and I like pain pills. So I was doing more than I should. My mom got me out of that house and took me away. Had she not done that, I think I could have gotten into big trouble. I'd been injecting Joan like crazy for pain, so the idea of shooting up wasn't frightening to me.

Did Ceremony break up at that point too?

No, but we'd gotten dropped from Geffen Records the week Joan died.

And didn't you tell me that your mom had just sued to get off the label?

Yeah. Our second single was ready to ship, and they pulled the plug the day they got the letter from my mom saying she wanted off the label. I didn't really care at that point—I was so consumed with Joan. I didn't quit the band until after Joan died. I just thought, *You know what? I really don't want to do this anymore.*

How did your dad find out you were gay, and how did he react?

He was the first one in my family to know. I was reading this lesbian book, and he saw it in my room. He picked it up and said to me, "Is there something that you want to talk to me about?" So I told him, and he was like, "Oh, I knew." He was really great about it, very supportive.

People have many misconceptions about Sonny Bono. His conservative politics would lead people to think he would never be supportive of your lifestyle.

First of all, let me say this about his political career: I am a Democrat; he knows that. We don't even talk about politics. However, I am extremely proud of him for what he's done, because it's a big deal. He had to work really hard. Even though we see things differently on a political level, on a personal level I am very proud of him.

I know he has not supported protective rights for gays.

He was talking to me at one point about gays having a minority status. I was very antigay then, because this was right around the tabloid time, and I was feeling, *Fuck anything gay.* But now, of course, my view is different. I think we do need to be protected. We are a minority. But I haven't really talked about that since with him.

You told me that when you were a child, your father, not your mother, was the one who made meals and ate with you.

Yeah, well, my dad wasn't as busy as my mom. During my whole growing up, my mom's career was doing a lot better than my father's. He had time to be more family-oriented. He still loves that.

It's funny. I was at my mom's this weekend, and something happened with her chef, and there was no food to eat. So I cooked spaghetti and meatballs, and my mom came in and said, "You look so much like your father right now."

He had more traditional values and more time to spend, which was really nice. It's hard to be raised by nannies and in chaos, and that's what my mom's house is like. It's still like that. I mean, it's great—I love to go there on weekends and spend time with her when it's really nice and quiet. But come Monday morning, the phones don't stop. So it was nice when I was growing up to have a place that was kind of normal. It kept me grounded in what was important in life, as opposed to getting caught up in all the Hollywood bullshit.

You don't feel comfortable with "Hollywood bullshit"?

Not really. I think people are always amazed to find out how much I am not involved in it, how I don't have any famous friends.

You never went to special schools?

I went to a prep school in Los Angeles, and I literally did not have one friend. I used to hang out with the teachers because I couldn't stand to be around any of the rich kids with famous parents.

How does this fit with the great bond you have with your mother? This is her world.

I think the closeness I have with my mother is not that part of her. She has a very flamboyant side that everybody knows, but there's another side to her that's kind of a homebody. I love watching movies or television with her or talking. It's weird because she's an extremely educated person despite having no formal education.

Education, unfortunately, wasn't stressed very much in my family. I think because they were so successful at not needing it, they didn't see the point in it for me. Not having it worked great for them: Look where they are now. My dad's a congressman, and he doesn't even have a high school diploma.

Was it hard for you when your parents broke up?

Yes, the adjustment of going back and forth between Mom and Dad was difficult. I don't do that very well even now. I like roots. I'd go to my dad's house, and I'd always cry when I got there the first day. Then by the time I was really comfortable, I would have to go back to my mom's house and start the cycle all over again.

What do you remember of your mother's marriage to Gregg Allman?

Gregg was a complete fuckup. He was the kind of guy who would say, "Oh, we're gonna do this great thing," and then not show up. My brother, Elijah—Gregg's son—just went to see him this past Christmas, and he's still up to his same tricks. He says, "I'm going out for a pack of cigarettes" and comes back three days later. I feel bad for my brother because I think it's probably the hardest on him.

My worst memory of Gregg is when he picked me up from school one day. I guess he was drunk, and he couldn't find his way back to Malibu. We got lost, and finally this guy said, "I'm going that way. Follow me." We followed him, and we ended up at this bar where Gregg got more drunk and picked up girls. We ended up getting home at around 11 or 12 at night. My mother was totally freaked because we were supposed to be back by 4. He was a big disappointment for a kid because he would just let you down every time.

How did you get your name?

My mom got pregnant with me during a movie she made called *Chastity.* I've never seen it, but I hear that it has some type of lesbian overtone. Nothing overt, but it's about a young girl discovering herself.

How did you meet your current girlfriend, Laura LaMastro?

The first time I ever met Laura was at a Halloween party. One of my dearest friends works with her at E! Entertainment. I was still with Joan, and Joan was healthy. I walked into Laura's house, and I remember her standing against this wall. I said, "Who's that? She is the best-looking girl I've ever seen in my life." But it didn't really go any further than that because I was happy with Joan.

And you saw her again after Joan died?

She was at a gig I played, and we talked a little. I was kind of ready to have something for myself again. She was able to talk to me in ways that my friends couldn't about what had gone on with Joan. She was so compassionate and open. At the time I thought she was an angel sent to help me get through my grieving. It was this instant connection. She was involved in a long-distance relationship at the time, and she was really hell-bent on staying in it. I was just kind of stuck with it and stuck with it, and then she broke up with her girlfriend. I don't think she broke up with her girlfriend to be with me, even though I think her ex-girlfriend probably thinks so.

At that point were you feeling any guilt about caring about somebody so soon after Joan?

I think the guilt came later. At that point I was just thrilled to be feeling again. Laura's a great girl. She has the best character of any person I've ever met. She is incredibly honest and loyal. She's really solid, and I adore her. So does my family.

Does either of you want to be a mother?

I do, but we're talking years from now. Laura doesn't really seem to want to have kids. But someday I would like to. The idea of actually being pregnant is really unappealing to me. But being a parent is not, so I don't know how I'll swing it.

Talk about your interest in journalism and the fact that you are now writing for *The Advocate.*

I think because I was in the closet and in denial for so long, it's great to be out and involved. I look at writing for *The Advocate* as a way to really do something for the community and to work and be involved in things that are important to me. It's creative, which is great, because I was really starting to miss that a lot.

You have this famous family. Do you think that being gay gives you something that is totally, uniquely yours? Elijah is not gay, Cher is not gay, Sonny is not gay.

Yeah, I guess it does. I don't say that I'm proud to be gay because I don't necessarily think it is something you should either be proud or ashamed of. It just is. Whenever I do something, people think, *The only reason you are getting to do this is because of your parents.* I've had people call Laura a starfucker. They say she just wants to be with me because I'm the daughter of Cher. Other people I've been with wouldn't even mention my mother's name, because it's not hip to give a shit.

I guarantee you, when people start seeing my name on *Advocate* articles, they'll say, "She got handed that on a silver platter because she is Chastity Bono." That's what everybody has always said about everything—from the work I do to the people I'm with. Nobody ever takes me seriously. Nobody ever says, "You got to make a record because you are a talented musician. You have a really nice girlfriend because you are a really nice person."

Are you relieved to be coming out at last?

I definitely feel that if k.d. lang, Melissa Etheridge, the Indigo Girls, and Janis Ian hadn't come out, I wouldn't be coming out now. I'm certainly too wimpy to be the first person on the block to do something. However, maybe my being one more person doing it is going to make another person do it. It's like that silly hair commercial: "Tell two friends, and they'll tell two friends, and so on, and so on."

Minnelli

Without question, Liza Minnelli

is one of the most fascinating, confusing, talented, funny, conflicted, over-the-top, conservative, warm, cold, fragile, hardy, fearless, fearful, thoughtful, and unrealistic human beings I have ever met. To this day I don't know whether she knew much more than she was telling me in our interview or much less. Swinging from denial to telling me secrets I never dreamed she'd reveal, Liza is, as the musical says, "a puzzlement." She's also utterly fabulous, out of her mind, heartbreaking, and great fun.

The nine hours I spent locked up alone with Liza in a Plaza hotel suite in New York City in the mid '90s is nearly indescribable. Not just because she was going though an enormous crisis at the time and shotgunned most of it into this interview, but because I like her so much and admire her struggle to such an extent that I'm concerned about what I dare reveal. Stranding me in several locations as she kept changing the venue of our meeting, our interview ended at 5 in the morning when the child of Judy Garland and Vincente Minnelli refused to let me leave her hotel room until I joined her in viewing one of her parents' old movies.

Weeks later, when we met again to do her cover photo shoot in Las Vegas, where she was performing at Bally's hotel, Liza seemed more subdued. Backstage I watched her handle fans, including one borderline man who snuck in by posing as a journalist. She knew he didn't belong there long before any of her handlers picked up on it. Taking control, she answered a few of his bogus questions, made him feel acknowledged, and then had him led out. Only afterward did she let on how shook up she'd been. Who would have known? Situations like this have haunted the superstardom of Liza Minnelli since she was a child, and she is a pro. She's also an overly generous host. Worried that people would be bored with Vegas, she arranged a table downstairs for what she called "the tits and ass" show. There are no words to describe what it was like for a cluster of gay and lesbian friends of Liza to sit with the Oscar and Tony winner watching half-naked people dance and sing to old show tunes. The epitome of this surreal experience arrived when a scratchy recording of Judy Garland singing "Over the Rainbow" came on. The table froze as Liza turned to us wide-eyed and innocent, gasping, "Oh, it's my mommy!"

A born and bred pleaser, gregarious but fragile, it would be difficult to blame Liza for trying everything under the sun to avoid the following interview. The subject—although I tried to disguise it—was rumors. Rumors about herself, her family, and her lovers. The context of these rumors was twofold: homosexuality and drugs. At the time of the interview Liza was back in the tabloids. An appearance on a British television series—looking very thin and acting very strange with a woman friend of hers—set things off. Was Liza gay? Did she have AIDS? Was she on drugs? What about the sexuality of her father, several of her mother's boyfriends, her own late ex-husband, Peter Allen, and a couple of her subsequent boyfriends? Given Liza's understandable resistance to such questioning, she turned out to be a good sport. Sometimes she told the truth, easily and bravely. Other times she bolted off into Lizaland, telling me riveting, non compos stories that made no sense at all other than to yank me off-subject—which was exactly what she wanted to do. Once, when I asked her about AIDS, and again, when I asked her about her rumored romance with cabaret singer Lana Cantrell, Liza threw a spoonful of vanilla ice cream across her fancy Plaza suite, nearly hitting one of those famous Eloise drawings.

I loved her spirit. I still do. And I got her message about the questions.

"Some people think that where there's smoke, there's fire, and my family has smoked its whole life, back to my grandparents and great-grandparents," says Liza Minnelli, responding at long last to questions about her family and homosexuality.

The Oscar-, Tony-, and Emmy-winning megatalent is sitting in front of a platter of ice cream and tea in a plush suite in New York's Plaza hotel. Painfully nervous but ultimately determined to open the door she's kept locked since she was practically born in a trunk 50 years ago, the chocolate-eyed offspring of showbiz royalty turns away from the dessert feast and sighs: "I've learned that when you try to set something straight, it's kind of a game, because you have to bring up the rumors. So there it all is again."

Being the keeper of the flame for her famous family, Minnelli has dealt in the past with gay rumors by refusing to acknowledge them at all—whether they were about her; her mother, Judy Garland; her father, director Vincente Minnelli; or her late ex-husband, songwriter Peter Allen. But tonight, with her ears still ringing from the enthusiastic shouts of a private party of businessmen—who paid six figures to see her perform downstairs in the Plaza's Grand Ballroom—Minnelli is ready to talk.

And with recent *National Enquirer* stories reporting LIZA'S STILL A PARTY ANIMAL and FRIENDS FEAR SHE'S HEADING FOR AN EARLY GRAVE LIKE HER MOM, it's probably a good thing. "I know how to deal with all this," Minnelli says, waving away the latest upsurge of drug-abuse and ill-health rumors. "I just do my work and wait it out. *She* deals with the rest of it, not me."

The *she* Minnelli is talking about is the star everyone knows as Liza. Created 43 years ago when a 7-year-old Liza danced on the stage of New York's Palace Theatre while her mother sang "Swanee," Liza the fashion, acting, dancing, and singing diva is not Minnelli the person. That person, who likes to call herself Liza May, has struggled most of her life to separate from Liza With a Z and all that jazz. Call it a coping technique, call it whatever—Minnelli doesn't care. The emotional girl the French have always recognized as "*la petite Piaf américaine*" knows one thing: It keeps her sane.

Through the years, as Minnelli's own accolades amassed and her stardom threatened to take on the huge shadows her parents left her in, many clichéd pitfalls opened up for her as well. Along with her three Tony awards for *Flora, the Red Menace; Liza at the Winter Garden;* and *The Act*—plus her Oscar nod for *The Sterile Cuckoo* and Best Actress award for *Cabaret*—Minnelli found herself battling the pain of broken marriages (Allen, Jack Haley Jr., Mark Gero) and substance abuse. It seemed the pressure of being *her* was just too much. "I was Judy Garland's kid. I didn't get that this was a disease yet," she says, referring to her addictions. "But when I did, I raised my hand. I asked for help. I did what I always do when I'm lost. I worked my butt off, studied, and learned about it."

"Liza's great because she's up for anything," says the Pet Shop Boys' Neil Tennant, who coproduced Minnelli's 1989 album *Results*. "When she's at the mike, you've got this whole show being done just for you. I think *Results* was possibly the best album we've ever made."

Singer Johnny Mathis, who joins Minnelli in a duet of "Chances Are" for her latest album, *Gently,* also enjoyed collaborating with her.

"I'd worked on several occasions with Liza's mom and was totally captivated by her magic," he remembers. "Working with Liza May was a joy." The album, released by Angel Records this past spring, definitely represents a turning point for Minnelli. As she herself puts it: "There is no glitter or pizzazz to my vocals. It's just raw me, singing as sweetly and honestly as I know how."

Sing out, Liza!

Liza, you're back in the tabloids.
Yes, they love me. I sell papers for them.

What does it mean that their stories about you always want you to...
Die?

Yes, and die in a way that repeats your mother's tragedy with drugs.
They are bored. Good publicity is dull. Do you know that they took that awful picture they used of me in the *Enquirer* [April 9, 1996] and ran it through a computer? You know how they can make you look beautiful? They can do the exact opposite too. When I'm not working, I never wear makeup. It's not good for your skin. There are no eyelashes... [*Stops for a minute, then goes for it*] Also, a few people should look up the word *menopause.*

Menopause?
Yes, it gives you tremendous mood swings, which nobody told me about. You start out loving somebody at the beginning of a sentence, and by the end you're going, "You son-of-a-bitch Communist bastard!" [*Laughing*] You really don't know what's happening to you!

Most people know about your battles with substances. What is recovery like?
It's the same for me as for anyone. Someone recovering from substance abuse in a small town and walking into church for that first sermon after she's back is like me going onstage the first time I'm back. It's just bigger, that's all. My parents were my parents—it was just bigger.

How did your parents raise you?
My parents were so wonderful, because my father would say to me, "Do whatever you think is right." My mother would say, "Do the right thing."

Yeah, but *that's* a lot of pressure.
That's true. My mother would say things like—which *was* pressure—"You're the proof that I am a good woman." That was too heavy for me.

How long ago did your mother say that?
She said it to me when I was a teenager and I was her friend. She

shared almost everything with me. That was the heaviest. That's why I ended up in Betty Ford, I'm sure of it, all those years later.

The pressure of being the best kid?

Yes, of having to prove she was a good woman. "I will never take pills," said I, who one day discovered I was taking a pill for my back (because I have scoliosis), a pill to sleep, a "terribly innocent, you can't possibly get hooked on them" diet pill, because I had gained seven pounds. Finally I said, "My God, I am taking pi-i-ills?" I never took a hallucinogenic in my life. I hated grass. I took coke only on weekends, because otherwise you can't sing—it freezes your vocal cords. That's when I did treatment. The first that really bugged me was that I felt I'd let my mother down—until I found out it wasn't my responsibility to prove that she was a good woman.

Why do you think you and your mother have had strong ties with gay men? The behind-the-scenes folklore about the '69 Stonewall rebellion is that it happened because the drag queens were grieving over Judy Garland's funeral.

I know. I just found out about that, and I am so proud!

***What?* You mean this is news to you?**

Yes, nobody told me this. So many people have said to me, "Why do you think you have such an enormous gay audience?" I kind of do this [*Minnelli is silent*]. Then they say, "Why do you think that your mother did?" [*Silence again*]

There has always been a link between your family and homosexuality. Do you remember how that subject was treated in your childhood?

I grew up with absolutely no prejudice of any kind. I was taught not to judge. And then somebody let me down badly.

What do you mean?

I married Peter Allen, and he didn't tell me he was gay.

You had no idea Peter was gay when you married him?

No! No!

Did he know?

Yeah! Everybody knew but me! And I didn't find out until I found out. And I found out...let me put it this way: I'll never surprise anybody coming home as long as I live. I call first. I do not believe in surprising anyone.

But, Liza, *this* is a different issue. Peter wasn't honest with you.

He didn't want to embarrass or hurt me. He loved me desperately.

Did it make you very angry?

At the time I didn't know what it made me. The betrayal was so huge. Peter was my first husband. He fought for me; he fought against my mom for me. We got married and got the hell out of there. We ran because we had to build our lives.

When did you find out about Peter?

Three weeks after we were married.

So you were really in the middle of breaking away from your mother.

Oh, yeah. Peter was my hero. We were great friends, we adored each other, and we had a wonderful sex life. When I found out...it's that terrible thing of the first lie leading to other lies, like "It was the first time" and "I'll never do it again" and "I was just curious" or "I was

drunk." It took a while to realize that none of it was true. I just didn't know what to believe. At first I fought because I didn't want to get divorced. But then, in my *mind,* I went to Detroit. And I started to look around until I found somebody I could fall in love with and get out of there.

How did you leave Peter?

I said, "Bye-bye, I'm leaving," I took the dog, and I left.

Did your mother ever know Peter was gay?

I don't know. If she did know, would she have let me marry him? [*Looks pained*] Na-a-ah!

When did you divorce Peter?

I lived with Peter for two years, then I married him for two years. I lived with him for two years because I had to know who I was marrying. [*Laughs uproariously*] Nutty, huh? You know how stupid I felt? We were married, so I stayed for two years because I really wanted to believe it would change!

Did Peter come to you when he got sick with AIDS?

No, Peter didn't tell me. I saw it happening for myself. He came to see me at Radio City, and there was something right here [*points to her face*], and I knew. I said, "Hi." My whole body wanted to scream. I said, "A-a-ah, the drapes are on fire!" and went into the other room and burst into tears.

Because you knew what was happening?

Sure. Then I heard he was coming to New York and had throat cancer. I knew that he'd come for treatments. So I called him up and asked him to go out with me somewhere. We went back to my house, and I put my arms around him. We just rocked. He kept saying, "I'm so sorry. I'm so sorry." I said, "You haven't cried about the 'throat cancer' at all, have you?" He said no. I finally said, "Now, I have to tell you two things: One, I love you. Two, you know that I have never said anything about you to anyone, and I'm not going to now." He said, "I know." I said, "Are we talking about more than throat cancer here?" He said, "Yes, darling." I said, "OK, that's all I want to know."

And that was it. Three days later he died. It was like he told somebody and he could die!

Liza, do you know that I actually heard two people tell me that you have AIDS?

Wha-a-at! [*Minnelli throws her ice cream–laden spoon across the room and laughs wildly*]

Oh, God, I'm sorry.

Oh! I just choked on my ice cream.

I think they said it because of those tabloid pictures of you looking so thin.

Do you know how hard it was to lose that weight? Do you know that I have to be at that weight for my hip replacement? Do you know that I fit into all of my costumes again for the first time in 15 years? This ain't anorexia, honey. It ain't bulimia, which is way too messy for me. But really, *why*? I wonder if the AIDS rumor is because of the drug rumors? Or maybe they say I have AIDS because I was married to a gay man who died of AIDS.

Who knows? Are you aware that people have said that other men you've been with (besides Peter) are gay?

I think most people assume I knew that they were. I hope they are not disappointed to learn that I didn't know.

You think you're letting people down?

Yeah. I think that people would want me to have known—they would have hoped that I wasn't that stupid. I just feel dumb about it.

And did you fall in love with a gay man again?

[*Long pause*] It's happened again, yes.

Was it a different experience from the one you had with Peter?

[*Another long pause*] It was different because it wasn't this huge, big secret, and he certainly had been with women as well as men.

What happened this time?

I should have been smarter because I had already been there. He said, "Listen, I've slept with a lot of women, and I've slept with a lot of men." I thought, *Well, I've got an even chance then, haven't I?* Then later I found out that he was scared and it wasn't really true. He'd been with many fewer women than men. I finally told him, "I feel like I lost for all womankind."

What did you do?

That's when I started to read up on homosexuality. I had a feeling it was biological, although you can dabble, I guess. I found out that they did a study on men who were in comas. They stimulated them while they were asleep with sexual images of women and sexual images of men. If they were homosexual, they got an erection with the male images. Now, that's not a choice! That's the deepest part of your brain. You can't lie about that. You can't lie because there is not a brain to lie with. That's not the "choice" part of your brain. That's not the part that decides how many pieces of furniture you need in a room. That is your soul.

The only *choice* you have is to lie about who you are.

[*Laughing*] Not if you're in a coma.

Does it feel better to know that it's not a choice?

Yes, because I don't feel rejected. Rejection is something I was not brought up to deal with well.

After your experience with Peter, did you wonder if you were gay?

Never.

You knew you were heterosexual?

Always. Romantically heterosexual. I am such a fool! Oh!

Do you ever wonder about all this homosexuality in your life if you're not gay?

I figure I inherited some of it. There have always been rumors about my mother, my father—everyone in my family at one time or another was said to have been gay.

Vito Russo, who wrote *The Celluloid Closet,* also wrote for *The Advocate.* In 1975 he reviewed a book titled *Judy* by Gerold Frank. Russo said that Frank should have gone into your grandfather's homosexuality but that he didn't because he promised you he wouldn't in order to get your cooperation.

Total cockadoodoo! I have read that everybody in my entire family is gay. Because there are people who want us to be like them. I don't care. [*Points to a chair across the room and pretends it's "the famous*

Liza Minnelli"] That's her over there with the sequins on. She takes all the heat. It is kind of interesting to watch what this poor chick over there goes through, because it ain't me. There's a separation. Liza With a Z is this person we made up. Fred [Ebb, her longtime lyricist] and I really do talk about *her* in the third person. It gives me a wonderful kind of freedom.

When did you start separating yourself from Liza the star?

My mama taught me. She said, "Anything that anybody says about this star over here, you can't stop them. They will say anything they want because they can. They like what they read; they don't want to know the truth. I know all about this. People don't want to know that at the end of a show when I sing 'Why, oh, why can't I?' and the curtain comes down, you come running onstage behind the curtain with my water."

I used to come out with a tray for her, and she would be this broken woman and look up and say, "Chinese or Italian food for dinner?" I'd go, "Uh..." She'd say, "Get off, the curtain's going up," and she would return to the pose she was in before the curtain fell. They don't want to know about the real woman. They don't want to know how really funny she was, funny about herself.

It must have been so complicated between you and your mother.

Oh, yes. My mother wanted to make this comeback, and she said, "I want you to do it with me." I said, "Why me? I haven't done anything." I tell you, in the course of a two-hour show [at the London Palladium in 1964] I went through what most women go through with their mothers for a period of about 25 years: competition. One minute I was onstage with my mom, and the next minute I was onstage with Judy Garland.

Really?

Yes. One of the promises I made my mom was that I would never sing any of her songs. And I kept it. I think she was worried that I might—if I wasn't good enough—try to use her stuff in order to work. It shocked me so. She said, "You will sing my songs, I know." I said, "No, I won't. I want to be a first-rate version of myself, not a second-rate version of you." She said, "Do you promise, Liza?" I said, "Yes, Mama, I do. I promise." And she started to cry.

Can we talk about your father and the rumors that he was gay?

I think it was because my father was so into the way things looked. He was an artist. People get confused about that. But recently I met a lot of his girlfriends. A group of them came to the theater that I was playing at. He had lots of girlfriends between marriages.

I'm sure you miss your close friend, clothing designer Halston, who died of AIDS complications in 1990.

I knew that my parents were going to die; you are taught that your whole life. But Halston? When I lost Halston, that was it for me. Like Peter, he too said, "I'm having a cancer problem." So I never got to say goodbye properly. Halston—I am telling you—when he died, I thought, *What am I going to do without this person?* He was my family! He was my brother. He protected me. He kept me away from everything. He kept me away from...

Drugs?

[*Laughs*] Yes, as opposed to what everybody likes to believe.

I read in one of those trash paperback bios about you that you and Halston did a lot of drugs together.

Let me tell you how all that got started. After I agreed to do Baryshnikov's TV special, Misha and I were trying to figure out something to do together. We would rehearse at Halston's studio. One day I asked Misha if he could do the Charleston. He said, "Is that like the bunny hop?" I said [*doing the Charleston*], "No, you step, boomp, step, boomp, step, boomp."

You were teaching Baryshnikov to dance the Charleston?

Yes. One foot of his was doing great, and the other foot was doing *Swan Lake*! Suddenly Andy Warhol arrived. He watched us for a while. Then he said, "Hi," and "Wow." That's *all* I ever heard Andy say, by the way. Halston told Andy, "They're doing a television show, and they are writing it right here." "Wow," says Andy again. Then the next thing I hear is Andy talking to someone on the phone. I hear him say, "You have got to come over! Baryshnikov and Liza are fucking on the table!" And Halston said, "For God's sake, Andy, get off the phone and stop lying. Stop talking like that! Who are you talking to?" But he went on with his conversation, telling all these lies about what we were doing. And, of course, whomever he was talking to wrote the book you read.

Well, according to that book, you've had sex with everybody.

Really? Like who? I love it. Tell me, I want to know!

Well, there was certainly Baryshnikov.

Yes, we had an affair, so that's all right.

Martin Scorsese?

Yeah, I got sued over that.

Peter Sellers?

Yes, but this is over a long period of time. I've read that I've been with so many people that I haven't even met.

The only woman I've ever heard that you were lovers with was one-time New York cabaret singer Lana Cantrell.

[*Screaming, throwing her spoon again*] Lana Cantrell! Oh, gosh! Lana Cantrell? Oh, honey. Wow, wow, wow! [*Giggling*] Oh, dear. She's a lovely woman but no, no, no.

Did you ever go through a stage of experimentation with homosexuality?

Of course.

Do you think most people do?

Yes, of course, and I certainly did as a teenager. My best girlfriend, Janet, taught me how to kiss. She said to say the word "pru-u-unes" because it does this [*puckers her lips*]. We practiced until she said, "That's good." I think she wanted to go further, and I was thinking, *Oh, that feels really good, but it's...* [*Giggles*] I could have definitely, definitely gotten into the feeling, the physical feeling. But what was making me giggle was that it was...Janet! [*Laughing*] I said, "Are we doing something queer here?" She said, "No, no, no, no." I thought, *Oh, yes!* I think there is a beauty to two women making love. It has always struck me as something natural, and for me that has to do with comfort and understanding. Plus, most guys who aren't gay are always turned on by two women, which I think is rather homosexual of them.

Why do you say "we" when you talk about gays or about the gay movement?

I say "we" because I feel part of this movement because of the privacy issue. I grew up never knowing what privacy was because my family was famous. There was no privacy, and I wanted it. I still fight for it every day. I know about keeping secrets. Because there are family secrets, and I don't talk about them. It was a promise I made to my mom. I must stand by that.

How does this relate to being gay?

Our movement's gone from one end of the spectrum to the other. It's now about celebrating, which is great, but this celebration shouldn't turn into a situation where we're forcing gays to talk about their private lives if they don't want to. Maybe a gay person's grandmother is dying and he doesn't want her to know. That's *his* business.

What did you think about your good friend Michael Feinstein's coming-out in *The Advocate* a couple of years ago?

[*Looks upset*] I think that Michael Feinstein did not want to label himself—and he said this clearly in print. He said, "You can say what you want about me. I just won't say it, because then it would come before my name, like *gay* performer, *gay* pianist. I will be labeled." It's like being called a "nonsmoking performer" for the rest of your life. It's limiting, and it's distracting. I think we need to take a few steps back and look with a new perspective at where we are.

And what will we see?

That we need a leader. We have got so many different factions, we ought to have a leader. We have to get together on one thing.

But gays are just people, and people are all very different.

I don't know how to say this, so let me try a metaphor. In a good closing number, everybody is wearing the same thing. And they walk forward—Bob Fosse did it best—in a unit. That kind of choreography will bring people to their feet. The audience goes crazy because the dancers are coming at you as a unit, together, alike. Usually Fosse would dress people quite normally so that the audience could relate to them. I look at an audience sometimes, and they are never affected or take it seriously when people onstage are leaping about in different styles. It looks like the troupe is not together! But they are. They are all in the same company.

So what should be their goal?

The goal should be to involve the people who don't understand. In a gay pride parade, the guys who wear dresses are the only ones the media report on. To be effective, we have to first get in the door. To get in the door, we have got to look like somebody on the other side of the door. If I want to go visit—let's say she was still alive—Mae West, I wouldn't wear jeans and a T-shirt. I would put on the best sequined dress I had, as much lipstick as I could, and 9,000 pairs of eyelashes. I'd get in the door because I'd be wearing what she would understand.

But a gay pride parade is primarily for gays and lesbians.

Yes, it's a celebration. We've celebrated, now let's get serious and get the rest of what we need. Get equal rights, get medicine, and get the cure.

Do you want to say something about your future AIDS hospice?

Yes, I want to build a hospice that agrees with alternative medicines. So from each concert I do, I'm putting some money aside. I already sing in hospices. That's terrific because then you see the power of music and the power of touch. It keeps me grateful and reminds me of what I am doing. Also it keeps me attached to all the people I've lost. It makes them not so terribly special. It reminds me I have enormous company in my grief.

Liza Minnelli

Rob

Halford

I remember sitting in a beer-soaked

rock hall in London called Hammersmith Odeon. If you were into heavy metal music, this was definitely one of your primo Euro venues. It was the late '80s, and I was there to cover Iron Maiden for *Creem* magazine. For anyone who didn't see *Almost Famous, Creem* was one of the first and purest rock and roll magazines in America. I was a regular contributing writer for *Creem*—as well as an associate editor for *Creem Metal* and *Rip* magazine—at the time.

Because rock and roll has always been completely international (German, Dutch, or Swedish bands can have number 1 hits in America and barely speak English), for the first time in my life I found myself travelling to England and Europe regularly, navigating my way through a world of macho men and deafening sounds. That I was a gay woman never came up. I certainly never mentioned it. The heavy metal rock world was all about sweaty hetero boys hitting on cute young girls who would never give them the time of day if they weren't in bands. If sex came up at all around me, it was usually because some band member on a tour bus needed me to help him find a condom because a groupie with legs that stretched to heaven had climbed through the window to be with him.

However, this particular intermission at Hammersmith Odeon stands out in my mind all these years later because of something very unhetero. I was sitting next to the lead singer of a multimillion-dollar heavy metal band, waiting for the headlining band, Iron Maiden, to take the stage, when he suddenly said something shocking to me. Throwing his black-leather-clad legs up on the seat in front of him, he announced, "Did you know that Judas Priest's lead singer, Rob Halford, is queer?" No, I had never heard any such thing. But it wasn't the gossip about Halford that shocked me. It was the fact that the forbidden subject of homosexuality had been brought up against the rugged terrain of hard rock. That stunned me. The singer then went on to ridicule Halford mercilessly while I sat there staring out at him stupidly from my closet. It was awful. Finally he stopped, noticing that I wasn't joining in his "homo roast." The lights went down. Iron Maiden came howling onto the stage, and I excused myself to go wait for them in their dressing room. I never again talked to this particular lead singer. But I never forgot what he had told me. Walking through the darkened backstage hallways of the dungeonlike Hammersmith, I marveled, *Somewhere, someone else in this raunchy rock world is gay.* At the time it seemed like a miracle. Dear God, what could his life possibly be like?

The significance of a heavy metal star coming out of the most Neanderthal-posing rock genre in music is incalculable. In the world of heavy metal (a term coined by William Burroughs in *Naked Lunch*)—with its devil-worshiping, electric-guitar-

dominated image; "get me some chicks" songs; and raunchy, heterosexual, blue-collar fan base—homophobia is rampant. What gay man would dare take this on and risk losing his career? Even Queen's Freddie Mercury went to his grave never making a public statement. But now, after nearly three decades of living his rock-star sex life in cautious silence, Rob Halford, onetime lead singer of Judas Priest, considered by many the archetypal metal band, bangs his head on rock's meanest closet door and breaks all the way out.

Long before sweaty mosh pits with rock fans slamming their half naked bodies together, long before the angry wail of heavy metal bands like Guns N' Roses, Metallica, Ozzy Osbourne, or Van Halen, there was Judas Priest.

Storming out of the harsh industrial regions of northern England, Judas Priest was a gang of five furious blokes with a very loud grudge. Typical of so many bands that change the face of rock forever (the Beatles from Liverpool, Led Zeppelin from Birmingham), Judas Priest came from an English landscape as brutal and oppressive as the band's own distorted guitar sounds. Connecting fiercely with the rage of working-class fans around the world who felt they had no bright future, Priest began its defiant push for success in 1969.

After two years of false starts and small record labels, the band replaced its lead singer with a theatrical lighting technician from Birmingham named Rob Halford. With his keen writing sense and ear-splitting leather lungs, Halford was the magic that launched both the band and an entire genre of rock called heavy metal—a bombastically amplified, guitar-driven wall of sound featuring a lead singer powerful enough to cut through it all. Like the shrill, grinding noises of the metal steel mills inhabiting Britain's cold north country, Judas Priest was a brazen force to be reckoned with.

Capitalizing on Halford's sonic howling and bondage-gear dress (complete with the Harley he drove onstage every night), Judas Priest sold millions of albums and filled nearly as many arenas with nasty beer-drinking, head-banging hetero boys. The band played so loud that they were said to cause involuntary bowel movements—so who would've ever guessed that the centerpiece in this macho commotion was a gay man?

"Yeah, but look at the homoeroticism in metal music," says Jon Ginoli, front man for the all-gay rock band Pansy Division. Ginoli and his band mates were instrumental in bringing Halford out of the closet after meeting him in a San Francisco bar in 1997. The bond they formed was so strong, Halford actually risked performing live with them at three gay pride events last year—although he still hadn't made up his mind to come out.

Part of the reason for Halford's indecision was his brand-new band and record deal. After a chance meeting with Nine Inch Nails lead singer Trent Reznor in New Orleans, Halford's newly

formed band, Two, signed with Reznor's label. This March, Two released its first album, *Voyeurs,* and in April commenced its first U.S. tour. To help launch the band, porn master Chi Chi LaRue was enlisted to direct Two's first video, for "I Am a Pig."

"When I first saw him," says LaRue, "I saw a big, tattooed, scary superstar—and the sweetest man I've ever met."

LaRue's observation is just one more dichotomy about Halford. Despite making deafening noises for nearly three decades, there was always one silence the rocker left unbroken. Now with this exclusive *Advocate* interview, that silence has been forever broken.

Why are you coming out now?

I really dwelled on it so long. *What am I gonna gain? What am I gonna lose?* I think it's true, when you become successful in the music world, you probably go more in the closet. You get *under the rug* in the closet because of the phobia that still exists in rock music. You could lose a record deal, a fan base. It's really difficult for any musician to come out.

And particularly in this genre of music—which you helped to create.

Yeah. Had I considered coming out five years ago, it would've been very difficult. But right now I'm experiencing the same emotions that my friends have told me they felt when they came out: this great clarity and this great peace. There have been no repercussions, no hate mail. I think people have had so many good times with my music that my coming out is easier for them to accept. It's like, "Well, look at the great music, look at the great shows—does it really matter?"

How did you hide your homosexuality from Judas Priest all those years?

Everybody in Priest always had an awareness that I was gay.

What? Priest knew you were gay?

Yeah, they knew because the way I started with Priest was through my sister, who was dating the bass player, Ian Hill. She told Ian of my singing abilities and, I guess, about me.

How amazing that they weren't afraid to have a gay man lead their band.

I never experienced homophobia from anybody in Priest. I think that if I'd sensed that they had a problem with it, I would not have joined the band—even though obviously it was the best thing that ever happened to me.

I used to contact your press people about doing an interview with you for *The Advocate.* Did you know about it?

Oh, there could've been things going on that I wasn't aware of:

calls to management, calls to the label, people saying we want to talk about Rob's sexuality. But Priest never got involved in social-political discussions.

Did you ever pretend to have girlfriends?

No, I never did that. I never went to a record-release party with a blond on my arm or that kind of stuff. I never felt that I was walking around creating a smoke screen.

From my own experiences traveling with heavy metal bands on tour buses as a journalist, I remember that often band members fell in love with a girl and brought her on the road.

That's exactly what I did.

With a boy?

Yes. Absolutely. That's exactly what I did. The guy I've had a relationship with now for the last three years will be going out on the road with me on this current tour—although we've gone beyond the sexual thing now; we're just platonic friends. But we live together, and we don't want to really let each other go. I've had only a handful of serious relationships. Fortunately, I could take these individuals on the road.

When rock magazines interviewed you on the road, did you hide your male companions?

You mean, "You better stay in the room and don't show your face until the interviewer is gone"? Naw, but it wasn't a brash act of "Hey, check this out about my boyfriend on the road with me." It was the typical Elton John thing. You know, Elton's lover is with him now on the road taking care of him. You're not so lonely with all those straight rock people around you, not knowing you're gay.

Tell me about feeling isolated with all those straight-arrow rockers.

It's horrible. The show ends, everybody goes to the titty bar or the nudie bar, and they all pick up a bunch of chicks and go up to their rooms. That's not me. I'm a gay man. So it was a very isolated, lonely kind of experience. You do this great show in front of thousands and thousands of adoring fans…

And so many of them are men!

Yes. Isn't it crazy? All those guys, and I'd go back to my room alone. It's 11:30; you close the door and watch *The Tonight Show* and fall asleep while everybody else is banging away down the hallway, doing orgiastic rock-and-roll things.

You never picked up any men?

Yes. You know, I had a few of the rock-and-roll groupie experiences with other gay men who were hanging out backstage. My gaydar would go off. But that was very isolated.

Were you aware of other closeted gay rock stars? Did you know Freddie Mercury [Queen's lead singer, who died of complications from AIDS in 1991]?

Well, Freddie… I just sometimes have these real emotional experiences and feelings about him, especially when I listen to his music. I worshiped him as a performer and as a musician. I just wished that we could've become friends. We came so close. I remember going to Mykonos [Greece] one time, and the plane stopped over in Athens. I was with a bunch of my gay friends, and we went to this gay bar in Greece. Freddie was there too. He was

in one corner, and I was in one corner, and we kinda smiled to each other and waved, "Hey, hi, how are you?" He was in Mykonos for two weeks on his huge yacht, which he'd festooned with bright pink balloons. It just kept going around and around the island. I wished there would've been an opportunity for us to get together. I was devastated like everybody else when he passed away.

When you first joined Priest, what was the climate like in the early '70s in England if you were gay?

The gay culture was established, but it was very underground; it was still being badly spoken of by all forms of politicians. You went to only certain bars, and it was all secret, and nobody knew where the bars were, nobody was in the streets. There was no trying to assimilate into society.

What made you create the leather look for Priest?

The imagery I created was simply out of a feeling that what I was doing before the leather and studs and whips and chains and motorcycles didn't fit me. Priest was going onstage in very flamboyant saggy pants. It was very extroverted and fluffy in its visual tone, but I didn't feel right. I've got great videos of me wearing outfits that I stole out of my sister's closet. I couldn't figure out what to wear. How do I dress with the music that sounds this way?

So I said, "OK, I'm a gay man, and I'm into leather and that sexual side of the leather world—and I'm gonna bring that onto the stage." So I came onstage wearing the leather stuff and the motorcycle, and for the first time I felt like, *God this feels so good. This feels so right. How can I make this even more extravagant, because this music is so loud. It is so larger than life.* So the first place I went to was a leather shop in London called Mr. S.

Who were they selling to?

To the gay crowd that's into the leather scene. But I remember going in there and seeing these harnesses and wristbands and cock ring–type things. I just introduced myself to the owners and explained what I was looking for, and they started to make things for me.

You never thought, *Oh, my God, I'm doing this gay-man leather fantasy in the middle of a hetero heavy metal rock show*?

Oh, yes, I did! I thought to myself, *Do you realize what you're doing here? I mean, you've got the whole thing going—the body harness, the handcuffs. You've got the whip, you've got the chains. This is like some total S/M fetish thing going on!* But nobody seemed to have a problem with it, and everybody was crazy for it, so we kept doing it.

You created an aesthetic in rock that attracts straight men too.

I guess that's true, because I met this guy recently, and he said, "When I was 13, I used to watch MTV, and you would be walking around in your leather stuff, and I'd always get an erection." A lot of men who are into leather are also into metal. They mayn't know they're gay until they see something that makes them feel hot.

Let me ask you about the anger behind all the heavy-metal raging. What is it an outlet for? What was Rob so angry about?

I think I was angry at myself. I thought that I was sexually dysfunctional, that I didn't fit in because I was still the gay man in an exclusively straight rock world. And I wanted to fit in, but I didn't want to fit in. It was confusing, and it was frustrating. And so it was great for me to have an opportunity to vent that way. I really don't know what I'd have done if I wasn't able to do that.

Now that you're out, will you miss screaming your pain away?

It's a relevant question, because I really get a lot of pleasure out of rip-roaring and screaming my head off. I recommend it to anybody. If you can't put it in words, then just let it come out that way. That's what people do at rock shows. They go crazy, you know, with mosh pits and screaming and knocking each other about—not in a destructive, violent way but in a cathartic way.

But now that I'm out about my homosexuality, I'm gonna be shouting my mouth off about having the same rights and being treated the same way as every other person on this planet. All of us are human beings, and we should not be denied the same kinds of things that the greater portion of straight society receives. That's got to be the next step on this journey for me. I'll stand up for it and make my voice heard for equal rights.

Do you want the right to marry?

Of course. There should not be a rule that says I don't have this right. It's so wrapped up in religion.

How were you raised with religion?

It wasn't really an important part of my life. You receive religious instruction in the U.K. schools—that's part of the curriculum.

What sent you on your spiritual journey?

Going through my sobriety stage, because I'm a recovering alcoholic. I've been through 12 years now. I know what makes me tick, whereas before I was clueless.

What made you stop drinking?

It was a cataclysmic event. Most of the men I'm attracted to [even now] are straight men. The boy I was dating back then had a cocaine problem. We had one of those bombastic physical attractions, and there was a tremendous amount of violence. We used to beat the crap out of each other in the drunken and cocaine rages that we had. And one day we were fighting, and I left for my own safety and called a cab. As I was getting in the cab, he came up to me and said, "Look, I just want to let you know I love you very much." And when he turned away, I saw that he had a gun. Moments later he put the gun to his head and killed himself.

What's *your* biggest devil?

Jealousy. And yet I'm the classic dysfunctional jealous person, because it's OK for me to mess around but don't *you* mess around.

What do your working-class parents think about your publicly coming out?

When I answered yes to being gay on MTV, it filtered through to the U.K. My mom was like, "Well, we saw the MTV piece, and we're really happy for you." Then Dad and I talked about everything other than that, and as we were winding up our conversation, he said, "I just want to let you know that I'm very proud of you. I think it takes a lot of courage, and I just want you to know that." *That* was the very first time he and I made that connection verbally. It was over the phone. I would've liked it to have been face-to-face so we could've given each other a hug and probably shed a few tears.

Were you aware of any other gay members in your family?

No. There was no uncle. [*Laughs*] There was none of that. So it was a pretty lonely, isolated kind of feeling.

Were you always thinking, *I'm a little different,* both in your sexual feelings and in the kind of music you liked?

Yes. My awareness of my sexuality preceded my love of music. I recall having real strong feelings around the age of 10, 11, 12. I had girlfriends. But there was never any sexual activity. I simply wasn't sexually stimulated by women. That's just the fact of being a gay man.

When did you get interested in rock music?

I loved all music. I'd been singing in the school choir, and I had a taste of what it was like to be onstage. So there was that kind of acceptance thing going on that may have had something to do with the fact that even though I might've thought being a gay man was wrong, I could be accepted because I had a voice. I could stand onstage, and people would clap. It had a balancing effect.

For your fear of being hated for being gay?

Exactly. So I left school at 16 and went straight to work for a large theater. I went from those high-school experiences in the straight world to the theater with gay men everywhere. I started to mix with my own kind, and I started to feel as though I wasn't the only one.

You mentioned being in a long-term relationship today that is no longer sexual. Do you want one that is sexual?

Sometimes I feel like Boy George: "I just want to have a cup o' tea." I tell you, I'm so over it. And maybe I'm getting close to middle age. We all know that part of our sexuality changes.

You sound bitter. I believe you can't be bitter without having once been a dreamer. Did you once believe you could have a long-term romantic, sexual relationship?

[*Laughs*] I tell everyone I'm not bitter, but I think maybe I am. Yes, part of me wants that, and part of me doesn't. A good portion of my relationships were with essentially straight men who suddenly went off and got married. They were just experimenting with me.

That's a drag.

Yes, I've been through all that crap, and it drives me crazy.

But you still want love?

Yes, that evil four-letter word, *love.* I think love is God's trick.

But maybe being completely out of the closet will change all this for you.

Yeah, I've been thinking it might come from that wonderful moment when you walk out of the closet. Now I've done that, and I've freed myself. Maybe that special moment is yet to happen, because I do believe that we are destined to find that one person. [*Starts to cry*] I admit it.

Well, you've gone through a lot to get here.

Yes, and it is a great feeling for me to finally let go and make this statement—and especially to *The Advocate,* because this magazine has brought me so much comfort over the years. Obviously this is just a wonderful day for me.

Rob Halford

"The [rock] show ends and everybody goes to the nudie bar, and they all pick up a bunch of chicks and go up to their rooms. That's not me. I'm a gay man... I'd go back to my room alone. So it was a very isolated, lonely kind of experience."

Mark W

ahlberg

The year was 1993, and I had just been hired

as the arts and entertainment editor for *The Advocate*. Jeff Yarbrough, then the editor in chief, called me at home, where I was resting between jobs. He told me it was his dream to get the controversial rapper Marky Mark (soon to morph into the talented actor Mark Wahlberg) for the year-in-review cover of *The Advocate*. Because I've been a published songwriter for many years and have a lot of music contacts, Yarbrough pushed me to use some of them and make some calls. As it turned out, one of my calls connected. Someone knew someone who could get me in contact with "Marky's people."

However, there were two problems. The first was that Marky was secluded in South Carolina's Fort Jackson, where he was costarring in his first film, Penny Marshall's *Renaissance Man*. The second was that while his famous Calvin Klein underwear ads had catapulted him up and onto the walls of many a gay man's bedroom, shocking charges of homophobia had sent him crashing down in a year-end melodrama with the community. Gay fans reacted like jilted lovers. Red paint obliterated Marky's 40-foot-tall Sunset Boulevard billboard. Boxes of soiled underwear were mailed to Calvin Klein's Manhattan office. It was an all-out public relations nightmare, and, not surprisingly, Marky didn't want to talk to the gay press. Who would listen to his side of the story anyway?

There are people who say no, and that's the end of it. Then there are those nos you get that are surrounded by hesitations and invitations. You don't really hear them. You feel them. Also, I admit, I'm very stubborn. The combination of all this plus the eager support of the magazine landed me in a motel room in South Carolina. I was there for two days before my constant haranguing eventually caused an exhausted and worried Marky to bang on my motel room door. "Judy?" he whispered through his deep neighborhood accent, "It's me, Marky. Open up."

Initially we were both so nervous to be locked up together in a tiny room with one bed and one chair, neither of us sat down. For the first half hour we stood there, shifting back and forth, talking in circles about the stupidest things imaginable. Marky went on and on about the marching maneuvers his movie character had to endure during the day at the military base, while I kept wondering why my tape recorder looked like one of the buttons had fallen off. Despite the awkwardness, the time was well spent, because I was learning how to understand him before the "hard" questions started. His speech was so full of the language of the streets, I literally wasn't sure what he was saying. But he was also so shy and sweet, I knew we'd be all right if we could just figure out a way to get started.

Finally, Marky took the lead. "Judy, you should sit down." He brought the chair to me and sat on the edge of the bed. "You want me to check out what's going on with the tape recorder? You worried?" We ordered pizza and edged closer and closer to the interview. When we finally got into it, everything came pouring out of him. It was instantly clear to me that this interview was as important to Mark as it was to *The Advocate*.

Years later I was at a huge fashion event in Los Angeles. It was star-studded, as they say, and I had slipped out early. Waiting for my car, a figure appeared in front of me with the streetlight silhouetting him. I couldn't see his face, but I knew his voice in a heartbeat. "Judy, it's Marky." We hugged. By then he was Mark Wahlberg, star of *Boogie Nights* and soon *The Three Kings, The Perfect Storm, Planet of the Apes,* and *The Truth About Charlie*.

"The interview was a good thing," he said, thanking me. "Before it, nobody had been listening to my side of the story. Once the interview came out, everything changed. It was a passage." Marky ("Mikey" to his dad) knew that accusations of homophobia can soil an entertainer's career. He was relieved to have had his say. And in his appealing, boyish way, he was also very grateful.

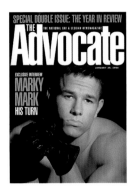

Marky Mark is exhausted. He's just spent the day marching around South Carolina's Fort Jackson, where he's been going through basic training in preparation for his role as a redneck Army recruit in Penny Marshall's new film, *Renaissance Man.*

Now, walking into the hotel room for an interview, the 22-year-old platinum-plus rap phenomenon has a face full of undelivered communications—and one of them is definitely dread.

The source of that dread? The certain knowledge that he is shortly to be grilled about a series of incidents that have led many members of the gay and lesbian community to denounce him as violent, insensitive, thoughtless, spineless, and homophobic. "Marky doesn't have hate for anybody," wails Miguel Melendez, the rapper's tour manager. "Nobody's listening to his side."

Oh, really?

Well, now it's his turn.

The future underwear model was born Mark Wahlberg, the youngest of nine children, in Dorchester, an inner-city neighborhood of Boston. "It was hard seeing kids right across the street having everything," he says in rough street tones, "being that close to it and not being able to have it." Rapping people on the head and taking their money became a way of life for Mark long before rapping to a beat did.

Although he and his brother Donnie were writing "stupid rap songs about food" long before Donnie's group, New Kids on the Block, took off for teenybopper heaven, Mark turned down the opportunity to be a part of the multizillion-dollar machinery, preferring instead to indulge in sports and camaraderie at the local boys' club.

After a brief stint as a bricklayer and some run-ins with the law, Mark found himself looking to music once again, this time as a means of expressing his darker side. "My brother had gotten enough money for both of us," he says. "So I wasn't doing it for the money. I thought I should share the shit I went through with the people who weren't seeing it every day, hipping them to what's going on and at the same time telling kids who are living these situations every day, 'Hey, nobody's out there to help you. You gotta help yourself.' "

His message of "you can overcome this shit" gave birth to the Funky Bunch in 1986. It was a relatively long birth followed by a quick signing to Interscope Records and a platinum debut album, *Music for the People,* in 1991. A second album, *You Gotta Believe,* was less successful, but a Calvin Klein underwear campaign more than made up for its sluggish sales. With a new workout video available in stores (*The Marky Mark Workout: Form, Focus, Fitness*) and his first feature film in the can, the kid who dropped out of school in the ninth grade is now working on a rap version of Shakespeare's *Hamlet* for the sound track of *Renaissance Man.*

"Marky wrote a great rap for the film," says Bronx-born director Marshall, who relates strongly to her star because they both came from tough neighborhoods. "Then he had to put his own ego aside and teach the other actors to do it, because his character would never rap. He was very generous about it." In addition to this rap, Mark is writing material for his third album, due out in March.

But now it's time for the rapper to face the music, not write it. As he moves tentatively to take a seat in the hotel room, Marky Mark knows full well that the questions he is about to be asked will be a bit more serious than "What's your favorite color?" "What's your favorite food?" and "What's your underwear size?"

What's going on between you and the gay community?

I don't understand all this bad press. I have always talked to gay magazines and done gay shows. What is going on here? This isn't right.

When people make accusations without asking me, it affects a lot of gay people close to me. That's why I say if people would listen to me instead of just looking at me, they would understand. Usually when magazines talk to me, they ask senseless things. Hell, if you're not asking anything important, why bother?

We didn't expect you to do this interview at all.

I have always said openly how I feel about gays, that they have a right to do what they want. With all this crazy shit going on in the world—which nobody wants to do anything about—why are people so busy worrying about what somebody is doing in their own home? I've always said that.

Let me start with what I've heard: You came to the defense of reggae singer Shabba Ranks last January when he condemned homosexuality on the British TV show *The Word.* He said it was against God's way, and you defended his right to say that.

No, no. First of all, this was a London tabloid TV show. I had come on, and they'd said some crazy things to me. They were trying to get me to take off my shirt. They asked me how I felt about my body selling more than my records, so I was kind of pissed.

What's this got to do with Shabba Ranks?

I was on my own, in the corner, sitting there while they were off interviewing Shabba. I didn't even see or hear what he said until I saw the videotape. Then I saw that he said he followed the Bible, and gays should be crucified. I was like, "Well, wait a second here!"

Suddenly people were at me with "You were endorsing him, and you and him were saying that gays should be crucified."

I said, "I didn't say anything except 'Leave me the hell alone' to the ladies on the show because they kept bothering me."

But you performed with Shabba Ranks, right?

Shabba Ranks was performing, and they were like, "We want you to go up and perform with him, spontaneously," and they pushed me out onstage and kept pushing me. There were cameras everywhere, so if you watch the video, you can see the lady and the guy pushing me.

They handed me the microphone and said, "Go! You're on!"

Mark Wahlberg

And I'm like, "I'm on? This isn't my show. What are you talking about?"

The music kinda broke down, and Shabba said, "I want to do this with Marky Mark. Come on up here."

So I did this little rap, and at the end a commotion started, and I was like, "Fuck you! Fuck *The Word*. Fuck everybody! I can say whatever the hell I want. Shabba can say whatever the hell he wants. And you can say whatever the hell you want!" And then I walked off and threw the microphone down.

You saw all this on the videotape?

Yes. Three or four days later we were in Hawaii, and people were asking me, "What were you doing, saying this and that on TV?"

I said, "What are you talking about? I never said anything on TV. I never had anything to do with this."

And they said, "Yes you did."

I said, "Play me the video."

I saw it and was like, "Man, that wasn't me who said it." I watched it, and obviously I hadn't been aware of anything that was going on.

But people were saying, "Well, Marky, you always said that you feel this way and that way. Why didn't you stick up for us?"

I was saying, "Wait a second. I was so mad at them telling me that I needed Oxy on my face! They were totally disrespecting me." The show is known for that. They were going crazy on me. So I was just sitting there in my own world. And when I watched it, I was like, "Wow!" I felt that I should have said something.

I should have told Shabba, "You can think what you want, but first of all, you're not God! So you can't say. Everybody has the right to do whatever they want. Who are you to say or even imply that you are the one to follow these commands? Look at all the shit that's going on today."

You didn't talk to him again until the two of you met at the Grammy awards?

Right. I ran into him at the hotel, and he said, "There are certain people who say you've gotten into a lot of trouble out of what happened. I didn't mean to implicate you in it at all."

I said, "I told them I wasn't involved. But what's wrong with *you*? Why would you say something like that?"

He was like, "Well, you know, I'm a man of the Bible," and he started saying the same thing that he said on TV.

I said, "Well, yo! If that's the way you feel, then that's the way you feel. But you don't have a right to be disrespecting people like that. First of all, you're not God, so you shouldn't be running around preaching things like that."

How did he respond?

I think, honestly, when I said it to him, he was taken aback and kinda got more into this pride thing about what he had said, like, "What is everybody going to say?"

I said, "So? What is everybody gonna say? That you're a tough guy 'cause you said this? That don't prove nothing. That don't make much sense."

I couldn't believe it happened. I had been sitting there like I was on *The Gong Show*! Then all this!

Suddenly people were tearing your Calvin Klein posters off their walls. Then I heard the story about you and Madonna.

That was a publicity stunt!

Was it?

Anybody who gets into a conflict with somebody and then calls their publicist five minutes later is going for a publicity stunt. I mean, I didn't go to the press about it, as appalled as I was that anybody would attack me at a Hollywood party with a bunch of professional people.

We heard that you called somebody a faggot at Madonna's party and that she threw you out. The New York chapter of the Gay and Lesbian Alliance Against Defamation [GLAAD] said you assaulted an executive from her label, Maverick Records.

The situation that happened was like this: Madonna was very upset about something that I had said about her in a London magazine. I didn't say what they said I said, but I did say I was a little upset by the way she was when I met her. I was a little disappointed.

We met briefly at a [Jean Paul] Gaultier AIDS benefit. I had commented on her outfit, kinda joking around. The magazine was a London rag, so I should have realized that they would make this the big quote on the cover! They tried to make it something that it wasn't.

So then you met Madonna again after the London magazine came out?

Sometime later I came to this *Truth or Dare* party and saw Rosie O'Donnell and said, "Hi. How ya doing?" I didn't know anybody at the party. I was by myself. I was there for 10 minutes. As soon as I said hi to Rosie, I went to the bathroom. By the time I got out of the bathroom, Rosie must have told Madonna that I was there.

Madonna approached you?

Madonna came trucking down the hallway with combat boots on. When she saw me, she came up to me and started going crazy.

I was like, "What's up, Madonna?"

She was like, "Don't fucking say hi to me. You know what the fuck you fucking did. You dissed me. You're a fucking asshole, a fucking fake."

I was like, "Well, first of all, Madonna, it wasn't what it was supposed to be."

She started going crazy, and I started laughing, which made her more mad. She was like, "Well, fuck you."

I was like, "Well, fuck you too."

She said, "Well, I'm going to get somebody to kick your ass." And that's when she went over to this record-company guy and this other reggae artist. And they came up to me and started saying stuff to me like "This ain't Boston; this is L.A." and insinuating that they had a gun, trying to egg me on. And I was laughing at them, blowing it off.

You stayed at the party?

I was sitting there talking to a guy from TriStar. He was like, "What's *his* problem?"

I was like, "I don't know." I didn't even get into what had happened with Madonna. I was laughing.

First of all, the London magazines have said about everything in the book about her. And if I believed any of it, I would never have even shaken her hand! So why would she just go berserk from something that she read in a London magazine?

So you had no idea that she was upset?

No, I just kinda said hello, and it was like *bang!* I was just walking around asking, "Whose party is this? Oh, the guy who did *Truth or Dare*? Oh, oh, cool."

Then these guys [from Maverick Records] came back again. There were some more threats. I said, "As you can see, I just came here to have a good time."

They were like, "Oh, we'll talk to you outside. I know you don't want to fight me." He was like, "I knew you was a pussy."

I said, "All right. Whatever."

We started to walk outside, and I seen one guy on the left and this other kid standing on the right side. He kinda came toward me from the right. He was, "Yo, you and my man could just go one-on-one. And squash it all now."

I said, "What are you talking about?"

And that's when the dude swung at me and kinda grazed me on the side of the head. So I swung back at him, and when I hit him, he fell down. Me and him were wrestling, and I was on top of him, and the other guy came and punched me in the back of the head. So I fell down to the ground, and we started fighting. And then some other guy with a beer came over and kicked me in the back of the head. Then everybody started breaking it up from that point.

Did you see Madonna again?

I was walking out, and Madonna came over on the other side of the fence and was like, "Get the fuck out of here. You're a fucking asshole. I told you you were going to get your ass kicked."

I was like, "Oh, fuck you."

And then some other big guy—who was supposed to be her boyfriend—comes running out, and he starts yelling and screaming at me in the streets. And then he started getting into it with some other guy—who was just standing there. And they started fighting. I was like, "I'm out of here."

This is definitely not the story we heard!

I left, and the next day was when I went and saw Penny [Marshall] again to read for *Renaissance Man*.

Were you afraid this would ruin your chances of getting a role in her film?

Yes. I thought, *Oh, God, I just met Penny. And they all ran and told this big bullshit story.*

Penny had already heard from Madonna. She asked me, "What happened?" I had to defend myself. I told her about the press thing, and she told me, "Yeah, well, Madonna's real sensitive to that stuff."

But it really hurt me too. As much as I try to go out and promote "do your own thing," I can't believe people would listen to that. You'd think people who know me would know I wasn't a gay basher.

So then none of this was about calling anyone a faggot?

No! Obviously Madonna had a problem with me. She was like, "All right, if you want to try to be smart and say something about me in the press, then I'm going to fuck with you"—which was appalling!

I mean, honestly, I had a lot of respect for her. I think she's very talented. She's very smart. She does a lot of good. As much as she promotes wild sex, she does a lot for AIDS research and stuff like that. I really give her a lot of credit.

You're saying this was really all about her ego?

All I said to the magazine was "She looked different than what I

expected." People say that kind of thing to me all the time. It doesn't bother me. So I really don't understand her.

I even heard a rumor that you called her brother a faggot.

Whose brother?

Madonna's.

It was never a gay issue.

So what happened is that all this got turned around into "Marky Mark hates gays and bashes them at parties"?

Well, of course! If your publicist calls the newspaper and says this is what happened, they will write that. It's like if I had gone to the police and said that those guys at the party attacked me, then that's what they would have written. But I was just so appalled by it.

Some of the press implied that you were gay-bashing because you were afraid people would think you were gay.

No way. I wouldn't have done an entire gay tour and all the other things I've done. I realized early on that the way [photographer] Herb [Ritts] shoots is more of a beauty type of thing and that it would make people look at me in that way. I wasn't bothered by that at all. I don't care what people think I am.

So you were as shocked as anyone when all this bad press came out?

It's so weird to have people saying, "What's the matter with you? What are you doing?" because I would always go out and do gay shows. They used to ask me, "What are you doing your show at a gay club for?" I was like, "Why not? They like my music."

The first time I ever did a gay show, I said, "That was the best show I ever did. They go out there and party and do what they want." Sure, the first time I was a little bit nervous. It's something that you're not that familiar with, but it was never something I was worried about, because a lot of people in my own camp are openly gay.

Really?

Yeah, but for me to say "I'm down with this one, and he's gay" and "Look at him, he's gay," that doesn't matter. Those people know how I truly feel about them as individuals. So I would never try to use them. It's like saying, "My best friend is black." You know what I'm saying? That's a bunch of bullshit. People just seeing how I am should know better.

Have you ever had a man come on to you?

Oh, yeah!

And how does that make you feel?

It's never been done in a way where there's been a lot of pressure. I remember somebody who works for my management company, he used to look at me and say, "Ooh, boy!" But I'm very comfortable around him. So we always play around and stuff. He gives me hugs, or he'll grab my butt and stuff like that. But I know him, and he knows me. So it's never really a problem.

Is it any different than having a girl you're not interested in come on to you?

I think I'm more comfortable around men, in general, than women. Women are very hard to figure out.

"For gays to go through these experiences and have people dislike them for something as simple as their sexual preference, to be able to come up from that and be proud of what they're doing—well, I've learned a lot from that."

Why?

Women are very sneaky. A man can kind of find out about a man. They're easy, as opposed to women. They're tricky. They trick you. I'm serious!

Do you mean tricky in a sexual situation, or do you mean that women in general are hard to figure out?

In general, in general. It's got to be in general before it's a sexual situation for me.

Why do you call women "bitches" in your songs?

Well, not all women are bitches to me in any way or form. I think I used it in a record more in a comical way: "It's Friday night, and I'm calling up my honey/ Bitch better have my money." See, I called her "honey." [*Laughs*] I think it's for people who relate to that language. These are the same women who will call you a dick.

So it's street slang?

Yeah, it's street stuff. You would never call your mother or sister or somebody else's mother or sister a bitch. We were calling the girls in Funky Bunch "our bitches," and we'd be their "hoses." But I know people get offended by it. If I ever said "bitch" around my mother, *crack!* [*Hits his head hard*]

So you have more trust and understanding with men than you do with women?

Yeah, definitely.

How do you feel about gay women?

Well, the straight macho thing is, Gay women are cooler than gay men. It's always, "Ooh, two girls is great!"

I remember this friend of mine—his girlfriend left him for another woman, and he was like, "Shit, you should have just taken me with you! Why did you have to get rid of me? I wouldn't have bothered you."

Do you ever go to gay clubs to hang out?

I did an interview for a gay writer who is a friend of mine.

Whenever I see him, we always go to a club or something and hang out. He said that he thinks that I'm gay and I just won't come out with it. I think it's just because I am comfortable around him and around the situation.

Have you ever had a sexual relationship with a man?

Nah.

And you don't ever see that happening?

Uh, not now. But you never know. You *never* know.

What are the advantages of having a large gay following, and what are the disadvantages?

As an advantage, you have loyalty and you have unity, which is very rare and something that I've learned a lot about from being around gay people.

For example?

It's like everything else. As you go through turbulent experiences, you see what going through them can do for you. It's like my situation in a lot of ways. Getting in all that trouble as a kid really helped me to figure out and know what I had to do to be a good person, to be able to go to sleep with myself every night.

For gays to go through these experiences and have people dislike them for something as simple as their sexual preference, to be able to come up from that and be proud of what they're doing—well, I've learned a lot from that.

You're inspired by the gay and lesbian struggle?

Definitely. Look, I always tell people, "You should pay attention to them. They're moving on! I'm telling you, they got their own thing, and they're still willing to work with everybody." I really respect that.

And what are the disadvantages of having a large gay following?

I think that them being so sensitive to me works against me.

Them?

The gay community—not being able to look at me for what I am and say, "Marky, what's up?" Obviously you're giving me that opportunity now.

I'm just trying to educate people and say, "It's cool to do what you want to do. You can set goals for your life and work on the big problems. Homosexuality shouldn't be an issue! Everybody should be able to do what they want to do."

What did you think when you first heard about AIDS?

Well, to me it was like AIDS wasn't here one day and the next day it was controlling everything. So I figured somebody made this shit, boiled it up in their basement, and designed it. Somebody who dislikes gays and people in the poor communities designed it to kill them. That's what I thought. But when I realized how big it was, I knew it was a bigger issue than that.

What made you realize that?

All you got to do is watch *And the Band Played On*. You gotta watch it, man. I watched that fucking movie, and I sat there and I cried. I know a number of people who have died, gay as well as straight. I watched AIDS kill them, and nobody cared. And that's what it's about.

You relate to the rage of feeling no one cared because the "wrong" people were dying?

Hell, yeah! So why not be even more sensitive and protective of yourself? I can understand and relate a lot to that.

Do you feel pressure from people who "wish you were gay"?

Yes, I've felt that. But in a lot of ways it doesn't make sense, because you're not going to be able to be with everybody anyway. So it doesn't matter what your sexual preference is. You can't say, "Cindy Crawford is married to Richard Gere, so I won't like her because I know I'll never get the opportunity to be with her." That doesn't make sense.

Is there something about this pressure to be gay that might be like what gays and lesbians feel when they're pressured by friends or family or society to be heterosexual?

I can relate to that totally, yeah, definitely. A lot of cases in life are different, but they're still similar.

Do you think gays and lesbians should always be out of the closet?

I saw this one case on *The Oprah Winfrey Show* where this lady wouldn't even talk to her daughter because she wanted to be with another woman. Yo, the daughter's doing what she's gotta do. That doesn't mean she's not the same person. You figure her mother could come around for her own kid! To turn on your kid! And even if it isn't your own kid, it's still wrong to say, "I'll never deal with that person because he or she is gay." That's wrong anyway, but to do that to your own kid? You've really got a problem. Those are the ones that should have God going *kaboom!* [*Does imitation of lightning striking*]

Because a lot of rap deals with aggression and violence, there's some concern that you could be into gay bashing. Are you?

No, but when I was younger, out of all the people we robbed, we probably robbed a couple of gay people.

So you were fair?

Oh, yes, we robbed anybody. I would have robbed my cousin if he had $20 and I wanted it.

Tell me about the Calvin Klein deal. How did it start?

I was running around in my underwear. I'd been dropping my pants onstage. That was kinda like my trademark. I did a fashion shoot for *Rolling Stone* magazine, and I'd been wearing Calvin Klein underwear. There was a picture of me with my pants hanging down and the underwear showing.

They saw the picture. Somebody called me and said, "Calvin Klein wants you to do this advertisement. They want you to model for them."

I said, "What? No thanks!"

They said, "No, they like the way you run around in your underwear and stuff."

I told them, "I don't want to do something against what I'm about." But then I actually had a phone conversation with Calvin and David Geffen.

David Geffen?

Yes, me and David Geffen are real cool. I talk to him all the time. I call him up for business advice. It's very rare that you will find somebody who will not only give you advice but good advice. I met him the first time at Calvin's house. They were like, "The only reason we want you is because you were doing your own thing, and that's what we want you to do for us. We think it's cool."

So I was like, "Cool."

They wanted what you were already doing, and you thought you'd have to do something that wasn't you?

Yeah! Exactly. And that's why I figure it worked out so well.

I went to Calvin's house, and Geffen was just hanging out. We were just talking. They were laughing because my pants were hanging down. I tried on some stuff. And then we talked again. Calvin said he would like Herb Ritts to shoot me.

I said, "Well, you can get me to do the pictures if Herb is going to take them! 'Cause Herb Ritts is the man!"

You were happy with the photo sessions?

There were some things I would have done differently. I just think that with the stuff being that powerful, we should have said a little bit more. I should have been able to get my message across a little better. It should have been a little deeper as opposed to light and sexy.

And now the contract has ended?

I think there's really not too much more to do. I think the second campaign wasn't half as good as the first one or even necessary, because the first one did it. I don't want to be a Calvin Klein model forever. Nothing lasts forever.

So the campaign didn't end because of pressure from GLAAD?

No, the contract was always over in December.

Do you think the campaign hurt you?

That's hard to say, because the campaign is what propelled me to this level where everybody knows me. But that's where the mix-up began. Everybody knew my music and my message, but then the sex thing started coming on—the shirt and the abs and that stuff—and it started taking away from the message. Then when the Calvin thing came out, it just went *boom!* People who knew me from my music knew what I was about, but everybody else just started with the sex thing.

Do you use sex to get your message across?

Sometimes my body gets them to listen; sometimes my music gets them to listen. But I'm not going to miss my opportunity to say what I have to say, because if I enlighten one or two or three people, I've done something. I've enlightened myself, so I've already accomplished—to me—a miracle!

Still, I'd like to say to all the kids, "Yeah, it's frustrating, but be patient. It's really important to find the right route. Try to love each other. That's all we can do."

Do you promote safer sex?

In my show I have a segment where I come out with a condom. I also tell kids not to have sex until they get older: "No sex is the safest sex. But if you're going to engage, please use a condom."

Do you have any members of your family who are gay or lesbian?

Listen, my stepfather's brother, who lived with us for three or four years, is gay. He wasn't really openly gay around us, but I thought that he was gay. He had a bunch of male friends who used to come around to see him. I don't really want to mention too much of his business, but he's openly gay now. He's very much like an uncle. He still spends Christmas with us.

Did his being gay matter to you?

Not at all. I felt uncomfortable that I might make him uncomfortable and not able to be himself. I was always telling him, "You gotta be yourself and do what you gotta do." He made the best chocolate-chip cookies ever!

Christmastime, I'm telling you, you gotta come over! He buys us the best Christmas gifts. Fly shirts and sweaters! I'm talking fashion! But I don't feel that I should have to say all this for people to believe me.

What has hanging out at Fort Jackson taught you about the military?

This Army base is bigger than Boston! They spend trillions of dollars on this stuff. But if nobody had an army, nobody would worry about people beating up on each other, so why not just put the money to good use instead and give it to the community!

I don't know. I'm an old peacenik. I never understood it.

You can call me a new peacenik, because it's like, Why?

Now that you've gone through basic training, what do you think of gays in the military?

Yo, brothers! Don't do it! I don't know why you wanna be in the Army. I mean, of course, it's your right to be there, but it's not that good of an idea.

I can't go into the Army because I don't have a diploma and I had criminal problems in my past. They wouldn't even take me. But I'm glad. I'm not trying to fight for that right at all.

I think everybody should have the right if they want to. But all these weapons? The more you got, the more shit's going to happen. And it don't take a genius to know that, because I didn't even get through the ninth grade. But, hey, I'm going back to get my GED, my general education diploma. I've been taking it for two years. I got one test left. I take it at the adult learning center in Boston.

You're being educated all over the place, aren't you?

It's so weird. People who aren't faced with things don't ever think about it. And that goes along with every facet of life. If somebody isn't poor, they're not concerned with people who don't have things.

It's the same thing with AIDS! If you don't know nobody with AIDS, you're not affected by it. I thought, *It can't happen to me*—until I saw somebody close to me dying of it. It was like, man, I started thinking about how I kissed this person before and did this or that. It made me think about it. Until you're affected by it, you really don't think about it. And that's fucked up.

I feel bad that you have to learn things by seeing them and experiencing them. I think to myself, *Wow, how many other things are going on that I'm not experiencing, so I don't know about them?*

Were you distraught when your parents split up?

Oh, yeah, definitely. I was going berserk when it first happened. I thought, *They have to live together because of me!* I realized afterward that if they couldn't be happy with each other, then they shouldn't be together. It's actually becoming harder for me now because my father is sick. He has cancer, and he lives by himself.

Are you doing anything special for your father now?

The most I can do is spend as much time with him as possible.

How does he feel about your success?

Oh, he loves it! He says, "Who'd ever thought it, Mikey?"

Mikey?

I always wanted my name to be Mike. To this day my dad calls me Mikey. Mikey Mike!

And your mother?

My mother remarried. There was so many problems going on. My brothers and sisters ruined my mother's life, and I did too, through booze and then drugs and all that stuff. I thank my mother every day and apologize for not listening to her. She should have kicked me in the ass one more time!

Where do you live now?

I'm a drifter. I have sneakers in New Jersey. I've got sneakers at my mom's house in Braintree, Mass., where my brother bought her a home. Donnie and I have always lived with my mother.

Is there anything that you regret, something that you would absolutely go back and do differently if you could?

Yeah, but then I don't think that I would be the type of person that I am. I don't think that I would have the heart that I do.

The only thing I'd do differently is to be a lot better to my mother. I would have kicked my other brothers' and sisters' asses for running my mother into the ground. But everything else I would just let be.

Is there anything I forgot to ask you?

[*Grinning*] Yeah, my favorite color is purple. I like steak, potatoes, chicken, fish, shrimp. I like to play basketball. I have an earring hole, but I haven't been wearing an earring. And my underwear size is medium.

Bar

bra

Streisand

I have never met Barbra Streisand

in person. Of course, I said this in the original introduction to our 1999 interview when she was the cover story for *The Advocate's* special "Best & Brightest Activists" issue. Because Barbra was in rehearsals for what she believed would be her last paid public performance—her New Year's Eve concert at the MGM Grand Gardens in Las Vegas—she only agreed to our interview if I submitted written questions. The world-famous perfectionist felt that she could reveal her enormous commitment to human rights best by taking her time and carefully writing out long, thoughtful answers.

She was clearly enthusiastic about the opportunity to share her most candid feelings with *Advocate* readers—something she had never done before—but only if we let her approach the interview this way. She needed to address the issues without constant interruptions from the whirlwind pressures around her at the time. We were assured that she would find time in the quiet of her evenings to write her heart out. So after pow-wows with *The Advocate's* executive editor, Bruce Steele, who suggested her for the cover, we agreed. Barbra's one request was that we run her full answers unedited and, additionally, that we not change or edit any of my questions—the ones we originally submitted to her—in the final version of the interview. The deal was struck. The writing and faxing began. When the interview came out, Barbra was delighted. She asked to have many extra copies distributed to her foundation, and was thrilled when we got word to her that then-president Clinton—her good friend—wanted extra copies sent to the White House. She also let us know that she looked forward to doing an "in-person" interview with the magazine in the near future. Satisfying as our interview had been, it suddenly felt like the entire experience had been some enormous exercise in trust—and apparently we passed with flying colors.

A few years later I met Barbra's son, Jason Gould, in New York City during the photo shoot we did for his *Advocate* coming-out cover story. One of the most difficult and carefully negotiated questions in Barbra's interview addressed how she herself had grown as the result of being the mother of a gay son. At the time of her interview, her son, Jason, had not publicly come out in print in America. Therefore, both my question and Barbra's answer never used the word "gay." Yet it was perfectly clear what the discussion was about. No one could possibly have missed it. Nor could anyone have missed the fact that no mother could have been more proud of her son.

Spending the day with Jason years later, it was obvious to me what a great parent Barbra has been. He has an amazing attention to detail, is full of bright ideas, and has boundless energy about the arts. Yes, like his mother, Jason needs to feel in charge, but also like his mother, he is driven by his quest for the truth. He questions everything. While Barbra is clearly more political in her approach, Jason is no less devoted to having his life and art make a difference in the world. After editing his interview, I came to appreciate Barbra's even more. She is an original. She set the standard for artists, activists, women, and "people who need people" years ago. And she's never backed off her standards. They are simple and clear. They're about telling the truth no matter what and finding a way to object loudly when that isn't happening. Barbra herself says it best in the following interview when she says, "Although I am an activist on many issues and I sometimes gather the courage to speak at rallies and other public gatherings, I still have always felt that I can speak more eloquently through my work than through any speech I might give. As an artist, I have chosen to make films about subjects and social issues I care about. One of the films I am most proud of in this regard is Serving in Silence. Col. Grethe Cammermeyer was discharged from the Army because she insisted on telling the truth about her sexuality.... I do think her case was incredibly unjust, and that is what made me want to tell her story."

Barbra Streisand has been challenging convention, prejudice, and bigotry since the day she made her Broadway debut in *I Can Get It for You Wholesale* in 1962. Unable to conform to the entertainment industry's pathetically limited standards of beauty,

Streisand simply changed them for everyone forever. Singing and clowning her way through the role of Miss Marmelstein, the fearless 20-year-old dynamo overturned every obstacle in sight and catapulted herself to superstardom using only her kooky Brooklyn personality and one of the greatest voices in show business history. She did it by knowing she was different and being herself, regardless.

Unsurprisingly, she's still doing that. With a Tony, two Oscars, three Emmys, 12 multiplatinum albums, 24 platinum albums (more than any other female artist), and 40 gold albums (more than the Beatles), Streisand is set to top all her past achievements with the October release of her new album, *A Love Like Ours,* featuring her current single, "I've Dreamed of You." She is also reteaming with Craig Zaden and Neil Meron, with whom she executive-produced 1995's Emmy award–winning *Serving in Silence: The Margarethe Cammermeyer Story,* on an upcoming television movie about a lesbian custody battle, *What Makes a Family.*

Recently setting the record for the largest one-day ticket sales of a single event, the 57-year-old phenomenon reports that this event—her New Year's Eve millennium concert at the MGM Grand Gardens in Las Vegas—may well be her last paid public performance. Which isn't to say you won't be hearing from her. For example…

Despite Streisand's busy summer recording schedule (and because she did not want to miss the opportunity to participate in *The Advocate*'s Best and Brightest Activists issue), she asked to have questions submitted to her so that she could work on them in her spare time. Although she said immediately that she liked the questions and felt she could handle them, we worried that something would be lost—her passion, her frankness, her humor, her rage, *something*—in the writing process. But we were wrong! As you can read for yourself, there's a reason why Streisand's magic has thrived over the years. Her power and integrity, her love and loyalty are inspiring. And fortunately, she's still absolutely fearless.

Equal rights: You were very visible and took a strong position when Colorado passed a referendum that deprived gays and lesbians of legal protection against discrimination. You were obviously driven to speak out against it. Can you talk a little bit about why and what kind of responses you got from people in general when you did this. Did you get any hate mail? Was there something in particular that you learned from taking this stand? Can you say something about why you think gay rights are not special rights, they're simply equal rights?

For me, one of the most disturbing elements of the right wing's political agenda is that it believes that there is one correct spiritual and moral path for all people to follow. The danger inherent in this is their explicit refusal to accept anyone who happens to lead a different lifestyle and the condemnation of those who differ. Homophobia is a disease which desperately needs to be cured. We need to get beyond this fear, ignorance, and bigotry, and move on to a mature society in which we recognize that all people deserve dignity and respect, regardless of their gender, color, religious beliefs, or sexual orientation.

I spoke out about my concern for the Colorado referendum because, by depriving gay men and lesbians of legal protection from discrimination, it set a very dangerous precedent. When I spoke out against the vote for hate in Colorado, I was attacked on many fronts. Many of my colleagues vacation in Colorado, and they were upset with me for saying that we should not go there. I received hate mail from people who were angry at me for just standing up for what I believed in. The most remarkable thing to me, however, in this instance was the incredible power of celebrity. The expression of my personal belief that people of conscience should not spend time and money in places that discriminate was suddenly elevated overnight into a call for a full-scale boycott of Colorado by people across the country. I was truly amazed that my remarks had such a large impact. Fortunately, through the hard work and dedication of local lawyers and activists, and national groups like the American Civil Liberties Union, we were able to challenge the constitutionality of this measure and ultimately defeat it on appeal.

The far right uses the phrase "special rights" as an excuse to hate and a way to confuse people into voting against measures which would give all people equal protection under the law. Gay and lesbian rights advocates do not seek to gain "special" rights, but rather they want to ensure that they are able to enjoy the same civil rights as everyone else. Activists have fought hard to get laws passed to secure the rights of people of different sexual orientations who are now excluded from protection. Through my Foundation, I have had the privilege of helping fund the important work done by many groups, such as the Human Rights Campaign Fund, Lambda Legal Defense, and the ACLU. They are the true champions in the fight for justice and equality. How I wish we lived in a time where laws were not necessary to safeguard us from discrimination. However, recent events like the murder of Matthew Shepard clearly demonstrate that this day has not yet arrived. And it is unfortunate—but true—that in our society today, even as we enter into a new millennium, unless antidiscrimination laws are passed and enforced, there is no inherent presumption that the civil rights of gays and lesbians will be ensured.

AIDS: In 1992 you made a passionate speech for AIDS Project Los Angeles in which you nailed all the people involved for not responding to the AIDS crisis appropriately. You talked about the homophobia involved and the terrible health crisis that mushroomed because of it. Can you update us on how you see people dealing with AIDS

"When I spoke out against the vote for hate in Colorado [depriving gay men and lesbians of legal protection from discrimination], I was attacked on many fronts. Many of my colleagues vacation in Colorado, and were upset with me."

today: the drugs, the safe-sex issues, the good and bad human responses you've seen coming from your professional peers, friends, and family?

The Reagan years legitimized bigotry. AIDS, which even then affected as many if not more heterosexuals than homosexuals throughout the world, was dismissed as a gay disease with an official homophobic wink, implying that those deaths did not matter because of who was involved. Luckily for all of us, however, in 1992 there was a change in leadership, and with a new president came a new understanding of the need to fight this dreaded disease. In his time in office, President Clinton has made many changes in government policy towards the gay and lesbian community. He has appointed openly gay people to serve in his administration, has supported the Employment Non-Discrimination Act, and has increased funding for AIDS research and prevention programs.

The entertainment community was generous and committed early on in the effort to bring awareness to this problem. Thanks to the commitment of people like Elizabeth Taylor and Dr. Mathilde Krim at the American Foundation for AIDS Research, a great deal of progress has been made in the past 10 years. Their recognition of and financial contribution to the cause, along with the hard work of a host of dedicated scientists, doctors, and activists, has helped create new drug therapies which allow people to live with HIV longer than ever before, and now the possibility of an AIDS vaccine lies within reach.

We are filled with the hope that someday, some way, we will see an end to this human tragedy, but the battle is far from won, and there is a long road still ahead. The most difficult challenge we face at this point in time is complacency. Since many people in the United States are able to live longer lives with the help of expensive drug therapies and aggressive treatments, we are getting used to AIDS and almost accept it as a fact of life. Although it is wonderful that many AIDS patients today are able to live long lives with HIV through these innovative drug programs, many people have begun to view these drug combinations as a cure for the disease, which they most definitely are not. There have even been cases recently in which the HIV virus mutated so quickly that it became "drug resistant" to patients' protease inhibitors.

We must be ever vigilant in the search for a cure. It is estimated that 31 million people worldwide are infected with HIV. AIDS is now affecting everyone—heterosexuals, women, people of color, and particularly residents of developing nations, where 90% of the world's HIV-infected patients live. And these people cannot afford basic medical care, let alone the tens of thousands of dollars per person per year that it costs to pay for new drug therapies. As the disease crosses into new populations, these communities need our support, just as the gay community needed the support of others when the AIDS epidemic was breaking out 10 years ago.

Gay marriage: You've already stated publicly that it's appalling to you that anyone would pronounce anyone's love invalid. Why do you think the fight for gay marriage is going to be one of the hardest gay men and lesbians will face?

I have said over and over again that I believe everyone has a right to love and be loved, and nobody on this earth has the right to tell anyone that their love for another human being is morally wrong. I will never forget how it made me shudder to hear Pat Buchanan say that he stood "with George Bush against the immoral idea that gay and lesbian couples should have the same standing in law as married men and women." Who is Pat Buchanan to pronounce anyone's love invalid? How can he deny the profound love felt by one human being for another?

It bothers me that so many conservatives resort to name-calling and stereotyping. I remember in 1994 when Newt Gingrich pitted President Clinton against so-called "normal Americans." This notion of "normal Americans" has a horrible historical echo, presupposing that there are "abnormal" Americans responsible for all that is wrong with America. Despite this rhetoric and hollow assumption, we are all normal Americans, with our joys, challenges, complexities, and triumphs. Unfortunately, however, as long as people like Newt Gingrich and Pat Buchanan continue in public life, the fight to codify gay marriages will be a tough battle to win.

I understand from Craig Zaden and Neil Meron that your production of *What Makes a Family* is moving along. Lesbian court battles are (unfortunately) filling many courtrooms today. Some refer to it as the "dirty little secret" of the gay movement. Do you think that gay marriage and other "legal sanctions" and support systems will help some of the women struggling with these custody issues today? What have you learned from your exposure to this painful subject matter? Outside of custody battles, do you think gays and lesbians make good parents? Do you think they have something special to give? Why?

For me, the issue of gay and lesbian parenting is very similar to that of gay marriage, in that I feel very strongly that no one person has any right to invalidate another person's loving relationship with another. The children of this world need love and attention, and they deserve to have parents who will love, cherish, and care for them. What makes a good family is parents who support, nurture, and love their children.

There is no one "perfect" model on which all family structures can be based. If we surveyed human history, we would see representations of every type of possible social arrangement. There is no "standard" to which all families must adhere. The idea that anyone can impose their image of what a "normal" family should be on others seems absurd to me. We all come from different backgrounds, cultures, and traditions, and have different understandings of what a family looks like.

Gays in the military: You have already made your feelings on this issue loud and clear (*Serving in Silence*). You said you were attracted to Grethe's case because it was "so unjust." Although "Don't Ask, Don't Tell" seemed to advance things a little at the time, today it seems to be causing a lot of human damage in the armed forces. Do you have any feelings about "Don't Ask, Don't Tell" that you could share with us?

Although I am an activist on many issues, and I sometimes gather the courage to speak at rallies and other public gatherings, I still have always felt that I can speak more eloquently through my work than through any speech I might give. As an artist, I have chosen to make films about subjects and social issues I care about. One of the films I am most proud of in this regard is *Serving in Silence*. Col. Grethe Cammermeyer was discharged from the Army because she insisted on telling the truth about her sexuality. Her story has always reminded me of a line from George Bernard Shaw's *St. Joan* that said, "He who tells too much truth shall surely be hanged." Don't they realize yet that one's competence at work has nothing to do with one's sexuality and it's nobody's business—whether that person be Grethe Cammermeyer, Eleanor or Franklin Roosevelt, or President Clinton. I do think her case was incredibly unjust, and that is what made me want to tell her story.

The Rev. Martin Luther King said once that "although social change cannot come overnight, we must always work as though it were a possibility in the morning." I do not agree with the government's "Don't Ask, Don't Tell" policy, and at the same time I know that changing policy takes a long time. I continue to look for the day when there will be no more barriers to employment in this country; when any person, regardless of gender, color, religious beliefs, or sexual orientation, will be able to serve in any occupation they choose, including our nation's armed forces. We have come a long way towards recognizing the civil rights of gay men and lesbians in this country, but we still have a long way to go before full equality is achieved.

Foundation giving: You have been very supportive of a plethora of good causes over the years. This support has been demonstrated both through your work, your actions, and your financial contributions to charitable causes. How does the Streisand Foundation function in achieving your goals, in terms of both gay and lesbian civil rights and AIDS?

The Streisand Foundation was started in 1986 with a concert at my home called "One Voice." I created the Foundation because it has always been very important to me to give back to the community. Not only is the value of giving charity a part of my Jewish tradition—in the Jewish tradition charity is linked to justice and an obligation to mend the world—but I also identify strongly with those who have suffered oppression. Since its inception, the Foundation has provided assistance to organizations working on a variety of issues, including civil liberties and Democratic issues, women's issues, civil rights and race relations, AIDS research, advocacy, service and litigation, children's and youth-related issues, and environmental issues. The Foundation steered the giving of over $13 million since 1986, $3 million of which went to gay and lesbian rights and AIDS causes.

I am thrilled my Foundation has been able to fund such groups as American Foundation for AIDS Research (AmFAR); AIDS Project Los Angeles (APLA); Human Rights Campaign; Elizabeth Glaser Pediatric AIDS Foundation; Project Angel Food; the American Civil Liberties Union (ACLU); Lambda Legal Defense; National Gay and Lesbian Task Force (NGLTF); Parents, Families, and Friends of Lesbians and Gays (PFLAG); Gay and Lesbian Alliance Against Defamation (GLAAD); Gay Men's Health Crisis (GMHC); and the Gay, Lesbian and Straight Education Network (GLSEN).

I hope you were able to read *The Advocate*'s cover story interview with Judy Shepard, Matthew Shepard's mother. There are no words sufficient to describe when any parent loses a child. But to lose your gay child that way is beyond belief. I have had two very nice phone calls with your son, Jason, over the last couple of years. We have talked at length about his doing something with *The Advocate* when he has a project he is particularly proud of. I mention this to "put it on the table" so that you know we talk. Since so many of our readers know Jason indirectly—through his movie work or through the one or two London-based interviews he has given— and know that you are his mother, is there some way you could say something about your own growth as a human being and an activist as a result of this crucial experience in your life? I am not asking you to talk about Jason. It's your evolution that would be so enlightening.

I would never wish for my son to be anything but what he is. He is bright, kind, sensitive, caring, and a very conscientious and good person. He is a very gifted actor and filmmaker. What more could a parent ask for in their child? I have been truly blessed. Most parents feel that their child is particularly special, and I am no different. I have a wonderful son. My only wish for my son, Jason, is that he continues to experience a rich life of love, happiness, joy, and fulfillment, both creatively and personally.

"It made me shudder to hear Pat Buchanan say that he stood 'with George Bush against the *immoral* idea that gay couples should have the same standing in law as married men and women.' Who is he to pronounce anyone's love invalid?"

ting

The first time I interviewed Sting it was 1985.

I was writing for a magazine called *Rock Express*, and he had just released his first solo album, *Dream of the Blue Turtles*. When he arrived at the Malibu motel room I was supposed to meet him in, he burst through the front door, threw himself across the bed, and wailed, "I just had a car accident on my way here!" Once we determined he was all right (he had banged his head on the windshield), Sting propped himself up on the bed, pointed to me and demanded, "Go for it. Ask me anything. I'm too vulnerable to be clever. You're going to get a great interview!" And I did.

Eleven years later *The Advocate*'s senior arts & entertainment editor, Anne Stockwell, came into my office and dropped an open magazine on my desk. The two-page spread depicted a beautiful library in Sting's 14-bedroom home near Stonehenge in England. "That's where you should go to do your interview with Sting," Anne said authoritatively. "That's where he'll really be honest with you. He'll be comfortable. He just made a movie where he played the seducer of both men and women. And his wife, Trudie Styler, made a terrific documentary about transvestites in Brazil called *Boys From Brazil.* Maybe you could interview them together."

Yes, I had seen this ultra dark movie, *Grave Indiscretion,* with Sting playing bisexual, and I certainly knew all the gay hearts that had skipped beats over him since his entrance on the music scene as the chief of Police—a band he left for an even bigger solo career. But how would I get myself all the way from Los Angeles to his 16th-century Elizabethan manor with the river Avon and 54 acres of beautiful land (think "Fields of Gold") all around?

As it turned out, it was possible. Because I was scheduled to do another interview in London that year, Sting's record label graciously offered to send a car for me to travel several hours outside of London to his breathtaking stone mansion in Wiltshire, a castle Sting calls Lake House. When I arrived, the Grammy-winning pop star was recording songs for his album, *Mercury Falling*, in a large, open living room with wires and amplifiers strewn around him. Trudie smiled, told me to wait for her husband to finish the song he was working on, then disappeared to go food shopping. The house was full of people. Some working on music. Some working on the 400-year-old home.

I lowered myself onto a lovely soft sofa in the Lake House library and just listened. A typically beautiful Sting melody hung in the air. While the recording continued, I scanned the fireplace mantle and studied the photos. There was a striking picture of an old ship docked in a harbor. The photo was slightly faded and sat in a sturdy wooden frame. Somehow I knew this was from Sting's past, when he was still Gordon Matthew Sumner, the son of a Newcastle hairdresser mother and milkman father. These were the years he worked by day as a teacher in Newcastle, a dank, oppressive shipping town in northern England. In the evenings he played music in his favorite black and yellow sweater, earning himself the nickname Sting—like a yellow jacket. When he met guitarist Andy Summers and drummer Stewart Copeland in 1977, the Police—and a whole lot of platinum-selling magic—was born. Now, over 20 years later, he had broken free of the band and become a superstar on his own. As a musician, an actor, a family man, and an activist, Sting was the ultimate success story.

I continued to study the photos until I sensed movement in the doorway. Sting stood in the library arch, hair mussed, face full of conflicting thoughts, eyes blurry with music: "Are we going to talk now?" he asked puzzled, turning his head back and forth between me and where he had been recording. "I don't know where Trudie is."

I explained where Trudie was. He seemed a little anxious. "Let's go out to the swimming pool and start there," he suggested. We walked outdoors on walkways of stone with weeds and summer flowers bursting through, then down several rows of steps that finally led to a sparkling blue pool with rubber children's toys and blow-up floats. Someone had left out two jars of delicious honey and a loaf of bread. Wordlessly we both began eating.

"Are you nervous about this?" I half-whispered after several minutes. He stopped chewing and laughed. "No…no. I…I mean, yes, but I want to do this interview." We both laughed at his response. "Do you remember me?" I ventured, a little embarrassed. He stared at me blankly. "Do you remember doing an interview in America years ago right after you had a car accident?" His eyes got big. "Was that *you?*" he said. "Oh, my God, *you* were there?" I reminded him about how honest and forthcoming he'd been in that interview as a result of banging his head on the windshield.

He reached over and turned on my tape recorder. "Let's see if I can do it again," he said grinning and rubbing his forehead. As the following interview with both Sting and his amazing wife clearly show, he definitely did it again.

"Really? Oh, who cares?" Sting says, pushing open the heavy wooden front door of his 400-year-old Elizabethan manor and walking out onto the 54 acres of rich English land it sits on. "Listen, if someone wants to say I'm gay because I kiss a man

on screen, it's not something I'm afraid of."

The 44-year-old songwriter-musician-actor is talking about his bisexual role in *Grave Indiscretioin,* a movie his wife, Trudie Styler, has produced and costars in with him. In the piece—a grim social comedy due in theaters this fall—Sting has two sex scenes with other men. "An interesting experience," he says with a grin.

Interesting experiences have pretty much driven the exotic life of Gordon Matthew Sumner. Born the son of a Newcastle milkman father and a hairdresser mother, he worked as a schoolteacher before changing his name to Sting—friends said he looked like a bee with his trademark yellow-and-black sweaters. Then, joining his blond good looks with drummer Stewart Copeland's and guitarist Andy Summers's, he helped to form the Police in 1977. After several platinum albums and Grammy awards, including one for "Every Breath You Take," the restless Police chief dissolved the band at the peak of its powers in order to follow his own headstrong rhythms. Although fans hoped it was just a sabbatical, Sting's first solo album, *The Dream of the Blue Turtles* (1985), was such a stunning success that it put to rest any dreams of a Police reunion.

Now, with his sixth solo album, *Mercury Falling,* already climbing the charts and a solo tour in progress, Sting's striking compositions have become an integral if unexpected part of the American landscape. His signature vocals provided the perfect noir atmosphere for this year's *Leaving Las Vegas* sound track, just as his canny musicianship has frequently proved to be key to the moods of other successful films, including *Sabrina, Copycat, Someone to Watch Over Me,* and *The Three Musketeers.*

"I first met Sting when he asked me to play the part of his lab assistant in a film he starred in called *The Bride,*" recalls Quentin Crisp, who later became the subject of a Sting song called "Englishman in New York." The composition, which depicts Crisp's bravery in the face of brutal homophobia, became Sting's metaphor for his own feelings of isolation after moving to America. "He's very courteous," Crisp says of the multiple Grammy winner (Sting won another Grammy in 1993 for "If I Ever Lose My Faith in You"). "I don't mean to sound condescending. I just didn't expect a pop star to be so gentlemanly."

Being a pop star is the one thing Sting doesn't do well. Although he still has a home in Malibu, Calif., he hasn't been there in many years. Instead he, Styler, and four of his six children share a 14-bedroom home near Stonehenge that he calls Lake House. It was there in his Wiltshire mansion, with windows on all sides and the river Avon running past, that Sting composed *Mercury Falling.* And it was in the Lake House library, with Styler occasionally joining in, that Sting spoke for the very first time with the gay press.

After doing *Grave Indiscretion,* do you think straight actors should play gay parts?

I was watching a gay TV show last night, and they asked that. They said, "There are enough gay actors to accommodate those roles." And the guy who was gay said, "Look, gay actors have been playing straights for years—Cary Grant and Montgomery Clift."

You're an activist. How aware of gay and lesbian civil rights are you?

A lot of my friends are gay, so my knowledge about gay rights has come through them. But in our world, gays are not terribly discriminated against.

What world is that?

In the entertainment world, people don't hide the fact that they're gay—not in England anyway. It's something that is a matter of course.

Even though there've been English actors like Ian McKellen and directors like John Schlesinger who've been able to come out without much damage, for a romantic lead it's still the last frontier.

I'm sure that frontier will be crossed, and I think that more straight actors playing gay is probably the way that will happen. The whole business of sexuality is very strange to me. I mean, we all have the gay gene, don't we?

We do?

Yes, I think we all have this gay gene. That's how we interact. Men couldn't live with each other if we didn't have the ability to be tender with each other or the ability to love each other. We *do* have that ability, whether it's spoken or not. Male bonding is nothing but erotic behavior. Football hooligans are homoerotic. Rugby teams are homoerotic. It's just that it's under a different guise—a disguise.

Were you aware of the gay following that you had when you were in the Police?

No! [*Laughs*]

You especially were considered quite the heartthrob. You didn't get letters from men?

No, I don't think so, but I'm flattered—deeply flattered.

When you starred in the film *Dune,* your character was homoerotic.

He was definitely that. The director, David Lynch, who's a strange man, had me in this costume, this flying-underpants-sort-of-wing thing, and it just looked like something out of a gay cabaret. Up until that point, the character was ambiguous, but after that he was gay, so I said, "OK, we'll go for it."

Have you worked with actors and musicians who are gay but closeted?

Uh, well, sure I have.

Do they tell you they're worried someone might out them?

I think that's unfortunate, to be honest with you. I think people should out themselves when they choose to. I don't think it's fair to basically abuse people—to abuse people's sense of timing and their sense of pride by actually feeding them to the bad press, feeding them to the wrong instincts of society.

You mean, when gays out other gays?

Yes, it's like the gays who are doing the outing are saying, "To be gay is bad. Look, we're going to punish you." I don't think that it's bad to be gay. People shouldn't be outed and punished because they are. People have a right to their privacy—gays particularly. So I don't like it.

Do you also see the other side: strength in numbers?

I think the straight community has to own up and say, "Look, gays have provided all these services throughout history, and it's not just choreography and hairdressing, it's war heroes and caregivers; they've fought in the armed forces and been decorated heroes, and they're *gay*. Admit it." There are similar issues in society that people should be honest about.

Like?

Drugs, for example. There are a lot of people who use drugs recreationally or for more serious reasons, and their lives are perfectly fine. They're not falling apart at the seams.

Are you talking about yourself?

I like to smoke pot, but this whole idea that to be the president of the United States you have to lie about your former drug habits is nonsense. It's a similar issue.

Well, yes, in that you feel shame about something you do or you are, and because of that, you lie.

Exactly. It's hypocritical, and that's sad.

You've always been candid about representing yourself as a very sexual person. I read how you do yoga to enjoy sex longer. Has your sexual appetite ever led you to a homosexual experience?

No, I haven't had a gay relationship—although I do have very close, loving relationships with the men I work with, other musicians. It's a very tight male community, a very close bond—and I love it. But it's not sexual.

How do you draw the line?

Well, thanks to the gay community, we men can actually follow our feelings and demonstrate our affection for each other without being afraid. I'm perfectly willing to hug the people I work with. I do it all the time. I think the generation before us—our fathers—they would shake hands, and that would be it. There would be no hugging or affection.

Do you think you suffered by not having more affection from your father?

I don't think I'm unusual for my generation. I don't think either of my parents really knew how to tactilely demonstrate their love for me, and I think that was hard on me. So I probably overcompensate. I mean, I'm constantly touching my kids, and they're constantly saying, "Leave me alone." [*Laughs*]

I believe your son Jake had a problem earlier in his life. He was in school, and no one understood what was wrong.

He is what's technically known as dyspraxic. He had a lot of learning difficulties, despite having a massive IQ. He is very bright but found schoolwork to be totally impossible. He's much better now; he's receiving treatment for what is a clinical condition.

When you were first dealing with this, did it give you any idea of what it might be like for a parent who has a gay child who isn't quite fitting in?

I don't see gayness as being something that's *wrong* with somebody. Jake had something that was wrong with his brain; it wasn't working properly. I'm not sure I would classify being gay as something wrong. I just think it's different.

But what *is* similar is that Jake had to deal with being different, right?

Oh, I see. Yes, he was feeling very put down, humiliated publicly. Every day was a humiliation for him. And he went from being an incredibly boisterous and self-confident kid to being this little mouse overnight, just by being in the wrong environment.

If any or all of your children were to come to you and say they were gay, would you be supportive?

[*Wide-eyed*] I love my children!

The number of kids who get tossed out of their homes over this is shocking.

That's beyond belief to me.

It can't be that different here in England.

But they're your children! They're a part of you.

Some people must not like that part of themselves. Have you heard the joke "Is he gay or just British?"

I don't think of that as a joke. Did we invent camp, or did we not? I think the British gay movement was probably a pioneer. Noël Coward thought of himself as one of the stately homos of England—even though it was against the law until quite recently. Homosexuals have a place in society. I think the British have a great affection for them.

Have you ever had any of your gay friends or actors come on to you?

No, I don't think so.

You don't *think* so?

Um…[*laughs*] Well, maybe they have.

When you did your gay sex scenes in *Grave Indiscretion*, did you feel anything for the other actor sexually?

I think that's very dangerous, because the easiest way to portray someone in love or someone in lust is to *be* in love or in lust. That's a very easy thing to fall into. If you're making love to a beautiful man or a beautiful woman—it's a quite attractive idea to your body.

So, Sting, did you like kissing the male actor or not?

[*Laughing*] OK. It wasn't entirely unpleasant.

Was that a surprise to you?

Yeah. I mean, I've been conditioned like most people. The idea that there are taboo areas of the body. To kiss someone on the lips is one of those areas. It's a symbolic thing. So all right, I did it, and the actor I kissed was the same as me: He'd never done it before with a man. Now we both have, so I suppose we're gay now.

Definitely; that's all it takes.

What I've learned from my gay friends is that there are all kinds of sexual relationships between gays. It's not just one thing, you know; it's a whole variety and intensity of sexual relationships that gays have. Gays are normally stereotyped for one act, and that isn't the only thing they do.

Which seems so strange to me. I mean, heterosexuals know there are all kinds of straight sexual acts.

[*Gasps*] There are?

[*Laughing*] Never mind. Let's get serious. What did you think the first time you heard about AIDS?

Oh, God, that *is* serious! I was terrified. I mean, I was intelligent enough to realize that a virus wasn't going to limit itself to gay men—even if it began that way. And, of course, it *didn't* begin that way, really—but that was the perception. My first thought was not *Phew! I'm glad I'm not gay, I won't get this thing.* I couldn't possibly subscribe to the idea that it's God's punishment for unnatural sexual behavior. That's nonsense.

You knew people who thought that?

They exist, sure. I think anyone with that mind-set should sit in a hospital room with some person in his mid 30s who is talented and vital and full of potential—and watch him die.

Did you do that?

Yes. It's a human being. It shouldn't be happening. I think there obviously *is* a cure for AIDS. There's nothing in existence that doesn't have an antidote somewhere. I'm an environmentalist. I keep saying, "There's a cure for AIDS in the jungle. It's nature's laboratory; the cure's there, we just have to find it." I keep hearing that there is a conspiracy to hold things back and into the hands of the people who can make money at it.

Do you believe that?

I believe it. There's so much money in the drug industry, and they're all fighting over patents. There's talk of plants in Africa and the Amazon that could hold this thing back. They're free, and you just have to find them. The whole idea of the drug industry and government bureaucracy all being hand in hand to keep this thing under wraps—it's wrong.

Have you ever written a song about it?

No. I don't write about issues unless I can find a metaphor to express them. I'm not a propagandist.

There was a movie of one of your tours—I think it was *Bring On the Night*—and somebody in your band or the crew called someone a faggot. Do you remember that?

Yeah, Branford Marsalis said it, I think. I remember the incident, but it was very much Branford being silly and daft. I didn't get any personal flak from that. [*Laughing*] But thanks for reminding me!

No problem.

There's a difference between serious psychotic homophobia and the sort of stuff that's learned in school yards. There's a difference. This mightn't be much solace to the victim, but there's a difference. But it *is* an insult, either way. I have to accept that.

I understand that there's maliciousness and there's carelessness, and I certainly didn't expect you to stand up in the tour bus and say "Get out!" to him [*Sting laughs*]. Also, that was a while ago, and I think there has been some evolution around this.

It's just a matter of knowledge, you know, of education away from this stuff. I mean, you know, Branford's been called a nigger. So he knows. He knows.

Well, I did an interview with Jesse Jackson, and he spent most of the time telling me, "Do not compare *my* struggle with yours." A lot of black

people think that there's more damage done to them because they can't pretend they're not black—forgetting that hiding causes other kinds of damage.

Imagine being black and gay! I think they have a particularly hard time from all sides.

A couple of years ago, you and Trudie decided to get married after being together for many years. Gays can't make that choice.

It's not legal for gays to marry?

No.

But there are ceremonies.

No, we make them up.

Right, well, but that's the best kind of ceremony.

Maybe from your perspective because you have a choice.

That's true. Gays have a right to some kind of recognized legal state. I would support that.

What about another traditional activity for couples: raising children?

Obviously there are gay couples that are far fitter to raise children than heterosexual couples. You can't generalize either way. Who's going to judge? See, the fear is that being exposed to gay behavior will make you gay. But as Ian McKellen said: "I spent all my school life in English schools being given heterosexual literature, and it didn't turn me straight." So it's fear.

What is the fear really about?

I think prejudice has a lot to do with self-esteem. People who are prejudiced have very low self-esteem, whether they are racist or homophobic. It's really about themselves and their own inadequacies and their own lack of confidence about who they are.

Jonathan Pryce, who played gay in *Carrington*, told me that he had a friend whose son had come to him and said he was gay. Jonathan said the father went ballistic, which made Jonathan suspect that the father might be gay.

I think we touch on this in *Grave Indiscretion*. Alan Bates's character is very macho, and he's very upset about this effete poet who has come to his house. Also he has a dream in which he's having sex with Trudie's character, and then it switches, and he's having sex with me.

Yes, if people are truly comfortable with their sexuality, they don't care much about what others do.

With our own kids we have so many gay friends that we've explained it to them, and they seem to take it in stride. [*Styler joins the conversation. Sting addresses her.*] They're very natural about it, aren't they?

Styler: I think so, yeah. I actually took them to see a film by a friend of ours called *Trevor*, about a boy discovering he was gay. It was a great, gentle way to begin the discussion about homosexuality.

What did they ask you?

Styler: Jake said, "Do people that young have those kinds of feelings?" And I said, "Yeah, they really do." And he said, "How terrible to feel frightened about it." He really got it. [*Laughs*] Then he went on and on about what a great actor the boy was.

From your perspective, do you think being gay is biological?

Styler: I don't think it's a choice. You can't disguise your feelings. You can suppress those feelings. That's your only choice: to suppress or not to suppress them. But to actually *have* the feelings themselves is not a choice.

Sting: A man cannot disguise his arousal. Nor can he fake it. Unlike a woman. [*Laughs*] If it doesn't work, it doesn't work. [*At this point Sting leaves the room for a minute*]

Your husband says he's never gotten fan mail from gay men. Do you think that's possible?

Styler: Who knows? I think he'd be oblivious to it. I think if people come on to you and you're not looking for it, you have no reason to really consider it. But it would not surprise me if they wanted him. He's a beautiful-looking man.

When you two fell in love, you were both with other people. I read that Sting said, "Trudie was the culprit and the savior." What does that mean?

Styler: I guess the "culprit" meant the other woman, you know? And the "savior," if you use that word, could be a bit of a theatrical way to describe that he was not happy. We got together after a couple of years of struggling through his unhappy divorce, but that struggle was a good thing for Sting to do. Then our lives became blissful; we're very happy. But the British press aren't very forgiving.

Oh, really? It was all in the press?

Styler: Yeah. Huge. The tabloids were nasty for a while. The British press is known for its hypocrisy. I'd had a very good acting career up until the point that I met Sting, and when the press exposed me as this leggy blond who had invaded this seemingly happy household, my work took a severe nosedive.

Trudie, when you produced the documentary *Boys From Brazil*, about transvestites in Brazil, did it cause you to wonder about your own sexuality?

Styler: Well, because these are people who are marginalized, outcast, people of the night, it was more a human rights issue to me. I would think, *What can I take for them? What would they like?* I found myself buying gold belts and jewelry for the boys, for the transvestites. I forgot that they were men, because they so identified with being women. And it gave me very strong feelings about myself, you know? What makes me heterosexual? Why aren't I homosexual? Am I bisexual? Are we all?

Have you known any lesbians?

Styler: I have a colleague who works with me in New York who's a lesbian. She's quite out. She flirts with me a lot, and I flirt back with her.

How do you feel about that?

Styler: Great! It's wonderful. Whenever I'm going out, I say, "Hey, Linda, how do I look tonight? Does this do it for you?" And I feel great if it does.

Do you think women are more affectionate and open to the idea of loving other women?

Styler: Oh, yeah! It's OK for two little girls to walk around holding hands and kissing each other. I'm a great flirt; I'm a great flirt to men and women. I love that physical contact and affection. [*Sting returns to the room*] Hi, [*laughs*] I've just come out.

Sting: Oh, good. So did I.

I'm sorry, but you really didn't.

Sting: Really? No, I'm sure I did.

No, you just said you felt a little something when you kissed the other actor.

Sting: I thought you said that was gay enough.

Styler: It's gay enough for me. But we shouldn't joke. Really, people are put through so much if they're gay, famous, and thinking about coming out. People are afraid of the consequences, so they suffer in silence. Ideally they should be able to come out and say, "This is what I am and how I want to conduct my life sexually. There. I said it. You have it. Now, fuck off and leave me alone."

Oh, that would work!

Sting: But I think it backfires. It backfires on the very people who have been victimized by the press.

What do you mean by "backfires"?

Sting: The idea that if you're gay, you should support the gay community and come out and say, "I'm gay, and my life is this way, and it's always been this way, and society won't be ruined because of my behavior"—it's a nice thought. But using the press as an ally is like holding a wolf by the ears. When you let go, it bites you.

Styler: I think you illustrated it by dear Nigel Hawthorne, who the theatrical set has known forever is gay. He does a movie [*The Madness of King George*] and becomes a big star overnight. He does an interview with *The Advocate* in which he mentions that he is gay, and the tabloids pick it up over here and headline, QUEEN GEORGE. Poor Nigel's life is now colored with that, because when he goes into a restaurant to eat with a friend, they'll be outside waiting for their photo op. It's like what they said about my transvestite movie: "These people should be shot with something more lethal than a 16-millimeter camera." There's the glorious tabloids.

Sting: The tabloids at their best.

But really, be honest. The tabloids may appeal to our baser selves, but if you see some juicy headline, don't you go, "Ooh, wow, look!"

Sting: [*Laughing*] Oh, yeah. We were thrilled with the Hugh Grant story.

Styler: We loved it! It was amazing.

Sting: We heard it two hours after he got arrested. I thought it was going to be a man that he'd been caught with.

Styler: Sting thought she was a transvestite.

Maybe you two will wind up in the tabloids for doing this interview.

Sting: I don't care, but I've never even had a gay man come on to me.

That can't be. You must have been asleep.

Styler: [*To Sting*] But you know that someone like Franco adores you.

Sting: Yeah, I flirt; I flirt a lot.

Styler: He's very flirty. He's like me.

Sting: And I'm not just a passive flirt either. I flirt with gays too.

Styler: And you enjoy it too.

Sting: Oh, yeah, I love it. I have a great time.

Did this interview make you think about your sexuality in a new way?

Sting: Yes, I was taken aback a couple of times, and I thought, *I must consider this afresh.* I think people are afraid that if they interact or flirt with gays, they will become gay by osmosis. It's ridiculous. It's so completely self-centered to imagine that you are the object of desire for all gays.

Vidal

I remember a very foggy, nasty morning

in Los Angeles in 1995. I arrived at the Beverly Hills Hotel and found an exhausted, moody Gore Vidal circling his hotel suite, looking suspiciously at our photographer. "You're going to move everything in the room?" he asked incredulously. The photographer ignored him and continued pulling furniture off to the side, leaving nothing but one chair and a floor lamp in the center of the room. Gore turned on his heel and walked into an adjoining cove, sat down at a writing desk, and put his head in his hands. "Damned media circus," he murmured to himself and refused to reenter the room.

I went into rescue gear. Suddenly I imagined the whole photo shoot coming apart. After years of trying to get the mighty novelist, playwright, screenwriter, actor, and congressional candidate onto the cover of *The Advocate*, I could see the battle still wasn't over. Without a good cover-photo image, the interview—that took months of hassling to finally bring in for a landing—would be nearly useless. How was I going to get this headstrong photographer and fiery activist to work together? I took a breath and entered the cove.

"Do you have arthritis?" I blurted. Gore lifted his head from his hands and stared at me in horror. If I hadn't heard my own voice say it, I wouldn't have believed it. Normally, I pride myself on knowing what to say to people to help ease them into the moment and the magazine. I have no idea where my censor was. I knew from the aching going on in my own back (due to the dampness of the morning) that anyone who suffered from arthritis would be having a hard time. But to have said it out loud? I could see in his eyes that he was wondering if anyone on the staff of *The Advocate* was sane—or, in the very least, well-mannered. Miraculously, maybe because I had shocked both of us with my obnoxious question, he answered. Yes, he hurt. He had also been up late with friends. His head ached. Slowly, carefully, we began sharing information about how we were feeling, conferring, giving each other advice and bonding. Coffee arrived, and we continued talking for at least an hour.

The Advocate's art director at the time, Ron Goins, arrived in the doorway, and wordlessly we followed him into the main suite. There, Gore walked without further ado over to the lone chair and lamp. He sat down, folded his hands, and allowed several rolls of film to roll by, capturing his stoic image. At one point, he glanced over at the floor lamp, then up at the photographer, and with typical droll humor, mumbled, "You're really married to the lamp, aren't you, dear?" The photographer, deep in his own thoughts, never heard the remark, but everyone else did, and we laughed long and hard, releasing the morning's tension in a gregarious burst.

After that, Gore suggested a walk in the nearby park for some outdoor pictures. We left most of the crew behind to gather up the equipment and walked arm in arm into the hazy sunlight. The changing weather was a relief and an obvious mood lifter. Suddenly Gore began talking about how he hated leaving his home in Italy, even for a brief publicity tour like this one. (He was in the States for the release of his memoir, *Palimpsest*.) He thought the U.S. government was tragically behind in its thinking, often overstepping its boundaries. In retrospect, this conversation prepared me for his recent support of the late Oklahoma City bomber Timothy McVeigh, a man with whom he says he shared some views about the federal government and the erosion of constitutional rights in this country. As for homosexuality and labeling, this too was something Gore blamed on the shallowness of American culture. "Europeans in general don't go in for compartmentalizing. This is a relief to someone like me who finds it appalling that people need to limit themselves and others with this useless, confining language."

Over the years since our interview, Gore has sent me handwritten notes from his villa in Italy. When Matthew Shepard was murdered in 1998, he read *The Advocate*'s coverage and offered to write a passionate perspective ("J'accuse!") for the magazine. With his usual flare and fury Gore charged "the highest-ranking member of the U.S. Senate, Trent Lott, with incitement to violence and to murder, specifically in the case of Matthew Shepard, and that Mr. Bauer [Gary Bauer, then of the Family Research Council] and others who have indulged in the same reckless demonizing of millions of Americans be equally charged." And thus the best-selling author of such wildly imaginative works as *Myra Breckinridge, The City and the Pillar, The Decline and Fall of the American Empire, The Best Man,* and *Palimpsest* continues to address the issues of our times.

I have come to realize that Gore may enthusiastically remove himself from his birth country (he was born in West Point, N.Y., and his grandfather was Oklahoma U.S. senator Thomas Gore), but somewhere in Italy he is always watching, criticizing, commenting, and concerned. Famously obstinate and cranky about the shortcomings of practically everyone ("There is no human problem which could not be solved if people would simply do as I advise"), he may not wish to be held in the affectionate esteem I continue to regard him in. But I'm somewhat obstinate myself, especially about people as fascinating, creative, controversial, and caring as Gore Vidal.

"A friend was surprised to hear me say that there was not one moment of my past that I would like to relive," writes Gore Vidal in his just-published book, *Palimpsest: A Memoir,* which Random House released on October 3, Vidal's 70th birthday.

"Apparently, I am unlike others in this...I am only at home in the present." Nonetheless, the past has a tenacious hold on the ageless novelist, playwright, and essayist, and though he confesses to not being at home there, he revisits it in *Palimpsest* with great wit, compassion, and an instinct for the dramatic.

Sitting for a photo shoot in his Beverly Hills Hotel suite, the handsome and aristocratic Vidal stares out a rain-drenched window and murmurs regret over the circus that has already transformed *Palimpsest* into a gossipfest. "The memoir he vowed he'd never write?" Vidal says, mimicking the media blitz. "Would that I had listened to myself about that."

Fortunately, he did not. *Palimpsest* (the term, as defined on the book's jacket, means "paper, parchment, etc., prepared for writing on and wiping out again, like a slate") was written from Vidal's home in Italy and covers the first 39 years of the multifaceted social critic's life. Among the book's many revelations is an exploration of Vidal's relationship with three key people who shaped his destiny: his grandfather, T.P. Gore, who was blinded as a child and was also elected the first senator from the state of Oklahoma; his mother, Nina, an alcoholic and subsequently a morphine addict who was prone to unpredictable behavior, alternately belittling her son's success and taking absolute credit for it; and his first love, Jimmie Trimble, a fellow student at a boys' school who had planned to become a professional baseball player but died in World War II at Iwo Jima when he was 19.

"That's really the whole book," Vidal says, his eyes looking stubbornly past the photographer's harsh lights to a faded photograph of himself with Trimble. Indeed, it is this relationship—fleeting, romantic, and tragic—that is the engine driving the narrative of Vidal's memoir, prompting him to go on a quest for his lost love, the one man who made him feel whole. "Would he still seem to me my other half?" Vidal writes. It is a theme that the writer has explored before, fictionally, in his third novel, *The City and the Pillar* (1948), which is dedicated to Trimble and was republished earlier this year with a new preface by the author.

"Even though he always said he'd never wrote this memoir, the surprise is, he really loved doing it," says Sharon DeLano, the senior editor at Random House who has been Vidal's editor for his last three books. "He had a fabulous time, and since this is only the first volume, he's truly looking forward to writing the rest of it."

Because Vidal's early professional career also included turns as a politician (he's been a candidate for Congress) as well as a screenwriter and an actor, his memoir is filled with luscious anecdotes about the rich and famous. Among those making provocative appearances in *Palimpsest* are Jack and Jackie Kennedy, Eleanor Roosevelt, Paul Newman, Marlon Brando, Jack Kerouac, Truman Capote, Greta Garbo, Anaïs Nin, Paul Bowles, Leonard Bernstein, E.M. Forster, and André Gide.

As one might expect from the author of the sly and sexually candid *Myra Breckinridge,* Vidal holds little back in addressing his own sexual habits in the memoir. He is honest, self-defining, optimistic, wry, and blunt. ("It was my experience, in the war, that just about everyone, either actively or passively, was available under the right circumstances").

Suffering patiently through the clutter and pandemonium his latest writing has unleashed, Vidal confides that every day he's away from Italy is a hard one. Still, the tireless pro knows all too well what must be done to secure *Palimpsest* the attention it deserves.

"I've yet to read a memoir by anyone I've known at all well that came anywhere near to the truth," he insists. "But then, over 90% of Americans admitted, in a recent poll, to being habitual liars. So truth *attempted*—it's not possible to achieve, but try anyway—disturbs our countrymen as well as persons. In fact, the truth teller is thought, often, to be a cold, hard person, lacking correctness."

You refer to *Palimpsest* as a memoir, not an autobiography. Does a memoir have a romanticized edge?

I decided to tell my own story as I remember it rather than as an autobiography, which must be real history with dates checked and everything accounted for.

Who will be angered by your memoirs? Do you have any concerns about this?

Angered? That sort of thing doesn't concern me. I do go to great lengths to avoid hurting the feelings of others. As I review the past it appears that I have never suffered from either sexual jealousy or professional envy, the two guiding passions of those I know—at least as recorded by their biographers. Or do the biographers project themselves onto their subjects?

Anyway, I'm in the debt of all these biographers in whose books or texts I appear, but they certainly spur memory. Finally, I seem to have caused distress in naming only three relationships when there must have been so many more. This is not coyness, as one dullard put it, but simply the refusal of anyone of my time and place to go on and on about his sex life.

Why do you name these three?

The three that I do discuss—Jimmie Trimble, at the beginning, then Anaïs Nin and Jack Kerouac—I would never have mentioned if a journalist hadn't worked out—and published—the fact that the "J.T." to whom I dedicated *The City and the Pillar* was Jimmie, while Anaïs and Jack each wrote at great length about me, obliging me now to return the compliment. The rest is my business.

What is the main thing you want readers to take away from *Palimpsest*?

I don't think that my disposition is of much use to others. I was born into a power family totally lacking in sexual guilt. What we wanted, we went for. As far as I know, none of us ever suffered from sexual guilt—a common malady, like hay fever, in the republic's amber fields of grain.

What would the young Gore make of your memoirs if he were given them to read today? What is the big picture?

Gore Vidal

The picture is to ignore as much as you can the world's view of you and get on with life and work. Americans, in general, are ignorant, bigoted, and deeply unhappy with their declining incomes. Their opinions are formed by the 1% ownership and its employees in the media, churches, and schools. I suspect that nothing that is generally believed to be true is remotely true. But then, if you're an artist, born in a cage, it's hard not to think of those surrounding bars as the world. So break out! Revolt! See?

When you wrote *The City and the Pillar*, you said, "I knew my description of the love affair between two 'normal' all-American boys...would challenge every superstition about sex in my native land." Has anything changed?

Since 1948 the old "either/or" superstitions remain as strong as ever, and some new horrors have been added, like "gay sensibility," so profitably plugged by *The Advocate* in the '70s and '80s.

You've been living in Italy since the mid '60s. We heard that you felt America made you uncomfortable about your sexuality. Is that true?

Comfortable about being a homosexual? But I'm not an adjective; I'm a noun, a male with all sorts of sexual possibilities, which should be of no more interest to the state—or anyone else—than a liking, say, for rice, not potatoes. Italians, Europeans in general (minus the giggling Brits, who are, simply, sweetly bonkers) don't go in for compartmentalizing. This is a relief.

You told *The Advocate* in 1977 that "boys who hustle here or in Italy can have very intense affairs with men, and then they will get married, have children, and give up sex with males.... They turn around and settle down and never revert." Is this still true in Italy?

I would only amend what I said in 1977 to omit that the *ragazzi* "never revert" to same-sex once married. Many do. With time, one picks up all sorts of useful hints about what people do.

What do you think about people who need to label themselves and others?

To be categorized is, simply, to be enslaved. Watch out. I have never thought of myself as a victim. I fear that the built-in defeatedness of those who meekly, stupidly allow themselves to be categorized may further narrow their chances to be human and useful rather than be flattened out into passive ciphers for that "either/or" slot so loved by our rulers. I have taken on great powers, and though I can't say I won every round, I managed to survive on my own terms. Is this example useful to those who feel—or indeed are—victimized? I hope so.

So it's important to take a stand?

Yes. Have you noticed the way a contemporary American, terrified of being incorrect, answers a question? "Well, like where...I mean...you know?...I *think* I'm coming from...it's well, like, *raining*." Then, of course, there's the new tic: "OK?"

You were one of the first people talking about bisexuality in the '60s. Do you think the "concept" of bisexuality has changed today?

I've said—a thousand times?—in print and on TV that everyone is bisexual. Some do this, that, etc. I have never labeled myself then or now as exclusively anything. But the press cannot cope with so extraordinary a concept. That means that what I conclude about everyone they say that I have said about myself. Of course, it is true of me too—and for the first time, in *Palimpsest*, I do discuss my sexual as well as my

emotional life—and the fact that the two are never the same for me, except in the case of J.T.

Is your overall need to remain fluid in politics and sexuality the real reason you prefer to be thought of as bisexual, or do you literally feel and act on your sexual attraction for women as well as for men?

The matter of sexual energy is not the same for everyone. Read "The Birds and the Bees" by me in *United States: Essays 1952–1992*. Now that *Newsweek* is onto my 40-year-old line "We are all bisexual," there could be a breakthrough—but I doubt it. This is a primitive culture where "either/or" rules. Anyway, I accept no labels about myself other, perhaps, than *failed revolutionary*.

This is why I've carefully developed a subtext to the memoir in which I recount the dogged promiscuity of three more-or-less contemporaries: Jack Kennedy and Marlon Brando, largely with women, and Tennessee [Williams] and me, largely with males, though in my case there was another life going on too.

What bonded all of you together?

Of the three, I knew Marlon the least, but the other two I knew quite well. Orgasm, rather than a meaningful, warm, mature relationship, was our common goal. Of course, we had greater opportunities than others, but I also think that we were simply behaving as normal males given, perhaps, unusual advantages.

You share your life with longtime companion Howard Austen. Would you say something that would shed light on your ability to have such a strong bond with someone after so many years?

I've lived with Howard 45 years. As the relationship is not sexual, we continue. I do my best to observe my own law: no sex with friends if you want to keep the friend. A sexual partner can become a friend. But a friend in the bed is either an enemy in the making or, simply, heartbreak. A poignant subject that I leave to all the other writers.

They say that every decade brings with it a different set of lessons. What does turning 70 mean to you?

Life does not notice the calendar. The body does its own thing until it stops. At 70, death is as much nothing as it ever was, and who can object to No Thing? The young, deprived of a full life, can honorably object but not the old.

The very first time you heard about a "strange cancer" that was killing gay men, what did you think? A joke? A plot? A nightmare?

My principal reaction to the "strange cancer" is that what little social advance has been made since World War II in the acceptance of—or at least in the reality of—the "or" of "either/or" as half citizens will be totally undone by Christian fundamentalists et al. This is happening, of course.

Where will it lead?

"Fortunately," we are due for a total economic collapse—now visibly under way—and our mangy tree of liberty will soon require a good deal of nourishment from the blood of patriots and tyrants, as Jefferson put it. Any group—real, the blacks; unreal but still believed in, the gays—must be willing to fight or be exterminated.

So you remain the fighter?

Now I reveal my true nature—I have always fought or been ready to fight, and I have no intention of ever giving way. *Ich kann nicht Anders*, as Martin Luther said—"I can do no other." But as my time is now limited, you get busy out there. It will be a lovely good war. OK?

Liz Sm

ith

That Liz Smith ever sat down

with *The Advocate* and talked openly and honestly about her public and private life is still somewhat unbelievable to me. And that we became good friends after the experience is even wilder. The reason I say this is because most of my early *Advocate* experiences with Liz's office were a bit stormy. Although she says she doesn't remember any of the flash floods, I do. And I also learned a lot from them.

Initially Liz's columns were very kind to me, featuring good mentions of my interviews with Mark Wahlberg and Chastity Bono. However, over time there were several dark moments as well. One occurred years back when I was arts and entertainment editor. *The Advocate* had put together its annual Sissy Awards issue. Now defunct (partially because of this particular incident), the Sissy Awards were the magazine's way of pointing out semi- or full-blown homophobic moments that had occurred during the year. For reasons I can barely remember and would never be so foolish as to defend, that year the staff chose Madonna as the sissy of the year for giving an interview in which she insisted, "I am not a lesbian."

We must have been out of our minds.

In addition to the zillion E-mails we got from outraged Madonna fans, we got quite a scolding in Liz Smith's column. After all Madonna had done for gays, AIDS, and *The Advocate* (she'd given us a marvelous two-part interview in the early '90s)—we should be ashamed. Of course, Liz was right. But like naughty children who couldn't admit to their mistake, we preferred to think that Liz had no humor. Over time I came to a different conclusion and must have written Madonna's publicist half a dozen apology notes. In this case, Liz's outrage had awakened me to the bigger picture and the consequences of doing something "smart-ass" without thinking about its impact on the very people who supported the magazine.

However, another tangle with Liz's column led to a different kind of disagreement, one that only got settled during the course of our long interview. The conflict was over the late congresswoman Barbara Jordan. Congresswoman Jordan, a hero to many, had never publicly spoken about her lesbianism. When she died in 1996, her memorial was attended by many, including her partner of several years. *The Advocate* felt an obligation to cover her life and death, to bring her accomplishments and humanity into the magazine's 30-plus-year history, to make her struggles and triumphs a part of our legacy and our reader's awareness. Thus, after much discussion, we did a cover story on Barbara Jordan.

When it hit the newsstands, we got a furious call from a representative of Liz. "This is despicable! How dare we discuss what Barbara Jordan had never herself publicly acknowledged?"

Over the years *The Advocate* has struggled to form a workable outing policy. In order to understand it, it is crucial to understand what outing is: Outing is the initial disclosure of a person's sexuality in a public arena without his or her permission. Using that definition, *The Advocate* does not out people. Our coverage of Barbara Jordan fit our policy. Newspapers had already reported that Jordan's partner of many years had survived her and spoken at her memorial. Therefore our cover story was not the initial disclosure. Both the memorial and the newspaper coverage were in the public arena. Thus, for us there was no reason to back off this important story. We felt the same way years later when pop diva Dusty Springfield died. It seemed wrong to ignore the life and death of such a talented, complicated, remarkable gay woman. So we didn't.

While it's true that Liz was initially unhappy with our Barbara Jordan cover story, we also heard from many, many young lesbians of color, writing us letters that included sentiments like, "Thank you for this story on Barbara Jordan. You have given me the courage to live. Now I have a role model who will inspire me for the rest of my life."

As you will see in the following interview, Liz Smith had the courage and tenacity to revisit her first response to *The Advocate*'s cover story on Jordan. The discussion in our interview served as a subtle blueprint of her own changes and evolving openness. Since the interview, I have sometimes heard other people criticize Liz's refusal to actually label herself. Frankly, I think they are completely missing the point. Not to respect how she chooses to reveal herself only detracts from her many profound, educational revelations. She is clearly telling us everything about a life lived during a different time in history. And we are lucky to have such a rich glimpse into our own past.

The late-morning fog hangs like a sullen mood around a Tex-Mex restaurant on 38th Street in Manhattan. Eleven flights up, Liz Smith leaves her famous home office and begins the descent to her favorite eatery—where I sit waiting and worrying.

This meeting and interview is long overdue. Sitting down with America's most powerful media columnist has been a goal of *The Advocate*'s for more years than Smith would ever believe. Unfortunately, sitting down with the gay press has never been high on her list. Then six weeks ago Smith's memoir, *Natural Blonde,* was published, and the landscape shifted forever for the unexpectedly shy goddess of gossip.

While it's true that Smith (and her assistant Denis Ferrara) have occasionally written glowing pieces about various *Advocate* cover stories over the years, there have also been those less-than-pleasant times when she's objected vehemently to our investigative reporting on the lives of Ricky Martin or the late Barbara Jordan. Why, she wondered, did we have to ask those questions? As the preeminent scoop detector of all time, she knew. Just as she knows today that talking to Mike Wallace or *20/20* or *New York* magazine will not be the same thing as sitting down with the gay press—certainly not after her revelations about two same-sex relationships in *Natural Blonde.* And yet she told us yes.

The waiters and I are alone when Smith—right on time, hands in pockets, head slightly bowed—strolls dutifully around the side of the restaurant and in through the glass doors. "Oh, they're not open," she notes, holding out a warm hand. "Sit over here with me." We sit staring out at the fog for an awkward moment. She glances at me sideways and asks nervously, "So? Will this work for you? Are you taping this? Do you need me to sit...?" I move my chair close to hers, protectively. At 77, Liz Smith—though she would be the first to pooh-pooh it—is a brave woman. After enduring years of attacks and outings by gay activists (and mean-spirited celebrities), she has managed to find her way through one of the most complicated lives and careers this magazine has ever examined.

A Texan who grew up worshiping the movies, Smith went to college, got married, got divorced, went back to college, and fell in love. "The only problem was, the object of my affection was a woman," she writes in her book. The year was 1946. Unable to express her feelings to anyone, including her parents, she buried them and threw herself into her lifelong journey in journalism. She was an editor at a movie fan magazine, a proofreader at *Newsweek,* a typist for Blue Cross, a Broadway press agent, a producer for CBS Radio, a producer for Allen Funt's *Candid Camera,* a producer for NBC live TV, a ghostwriter for Hearst society columnist Cholly Knickerbocker, an entertainment editor for *Cosmopolitan,* even a writer for *Sports Illustrated.* And of course, today her Liz Smith column appears daily in *Newsday* and is syndicated to millions of readers in more than 70 newspapers.

"Maybe you better roll your tape back," she says as a waiter leaves us some tea. "I think these interruptions won't make for a good beginning." I tell her that I haven't turned it on yet and pull out my questions. Her powder-blue eyes take me in carefully. She draws a deep breath and smiles. As if on cue, the sun begins burning away at the fog outside. Her hands tremble imperceptibly as she folds them in

front of her like the "well-bred girl" she is at heart. "OK," she whispers, more to herself than to me. "Here we go...."

Did you know that *The Advocate* is 34 years old?
Good God. You've become so established.

The whole movement is moving in that direction, though some don't like it.
That's good. You can't be in a revolution your whole life.

I know you don't like labels, Liz, but...
It's OK for you to say anything you want. I just don't want to label myself because I have never gotten my act together. It's just not accurate for me to label myself. I don't care what other people say; other people have said such terrible things. You know Frank Sinatra called me a big dyke from the stage of Carnegie Hall?

Was that terribly frightening for you?
No. I wasn't frightened; it just made me feel bad. He meant it in such an insulting way. And it was just evidence of the general homophobia and name-calling. Look, every gay person sleeping with someone of the same sex is not, you know, a ridiculous faggot or a big dyke. That kind of talk is just an insult. It's like saying "nigger."

Of course, but that's not the kind of labeling I mean. But let's first talk about gossip. Weirdly enough, I worked for a magazine called *Rona Barrett's Hollywood* years ago.
Oh, my God, did you really? Rona was a real entrepreneur by then. I knew her but not well.

You describe gossip as "news running ahead of itself in a red satin dress." When I was working on movie magazines, the editors made it clear that "Rock Hudson was married!" and in general, you were to take care of the stars back then. It was more about making them look good.
Yes, that's all it was about. Rona was much later, and I'm sure it was much more realistic.

No, not at all. You still take pretty good care of the stars in your column.
But look, let's discuss the Rock Hudson thing, because I became friends with him when I was doing *Modern Screen.* I loved Rock, and I was very attracted to him. I mean, every woman who met him was. He was just very sweet, charismatic, flirty, and really smart. So I knew him for years without knowing anything about him. Then I went to Rome with Elaine Stritch, as her secretary when she was making *A Farewell to Arms.* So I saw him again, and he was very good to me and took me out to dinner and everything. And then he started taking Elaine out to dinner, 'cause she was a lot of fun. And she started getting oozy-goozy about him. So did I.

This is when you were writing out your name as "Mrs. Rock Hudson" on pieces of paper?

[*Laughing*] Yeah.

He caused a lot of crushes, I'm sure.

Oh, yeah! So I came back to New York, and I got married again. I didn't see Rock for a long time. By the time I saw him I had heard all these stories about him. I decided, well, maybe he is gay; yes, I guess he is. Because I also heard some things about him in Rome, that he and another man were, you know, picking up guys and so forth. But he was married then, so I was confused. And then many years later he called me. He said he was being blackmailed by a lady that wanted a lot of money or she was going to sell a nasty story about him to the tabloids. And I was just flabbergasted. I knew this woman. So I sent him my file on her. He showed it to her, and she backed off.

Were you trying to protect him?

My purpose wasn't to try to heal his image. I just didn't approve of somebody blackmailing him. In the first place, it's a crime and it was evil. He would have been washed up. It's one thing for everybody to talk about him being gay, but it was another to have it be printed. He could not have gone on working in the movies. But of course the end of his life was so tragic. And he really never addressed AIDS, you know. He never really said "I'm gay" or "I'm homosexual" or "I like guys" or any of those things.

Did you ever confide in Rock that you had had an affair with a woman?

Oh, no. I was relentlessly heterosexual at the time. So I never even thought of doing such a thing.

Did you report about Rock getting AIDS?

You know, Rock didn't know what getting AIDS meant. He didn't know what he would do for the movement, for activism against AIDS. He didn't have to cooperate. And he didn't. But he didn't lie. So he became the poster child for the fight against AIDS. And so many people left him. And you know, honestly, I'm not bragging, but I think we were the first column ever in a popular periodical to write that there was this disease. I think it was in 1983.

I have questions about your second marriage. You don't have to answer, but was Freddie Lister gay?

Well, I don't know. Yeah, maybe. I never did discuss it. He wasn't the type that would tell me. Maybe it was part of our mutual attraction. He was like a kid, really. He was so wonderful and sweet to me. But I never once fooled myself that I was in love with him. I was just having a good time. It was a very strange interlude. I've been attracted to a lot of gay men.

You sure write about a lot of them in your book, although you don't always say they're gay.

I think gay men are very attractive and they're fun and wonderful. I lived with Joel Schumacher for a while. I knew he was gay. He was the sexual outlaw, because he too was living a very bisexual life when I met him.

How do you feel about *Natural Blonde* these days?

I've been pretty honest in this book. Oh, yes, I didn't tell all those romantic details in my relationship with Iris Love. And, yes, this has caused lots of people to just jump all over me. Well, I'm not going to write that. She's a sort of semiprivate person. I'm not going to reveal chapter and verse about every woman I've known. It's ridiculous. You can do that about the men, because you're not going to ruin their lives if you do. It's up to the women to say if they want this told about them.

Perhaps this is why when I read your book it felt like you were very lusty toward the men you were attracted to but very cagey about the women.

I felt that if you didn't understand what my relationship with Iris was, you were really stupid. I thought you had to be a moron not to get it.

Well, I think it bothered people when you called her your "friend." They wished you could have said "lover."

I probably wouldn't have said *that*!

What would you have said?

I'm just too Victorian to say that.

So what do we call our partners?

[*Laughing*] "My life's companion."

That sounds worse.

It's bullshit. It's like people using the expression "friends." Now I never refer to anyone as a friend, because it's a gay term for "lover." I have thousands of friends I've never been lovers with.

So what do we call our lovers?

Nothing. Maybe it will get to a point were we don't label. But I wish I had been a little more specific about my…about Iris. But again, it was my reluctance to be nailed into a box.

But your book was full of your male affairs. It was clear this was a big, complex box.

Yeah, but honestly, I'll tell you I had a reluctance to be bragging on how many relationships I've had. Because I have had a lot. I had a long relationship after Iris. With a man. And I just couldn't bring myself to put that in the book, because it sounded like I was trying to say, "I'm not gay. Let me out of this gay label." So I thought, I won't mention it. I won't say anything. [*Sighs and runs her hand through her hair*] Yes, now I wish I'd said more. Because, I mean, I think I mystified some people.

How does Iris feel about it?

Iris doesn't care. That's different. You know, um, she doesn't get it. She doesn't live in the real world. She's an archaeologist and sees her sexuality as a given through history.

Oh, I like that.

Yeah, so she doesn't care, and she doesn't care what people say about her. But there are other people who are private people who, you know, now they're married; they're grandmothers. I'm not going to tell all of that. If they want to write a book, all about their affairs with the infamous Liz Smith, that's OK.

Did Iris like what you wrote about her in the book?

I don't think she thought I gave her her due. I read her what I was writing, and she kept giving me things from her curriculum. [*Laughing*] And I said, "Iris, this book is not about you; it's supposed to be about me in relationship to you." So she read it and said, "Well,

I don't like it; you make me sound like I'm just some busy little kid or something." So I went back and tried to make it more to her liking. I think she still feels it's rather dismissive. But that's why I say to you, I wish I had said more.

Well, you thought she was important enough to talk about, even though it meant revealing more about yourself.

Yes, I think she is secretly pleased. She is a remarkable, fabulous character. I always said that I never had to have children because I have Iris.

Well, that happens…

I think a lot of female relationships embody that. One of them is the parent; the other one is the child. And of course, there are a lot of heterosexual marriages too that are like that. I hope I'm more grown-up now. I don't want to be Iris's parent. I don't want to be anybody's parent. Now I want to be an independent person.

One of the most moving moments in your book is after your first affair with a woman in college [in 1946]. You try to tell your raw feelings to your parents so that they can understand you, and…

I couldn't talk to them. And I realized it wasn't ever gonna change. So we got into this "don't ask, don't tell." And that just wasn't about women; that was about men too, because they were horrified when I got a divorce. They almost never forgave me for that. So I really never told them about anything. As far as they knew I didn't have any boyfriends or girlfriends. Whether I was living a celibate life or not, they just didn't want to know.

They shut you down, so you shut yourself down. I wonder if this affected how you dealt with other people in your life? Did you feel that in order to have access to friends or celebrities, you had to do what you did with your parents: not share your whole self?

It certainly affected my relationship with them. As I say in the book. I don't think I was ever really myself with my parents again. It took me a long time to get over that. But I just told myself, *Well, that affair must have been an aberration.* So I went to New York, and I got married again. I immediately had an affair with some guy I met in New York. You know, it was not a time for revealing yourself. Times change, things change. I'm 77 years old now. It's all academic, what happened in the past. I'm not living with anybody and don't know if I will be ever again.

That's what is so important about your life. It represents so many half-hidden lives lived at a time when there was no visible support anywhere in society for wondering about and exploring your sexuality. It's one thing to be a 15-year-old lesbian today who walks across her living room while Ellen DeGeneres is beaming out of a piece of furniture, a television, announcing, "I'm gay."

And her mother is supporting her!

Yes, these are different times. It's easy for people today to look at you and say, "How come she didn't tell more about her gay life?"

Well, another reason why I didn't tell more is that I didn't know what I wanted to tell. I mean, I had been accused of being hypocritical for writing about the private lives of other people without revealing my own life. Bullshit! I don't see reporters stating their sexual preferences before they write something. And look, I'm not writing any gossip that's so torrid and sensational that I thought that my own personal life was important to it.

Let's talk about gay and lesbian struggles from your point of view.

There are those who still want to be in the streets with guns fighting and soul-kissing in a parade—things I don't like. But I am an old-fashioned person. I was born in 1923—before public behavior became an art form. I'm not crazy about any displays of physical intimacy. I don't like it.

Well, Liz. I think you were pretty brave to be in college, with no reference points at all, and realize that you were in love with a woman.

That was a really emotional, romantic, unrealistic experience for me. And it wasn't unrealistic because it was a woman. It was unrealistic because she was engaged to be married and I didn't know what I was doing. I was in the middle of getting divorced. I was stunned by it. And blown away by it. It took me about two years to get over it. And I didn't have any help getting over it. I didn't know where to go. It didn't occur to me to see an analyst.

It happened to me too. I fell in love with a friend. She wasn't gay. Suddenly I was left all alone with my gay feelings. This was back in 1971…

Well, try 1946 or 1947!

I can't imagine. That's why you're amazing. One thing each new generation has to ask is: "How did people do it back then? How did they figure out how to live and love?"

Well, remember in my book, I had met those nurses [in Ottine, Tex.] who were older than me, and they were gay.

Did you think they were gay at the time?

I didn't know until later, after I met gay people. I knew that those nurses were having a perfectly wonderful time. But I was just ignorant. They liked me. I was like a pet or mascot or something. None of them ever decided to "enlighten me." They weren't attracted to me, and I wasn't attracted to them. I was just so interested in them because they were so vital and grown-up and kind of cynical and they had been places. I was mostly fascinated by their philosophy about how they approached these poor people who had been left paralyzed. They kept trying to get me to give up my emotional approach to working there, because it was so hurtful for me. I was so full of pain and empathy. And they kept saying, "That doesn't help the patient." But they were the first gay people I'd ever seen. Later I went back in my mind and identified them as gay. And I do remember that they kept using this expression, "Gay, gay, gay." That was a long time ago. That was 1945.

What about when you got to New York in 1949?

When I came to New York I went to a gay bar on the second night I was here. My friends Scotty and Floyd took me to this really famous gay restaurant, but we didn't know that. We just thought that everything in the Village was like that. I was just interested as a social phenomenon. And it was all men.

Well, women must have been totally invisible back then.

There were never any women. The guys were so great-looking. But I didn't think much of gay bars.

Did you think back on the woman in college?

I felt that the experience I had in college was a really…I don't mean it wasn't real, but it was a delayed adolescence on my part. I had already been married. He was a wonderful person and still is.

"I just think my own nature prevents me from going hog-wild or from being any kind of role model. So they can call me whatever they like. I just don't want to call myself anything."

But I didn't want to belong to somebody else. I didn't know who I was. I was yearning to be free. I couldn't stay married, because he wanted to immediately have children. And I was going, "Wait a minute! I didn't get into this for that. I got into it because it was exciting." He was gorgeous and a wonderful person. But I wasn't really ready.

Do you think you've ever felt like you belonged to someone?
Oh, yeah, I have. I've gotten better through the years. I think I'm a serial breakup artist.

You mean a serial monogamist?
Is that what I am? Maybe so.

What did you feel when you gave yourself to someone else?
Well, I don't think it is a good idea for me. I think I am more apt to get into a co-optive relationship, where the person is too important to me. And I think some of them never knew what I was talking about. In other words, I loved them and maybe they loved me, but it wasn't the same for both of us. I had to go to therapy to get over all of that, to get over all of my romantic ideas about two people becoming one. Two people better not become one!

Well, we're fed a lot of stuff about romantic relationships...
Yeah, I was raised on the movies and books. I was thinking that my romantic interlude in college was right out of *Romeo and Juliet*.

Yes, that extra spice of the forbidden.
And the person is is not gay and went on to be happily married—I'm told. [*Looks around the restaurant*]

Am I drilling you too much?
No, no. I'll tell you something. I think one of the bad things about the whole gay experience is that it jerks everything out of perspective. People only perceive that, and they think you don't have any other life. You don't have any other intellectual life. You don't have any spiritual life. You aren't interested in history. You're only interested in gay history. It's like you're not a fully realized person. And I'm always trying to be fully realized person—in spite of my sexual

confusions, which I thought were the least interesting thing about me. The great fallacy about sleeping with a woman is that people think you are attracted to every woman you meet. I hate that. It drives me nuts. I'm not; I'm attracted to very few people. Oh, and they think that you'll corrupt children. That's my favorite!

Do you think there is ever a good reason to out someone?
I do think there is the hypocrisy factor. If Barney Frank had stayed in the closet pretending he was straight and voting against gay rights, that would have been the reason to out him. But he's a really brave and fabulous person. And he even survived, you know, a scandal about himself—not the scandal of his homosexuality, but something else. And he's a remarkable, fabulous person for it. Also, think of the Larry Flynt campaign to bring down the Republicans because he felt that they were so hypocritical about Clinton. Larry will never get the credit for doing this really incredible thing. He saved Bill Clinton from being thrown out of office. The whole Republican arm just backed off. They saw that he was going to really let them have it.

You were outed.
Well, let me tell you something about my period of being outed by Michelangelo Signorile [in his "Gossip Watch" column in *OutWeek* magazine in 1989 and '90]. He said he had of all this so-called information on my life, and he would write whole columns where he said, "Fuck you, Liz." And he carried on for about a year. And honestly, what do you get if you out somebody who's extremely confused and maybe they haven't made up their mind yet? I mean, I wasn't going to just throw my private life into the public arena because somebody said I should. I was still—and still am—living a very diverse kind of life. I didn't feel I had to do what he said.

They say if you throw somebody into a swimming pool before they're ready, they don't learn to swim very well and they are afraid of the water forever. [*Liz laughs*] If you out somebody, they will never be a strong, confident role model or spokesperson.
Yes, he was determined that I would become some sort of poster child for gay liberation.

Well, this came at a very angry time in gay history. People were dying of AIDS and no one was coming forward to help, including lots of closeted gay people—which made activists like Michelangelo furious.

I couldn't imagine that somebody with two of the most beautiful names from the Renaissance could be such a jerk. I kept thinking, "What would I do if I were going to declare my sexual preference? Would I write it at the top of my column every day?" [*Laughing*] I don't like labeling. I hate that stuff. I mean, as soon as you get somebody in a little box, in America they slap the box shut on you. A person's capabilities are intensely limited. I've said this before, but I loved when my friend Rita Mae Brown, on her 40th birthday, stood up at her big party in Virginia and said, "I want to announce I'm resigning from being a professional lesbian." I didn't go to this party, but later I said to her, "Why did you do that?" She said, "I'm just sick of being described as a lesbian writer. I'm a writer who happens to be a lesbian." I thought that was really great. She had real regrets, I think, that she outed herself and outed other people—whom she made very unhappy. And she feels, I think, that maybe she limited her own career and limited theirs.

But we constantly label ourselves. I say I am a woman, a writer...

Saying someone is gay is not the same as saying that she has red hair.

Why?

Because there is so much homophobia in business, in government, in international affairs, everywhere. So why do that? Let people define themselves. I'm not living my life to be an inspiration or a role model. This is not something you should do until things improve.

But how will we improve them without visibility?

Things are improving. They are improving in spite of all the people that drag their feet—like me. [*Laughs at herself*]

Thank you for saying that. But what if Ellen hadn't come out?

I don't know that I think that Ellen changed anything. I think things were just changing.

But she pushed it along further. You know, Liz, when *The Advocate* did a cover story on Congresswoman Barbara Jordan after she died, you were upset with me for printing the facts of her personal life.

I don't remember.

And yet we got mail from young black lesbians saying "Thank you for giving me a reason to live and the courage to be out. If I'm not out, people won't know that I exist." That's the other side of it.

I'm perfectly willing to acknowledge that there is another side of it. But I still don't think that anybody has the right to call somebody something that might ruin them or their family, ruin their children, cause them to be discriminated against. You have to let them do it themselves. If Ellen changed a lot of things for a lot of people, great. I admire her very much; I think she was very brave. But God, occasionally she must wish she could get in a hole someplace.

[*Laughing*] Oh, yes, she does.

Whatever her real identity is, there is also a more complicated identity to her. Diane Sawyer said to me the other day, "Don't you feel that you gave up something private that you can never get back?" And I said, "Yeah, I do. And I'm not so happy about it." But

maybe in the end it will be a good thing—if you really believe that people are only as sick as their secrets. Psychologically it is good to "dare to be true." I always thought that was the greatest motto. But I never felt I could live up to it.

But you're doing this interview.

OK. But I'm, you know, half-dead with old age here.

What about all the women who are in their 70s who've read your book and can now say, "I exist because you did this."

What's really great is this congenial, generally tolerant reception I'm getting. I haven't had—so far—a single bad question, bad comment, any sort of negative, moralistic, preachy "aren't you ashamed of yourself" thing said to me. And I fully expected that I would. [*Shrugs*] Next week, tomatoes wherever I go.

I don't think so.

I mean, I'm amazed that these ordinary wonderful Americans are just sitting, just dying laughing at everything I say about myself and this book when I go on tour. And I seem to be beguiled. There's no fool like an old fool, I guess.

Perhaps dialoguing with these "ordinary Americans" is giving you the one thing your parents robbed you of: the chance to share your whole self.

Maybe that's true. [*Smiles*] If so, that's very good. That's great. And if it happens that my doing this is any kind of inspiration to anybody, great. Although I admit it's late.

It's never too late to tell.

[*Stares out the window a minute*] I'm thinking back. I'm trying to think about this Barbara Jordan thing you brought up. I guess the thing about Barbara Jordan was that she's such a hero to me politically and ideologically. I didn't know anything about her private life. I didn't care. I thought she was a great woman. And my impression is she never said anything about her sexuality...

She didn't, not publicly.

She didn't say anything? I suppose her friends knew.

And her partner, it was reported, was at her funeral.

So I guess maybe I felt she should have been left alone, but...well, I mean, she was dead. She couldn't be hurt anymore by anything. And nothing could damage her great reputation. So I suppose if she became a great role model for these young black women, well, maybe it made sense.

We felt the same way about doing a cover story on Dusty Springfield after she died—although, of course, we tried to talk to her while she was alive. I felt we needed to tell her full story because otherwise we lose a part of her—and our—history. I'm happy you wrote your book because...

No, I'm glad that I went through this whole thing too. I would say to myself, "What should I do about this thing about my private life?" I'm not that certain about what I really think.

When you look back on your relationships, which ones do you think were the best for you? The ones with men or the ones with women?

Well, this is just a cliché, but I think that my relationships with women were always much more emotional and more emotionally

"I'm not going to reveal chapter and verse about every woman I've known. It's ridiculous. You can do that about the men, because you're not going to ruin their lives if you do. It's up to the women to say if they want this told about them."

satisfying and comfortable. And a lot of my relationships with men were more flirtatious and adversarial. I just never felt I was wife material. I always felt that I was a great girlfriend.

And you didn't have to feel like a wife with another woman?
No. I didn't have to play that role. And so maybe that was more natural for me. But, you know, men are a lot easier to have relationships with than women because men will seize these occasional opportunities and go forth. Women are not—at least the women I've dealt with—like that.

So it's more complicated to get together with a woman?
I can't really say. I never… [*Laughing, embarrassed*] As I say, I'm a serial failure at maintaining a relationship.

Now, when you say failure, are you saying that you would prefer it if you *did* have a relationship?
I mean four years was about as long as I ever stayed with anybody, except for my 15 years with Iris. And Iris became like my child and she still is. She has a very a childlike nature. And we are still companions and friends. We travel and so forth. Sex was the least of it.

Is it any different for you to know that you are talking to the gay press versus all the other press you've done?
No. You're just as cute and nice as Mike Wallace any day.

[*Laughing*] But you've never talked to the gay press before.
That's true. Well, I hadn't written my memoir either. And the great thing about this, the pragmatic thing about this is that it's created a sensation. I thought it would just sort of pass, like people would say, "Oh, well, I already knew that." But it created an enormous sensation, which I suppose has sold the book. But it's not a book about my sex life. Maybe I'll go back and write a whole book on my sex life. [*Laughing*]

Then we'll have to do another interview.
I don't want to act here with *The Advocate* as if I think I have all of the answers, because when you made your argument a while ago about why it's important for people to come out, I understand the point. I just think my own nature prevents me from going hog-wild or from being any kind of role model. So they can call me whatever they like. I just don't want to call myself anything. I think I have really bent over backwards to try to help victims of injustice in my columns. I'm trying to right wrongs whenever I can. The column has helped to raise millions of dollars for AIDS. On the other hand it irritates me when people say I use the column to promote all kinds of gay causes. You bet I do.

Speaking of your causes, it was very interesting to me to read in your book how your heart went out to black people while you were growing up in Texas. You've always been for the underdog.
I think I was always sort of a softhearted sap. I hated that intolerant thing that was all around me when I was growing up.

You probably already knew yourself, knew something about your own uniqueness and what the world was going to do to you for it.
I like your suggestion. A unique person. [*Laughing*] I take that as a compliment.

Certainly your parents weren't like you.

They had a natural barrier around them, which was from the Southern Baptist religion. [*Sighs*] I really wish everybody would leave everybody else the hell alone. I know that's a stupid thing for a gossip columnist to say, but I'm not a very good gossip columnist. I think I'm a pretty good social barometer and observer, though.

You say to leave everyone alone because you have been hounded and outed. At *The Advocate* we constantly struggle about what to say or not say about someone's sexuality.
I think it's perfectly logical for you all to try to encourage people to talk about themselves. That's what you should do. *The Advocate* in particular is in this ethical dilemma all the time. But, you know, if you went around outing people, I think you would suffer. The magazine wouldn't be the icon and responsible thing that it is. And others can become role models if they want to. I think a lot about Ellen. I wonder if she wanted what ultimately happened to her.

She couldn't tolerate being a lesbian and lying about it.
Hmm, that's pretty special.

Remember when you wrote that some TV icon talk show host was coming out and all hell broke loose?
You know, we printed that item in the column, and it caused us a lot of trouble. I would have never printed that until I was absolutely certain that it was going to happen. We didn't say whether it was a man or a woman. We had about seven people nominate themselves as this person and tell us in the most irate tone that they weren't going to come out. And we said, "Great, we never said you were."

Did the person that you were talking about decide not to…
They also called me [*laughing*]…yes, decided not to come out.

Why did you think they were?
Somebody so close to them told us. And it was so dumb of us to do that. It was dumb, very damn foolish. I don't know why I did it. Don't do blind items.

In your book you talk about some unknown man who kept calling your office and insisting you and Barbara Walters were lovers.
Yes, he was really on our case. I would tell Barbara about it and she'd die laughing. It's true, heterosexual people have so much certainty about themselves. She could take is as a joke and enjoy it. The other night at this birthday party, Barbara stood up and made this speech. And the room is full of all these different celebrities, including Matt Drudge and Prince Edward of England. It was a very eclectic group. So Barbara got up and said she was announcing that I was not a natural blond and that we were lovers. And the audience started laughing. It was very funny and defusing. And then I got up and said, "Actually, I've slept with everyone in this room." There were 400 people. So you know, you have to have a little sense of humor about it. And nobody cared.

Why do you want Hilary Swank to play you in a movie?
If you ever see her outside of *Boys Don't Cry,* in her real-life self, she is very voluptuous and adorable and really pretty. But they'll never make a movie of my book. [*Laughs*] It doesn't have any ending. I'd have to end up with Ellen or with Rob Lowe. We need a socko ending to the Liz Smith story.

Picture Credits

Photographer Biographies

The following photographers made generous contributions to this book and have photographed numerous *Advocate* covers over the years.

LYNN GOLDSMITH

Lynn Goldsmith is a multi-award-winning portrait photographer whose work has appeared on and between the covers of *Life, Newsweek, Time, Rolling Stone, Sports Illustrated, People, Elle, Interview, Us, Bunte, Paris Match, Out,* and *National Geographic.* She has produced seven of her own photographic books: *Bruce Springsteen, The Police, New Kids on the Block, Circus Dreams, PhotoDiary, Springsteen: Access All Areas,* and *Flower.* For *The Advocate,* Goldsmith has produced dynamic cover portraits of Guinevere Turner, Dennis Rodman, Jason Gould, and Ani DiFranco. For *Celebrity: The Advocate Interviews,* she contributed the portraits of Barbra Streisand and Rob Halford and the cover image of Mark Wahlberg. Goldsmith can be contacted through her Web site: www.lynngoldsmith.com.

GREG GORMAN

For nearly two decades Greg Gorman has continued to master the art of photography. With work that encompasses personality portraits and advertising campaigns as well as magazine layouts and fine art, Gorman has developed and showcased a discriminating and distinctive style in his profession. In 1990 CPC Publishing released his first solo book, *Greg Gorman, Volume One,* which features his stark black-and-white personality portraits in addition to his more-personal work with male and female nudes. This book followed the 1986 photographic anthology *Visual Aid,* published by Pantheon Books. In 1992 Treville Press published *Greg Gorman, Volume Two,* a collection of his male and female nudes. *Inside Life,* a career retrospective of Gorman's work, was released by Rizzoli International Publishers in 1996. In the fall of 2000 Powerhouse Books published *As I See It,* a book of his fine art male nudes. For *The Advocate,* Gorman has created iconic cover portraits of Greg Louganis, Martina Navratilova, Eric Roberts, Janis Ian, and Johnny Depp. For *Celebrity: The Advocate Interviews,* he contributed the portrait of Mark Wahlberg, which he originally shot for Wahlberg's 1993 cover story interview. Gorman's fine art work is represented worldwide by Fahey/Klein Gallery in Los Angeles, and he can be contacted through his Web site: www.greggormanphotography.com.

BLAKE LITTLE

Ellen DeGeneres, Jack Nicholson, Brooke Shields, Tom Cruise, Sandra Bullock, Gwyneth Paltrow, and many others have all revealed themselves to Blake Little. In his 17-year career, Little has created a body of work acclaimed for its ability to capture the emotion and beauty of his subjects. He is one of the most distinguished entertainment and advertising photographers in New York and Los Angeles, creating imagery for such diverse clients as Pepsi, DirecTV, MCA Records, Got Milk? and the award-winning Virgin Shaglantic campaign with Mike Myers. His first photography book, *Dichotomy,* was published in 1997. For *The Advocate,* Little has created memorable cover images of Melissa Etheridge, Nathan Lane, Boy George, Amanda Bearse, and Mitchell Anderson. For *Celebrity: The Advocate Interviews,* he contributed the portraits of Steve Kmetko, Chastity Bono, and Gore Vidal as well as the cover image of George Michael. Little is represented by G. Ray Hawkins Gallery in Los Angeles and Wessel + O'Connor Gallery in New York and can be contacted through his Web site: www.blakelittle.com.

Acknowledgments

I want to thank the entire staff of LPI (parent company of
The Advocate, *Out*, *HIV Plus*, Alyson Publications, and
Advocate Books). Over the past years their hard work has
helped to make it possible for me to interview the
celebrities on these pages. Without their relentless support;
encouragement; and editorial, photo, and design skills,
these interviews could not have been successful. That the
interviews still hold up—despite many personal and
professional changes in the lives of the stars—is a tribute
to everyone involved.

I want to especially thank Liz Smith for her generosity and
encouragement in this project. And lastly (but mostly), I
want to thank my great love of 13 years, Suzanne, for always
thinking I can do it—whatever it is.

—JUDY WIEDER